Back to Work

Back to Work

HOW TO REHABILITATE OR RECONDITION YOUR HORSE

Lucinda Dyer

Trafalgar Square Books

North Pomfret, Vermont

First published in 2007 by
Trafalgar Square Books
North Pomfret, Vermont 05053

Printed in China

Disclaimer of Liability
The author and publisher shall have neither liability nor responsibility to any person or entity with respect to any loss or damage caused or alleged to be caused directly or indirectly by the information contained in this book. While the book is as accurate as the author can make it, there may be errors, omissions, and inaccuracies.

The author has made very effort to obtain a release from all photographers responsible for the photographs used in this book. In some cases, however, the photographers' whereabouts may not have been known and therefore they could not be contacted.

Library of Congress Cataloging-in-Publication Data

Dyer, Lucinda, 1947-
  Back to work : How to rehabilitate or recondition your horse / Lucinda Dyer.
    p. cm.
  Includes index.
  ISBN 978-1-57076-366-3
  1. Equine sports medicine. 2. Competition horses—Wounds and injuries. 3. Competition horses—Diseases. 4. Competition horses—Training. I. Title.
  SF956.D94 2007
  636.1'08971027—dc22

                        2006038871

Book text and jacket design by Heather Mansfield
Typefaces: Warnock Pro and Gill Sans

10 9 8 7 6 5 4 3 2 1

To Reason & Raf

Show me your horse and
I will tell you who you are.
—English Proverb

CONTENTS

Introduction

⟋

This is the book I needed but couldn't find. When it came time to put Reason, my then 17-year-old dressage horse back to work, I soon realized that I had no idea where to begin. I was utterly and completely lost—and terrified that I might unwittingly do something that could re-injure him.

I scoured the Internet and spent hours Googling phrases like "re-habbing dressage horse" and "bringing horse back from injury." Nothing. What I needed was "The Plan"—a simple, straightforward, impossible-to-screw-up, "On Day One, do this, and on Day 83, do that" plan.

Fortunately, I had a veterinarian, Dr. Matt Povlovich, who was both knowledgeable and endlessly patient. He answered a neverending stream of questions from "Is the driveway too hard for him to walk on?" to "How big is a big circle?" and never laughed. My friends Amy Crownover and Susan Kaestner, who were in the final stages of rehabilitating their own horses, were a constant source of strength and good naturedly endured my frequent bouts of paranoia—"Are you *sure* he doesn't look off?" Add in the unending kindness of barn owner, Lorraine Ferrell, and nursing skills of my trainer, Laura Galoppi, and I was able to put together a plan that saw Reason return safely and successfully to work. I was very lucky.

What was needed, I decided, was a book that would provide both foundational plans for returning a horse to work and insights from riders who had actually "walked the walk"—quite literally, considering the weeks of hand-walking involved in rehabbing a horse. These plans would be "rehab road maps" that could be customized by a reader's veterinarian to fit any horse's injury, riding discipline, age and temperament. The stories from riders who had "been there and done that" would, I hoped, provide both information and inspiration.

When I began *Back to Work,* I saw it as a user-friendly source book—an "everything you ever wanted to know about rehabilitating your horse" sort of thing that would include lots of tips from vets and other experts. The stories from riders would be weighted toward the details of rehab—how long they trotted on Week 16, when they reintroduced leg-yields or began cantering small fences. I wanted lots of facts and became obsessed with dragging them out of everyone I interviewed. But, as I began to talk with riders who had successfully rehabbed their horses, a common thread began to emerge. And it had nothing to do with the minutiae of their trot programs.

It was the *experience* that we talked about for hours on end. We cried and laughed (a lot) and compared notes about what an extraordinary journey it had been bringing our horses back to work. How it had changed us as people and deepened the bonds with our horses in ways we could never have imagined.

So while information is the foundation of this book, *inspiration* would become its heart.

Note to Readers
Because riders from a variety of disciplines—and who have experienced differing scenarios in terms of injury, treatment, and rehabilitation—have contributed to *Back to Work,* some of the details included in their stories may well be a mystery to readers. What's a USDF silver medal? Is Preliminary Level eventing higher or lower than Novice Level? What's a

Medal Final or the Tevis Cup? When would my horse need fascia release surgery? What are "Ace," Banamine®, and xylazine?

To help untangle this web of equestrian and veterinarian terminology, I have provided a resource section (see pp. 365–378) that offers information about the associations that govern dressage, eventing, endurance, and hunter/jumper competitions; basic explanations for various surgical procedures, veterinary treatments, and commonly used medications and/or supplements; and a listing of products and books that contributors to this book found helpful as they brought their horses "back to work."

The photographs in this book were taken by many different people—both professional and amateur photographers. Their images help bring the stories I've included to life. They are listed on pp. 381–2.

Chapter 1

Early Planning

You see it in your vet's eyes before the words are even spoken. This is something that will not be better after a few days off or a dose of anti-inflammatory medication. You hear yourself saying, "I don't care if he ever competes again, I just want him to be okay." You throw all your energy into making decisions about treatment options. Whatever it takes, you'll see it gets done. And when it's done, you find yourself face-to-face with the fact that the training and competition goals for which you've worked so hard are now on hold—perhaps, for a very, very long time.

But there is still work to be done and new goals to be met. Ask any of the riders profiled in *Back to Work* and they will tell you the time spent rehabilitating and reconditioning a horse after surgery or an injury is a time that can bring great rewards.

Having a plan—one that you and your veterinarian design specifically for your horse and his rehabilitation needs—will allow you to set these new goals and focus on the months to come. Bringing a horse back to work takes as much organization, commitment, consistency, and dedication as preparing for any show, event, or endurance ride. And the rewards can be just as great as those from competition—perhaps even greater.

Planning Ahead

Successfully rehabilitating a horse takes not just time, but planning. Can your barn accommodate the needs of a horse that will be stall-bound for weeks or even months? Are there flat areas with good footing appropriate for hand-walking and early under-saddle work where your horse is stabled? How will a daily commute, perhaps multiple times, to and from the barn affect the other commitments in your life? Who will bandage, medicate, cold-hose, walk, or ride your horse if your child is ill or you have to make a business trip? You will have to ask yourself these questions, and many others, as you put together a rehabilitation program that is both manageable for you and beneficial for your horse.

Meet with the Vet

Schedule a sit-down appointment with your veterinarian to customize a rehab program. (If possible, include your barn manager, trainer, and any friends who will be pitching in to help hand-walk or ride your horse.) Remember, just as you would pay for a consultation with your doctor or accountant, let your vet's office know you expect to be billed for this time.

Bring a list of questions and concerns and be honest with yourself. If you work full-time or have a family (or both), don't accept the schedule your veterinarian has designed if you cannot reasonably follow it. Ask for a "Plan B."

Take detailed notes. If individuals integral to your horse's recovery are unable to attend the meeting with your vet (such as your barn manager or trainer), make certain they receive a copy. The notes can also serve to remind you of schedule specifics, should the need arise. Issues to discuss with your vet:

- Try to gain a complete understanding of the nature and extent of your horse's injury and how it will be treated. Specific information should be included on the "discharge plan" from the clinic or veterinarian. Be sure to obtain a copy for your reference.

- If you are bringing your horse back from surgery, ask how the area should heal and what behaviors and/or symptoms might be signs of trouble.

- If your horse is rehabbing from a leg injury, ask the vet to show you exactly what to look for when you check his legs each day.

- Request instruction in any related icing, wrapping, and medication administration.

- Try to get an idea of the prospective timeline and how to determine if your horse is ready to advance or if you are asking too much of him in the course of his rehab.

- If you are worried about hand-walking or turning out a horse that's stall-bound and has way too much energy, ask your veterinarian about sedation options.

- Ask for a general schedule of recommended progress reports and veterinary check-ups.

Meet with the Barn Manager

If you board your horse, schedule a time to go over any concerns the barn manager at your facility may have regarding your horse's injury and time off. "When it comes to working with boarders whose horses are coming back from an injury or illness, I can never be given enough information," says barn manager Susie Symmes. "The key to making it all work is no guessing ('Did Jane want us to hand-walk her horse today?'), organization, and good communication between boarder and barn manager." Issues to discuss:

- If the barn manager was unable to attend the meeting with your vet, explain the nature and extent of your horse's injury and how it will be treated. (Provide a copy of the "discharge plan" from the clinic or veterinarian for her reference.)

- Stall rest and turnout restrictions. How will your horse adjust to his friends being out while he's alone in his stall? Can your horse be turned out in a size-restricted turnout space or possibly moved to a stall where he can see other horses? Should he be sedated when he is turned out?

- Bandaging to be done by the barn staff. (Note: Expect to be charged for this service.)

- Medication and its administration and dosage schedule.

- Changes in your horse's feed or supplements.

- The schedule for your horse's time off and return to work.

- Cold-hosing, hand-grazing, hand-walking, or riding to be done by the barn staff. (Note: Expect to be charged for these services.)

- "Outside" friends (those who don't board at your barn) who plan to help hand-walk or ride your horse should sign the barn's liability waiver and turn it into the barn manager.

Susie Symmes

Susie is the barn manager and dressage trainer at Eleazer Davis Farm in Bedford, Massachusetts. This 26-stall facility is home to horses and riders that compete in eventing, dressage, and combined driving.

Susie has been riding since she was 10 and working as a barn manager for nine years. She has competed in dressage through FEI and currently shows her Danish Warmblood mare, Anastasia, at Fourth Level.

Additional Hints

- Take photographs of injured legs and note any pre-existing blemishes, scars, etc. This should prevent panicked moments of "Was that bump always there?" or "Did his leg always look like that?"

- See what lies ahead—do you have a vacation scheduled, business trips, anything that would mean a break in your horse's rehab? Make arrangements well ahead of time to have your trainer, friends, or barn staff work with your horse. Write out a schedule, make copies for everyone involved, and reconfirm it at the beginning of each week.

- If you plan on using massage therapists, acupuncturists, or chiropractors during your horse's rehab, meet with them to set up a treatment schedule.

- If necessary, schedule a "walking" lesson with your trainer. You may have weeks of hand-walking ahead—make certain you can do it safely (see Hand-Walking, p. 280).

- Keep a journal. Record what your horse does each day (i.e., "Added five minutes of trot. He felt like a wet noodle.") and how he works ("Suddenly he became stiff to the left"). When a friend hand-walks or rides your horse, ask him or her to make an entry (see Keeping a Journal, p. 11).

- Consider buying a heart monitor (see Rehabbing with a Heart Monitor, p. 302).

- If friends or barn staff will be tending to or wrapping your horse's injury, make up a kit containing any supplies (Vetrap™, DMSO, gauze, etc.) that will be used. Keep everything together and in one place.

- If you will be sharing the responsibility of administering medication to your horse with friends or barn staff, make up a chart that can safely hang on your horse's stall that lists each medication, the dosage, the day and time it was given, and who administered it.

Maintaining a Health File

"Keeping a horse sound and healthy starts with keeping track of details," believes Kirsten Johnson, co-owner of KESMARC (Kentucky Equine Sports Medicine and Rehabilitation Center) with her husband, Hub. The most famous sport, performance, and race horses in the world come to KESMARC's Versailles, Kentucky, rehabilitation facility, which includes equine swimming therapy, an exercise gym, a solarium, and equine hyperbaric oxygen therapy.

"At KESMARC, we need to keep track of information on some 75 horses at any one time. Maintaining a complete and up-to-date health file for your horse means you have essential information at hand anytime it's needed."

Kirsten recommends your horse's health file include:

- Medication records. Document the name of each medicine, when the course of treatment began and ended, the daily dose, and any problems that might have been encountered.

- Good quality baseline X-rays of all four feet on correct angles; the front feet being the most important. Front navicular radiographs, and hock radiographs, should be included. Since X-rays are normally kept at the vet's office, ask if it's possible for you to have copies made for your health file.

- Copies of any ultrasounds taken—for any injury.

- A current Coggins certificate.

- Vaccination records.

- Copies of dental records.

- Deworming schedule.

- A list of all supplements. Note the name, the daily dose, the period of time it was (or has been) in use, and any positive or negative effects on your horse.

Keeping a Journal

A journal allows you keep an accurate record of your horse's progress throughout his recovery and return to work. There is no guessing about how many minutes you trotted last week or when he had his last ultrasound. Writing in a journal is also a great way to vent your frustration when you hit a setback or to celebrate when you take a big step forward.

Max Corcoran, head groom for international eventer and three-time Olympic medalist Karen O'Connor, finds that keeping journals is an invaluable tool in caring for the horses of "Team O'Connor." "I use a big, eight-inch by 10-inch, week-at-a-glance planner. I record what a horse did that day (how long he was hand-walked or ridden), any medication he received (medicine name and dosage) and vet or farrier appointments. I also make a note of how he felt—was he stiff, tired, anxious? Maybe he felt great—make sure to record that as well."

Writing this book has reinforced my belief that one can sometimes best learn from others' experience—whether bad or good. In addition to the general recommendations in this chapter (and the more specific tips from experts and riders you'll find in chapter 5), I might further add that when faced with something as overwhelming as a horse's potentially career-ending illness or injury, you should *talk* to people. Find other riders who have survived similar challenges and ask them to share their stories—talk with barn mates, post questions in your association's chat room, and contact the authors of articles on the subject. Be "all ears" (and "eyes")—the most important thing you'll find is a community of people who understand your struggle. Read on, and you'll see that you and your horse are by no means alone. And *that* can be half the battle won.

Chapter 2

Colic Surgery

Introduction

by Bob Grisel, DVM

The word *colic* simply means "abdominal pain." Although there are many causes of abdominal pain (such as abdominal trauma, kidney disease, peritonitis, bladder stones, etc.), we will use the term *colic* to refer to only those problems that directly involve the gastrointestinal system for the purpose of this chapter.

From the primary (ambulatory) veterinarian's standpoint, there are two major types of colic. Those that:

1. Can be treated at the farm
2. Require referral to a surgical facility

Most horses will respond to conservative management "in the field" (that is, "at the farm"). Conservative management might involve administration of anti-inflammatories (e.g. Banamine®), sedatives (e.g. xylazine), oral laxatives (e.g. mineral oil), and oral and/or intravenous (IV) fluid therapy. In more severe cases, horses might warrant referral and transport to a hospital. Once at the referral facility, the horse may undergo further conservative treatment (such as extended intravenous fluid therapy) and/or surgery in the form of exploratory laparotomy (surgery via an incision into the abdominal wall).

It is the primary veterinarian's job to recognize clinical signs that separate potential surgical and non-surgical colics and determine if and when transport to a referral hospital is indicated. The most common parameters evaluated by the veterinarian are:

- Degree of pain
- Duration of pain
- Heart rate
- Gut sounds

Dr. **Bob Grisel** began his equine veterinary training at the age of 13, working for a racetrack veterinarian in southern Florida. After graduating from the University of Florida College of Veterinary Medicine, he completed residencies in equine surgery at San Luis Rey Equine Hospital and the University of California—Davis and was on the teaching staff at Oregon State College of Veterinary Medicine.

In 1997, Dr. Grisel founded the Atlanta Equine Clinic (www.atlantaequine.com), a state-of-the-art, full-service, equine diagnostic, surgical, and emergency care facility with offices located in the Braselton and Alpharetta areas of Atlanta, Georgia. Dr. Grisel regularly trail and pleasure rides his Quarter Horse gelding, Four-Stroke. His daughter is learning to jump and competes in dressage on her Arabian gelding, Bourbon, and his son competes in 25- and 30-mile endurance rides on his Arabian gelding, El Dorado.

- Mucous membrane (gum) color
- Rectal findings

In some cases, peritoneal fluid (fluid from the abdominal cavity) is analyzed to assess intestinal viability. A horse requiring referral might exhibit one or more of the following in the face of appropriate conservative management:

- Extreme (and sometimes violent) pain
- Abdominal pain that has persisted for over 24 hours
- An excessively elevated heart rate (sometimes over 100 beats per minute)
- A complete absence of gut sounds
- Compromised (dark red, purple, or black) mucous membranes
- A problem diagnosed via rectal palpation that is unlikely to resolve without the aid of internal surgical intervention

Once the horse reaches the surgical facility, it is the responsibility of the referral veterinarian/surgeon to pursue an appropriate course of action. In many cases abdominal surgery is indicated in an attempt to save the horse's life.

From the referral veterinarian/surgeon's standpoint, there are two categories of surgical colic:

1 Uncomplicated
2 Complicated

When intestinal colic develops, the lumen of the bowel first becomes obstructed. This might occur as a result of an impaction of ingesta, a displacement, or via strangulation from another structure (such as a lipoma or another piece of bowel). As long as the blood supply to the intestine itself is adequate, the bowel remains alive and viable. This situation is referred to as an *uncomplicated* colic. It may require surgical manipulation to resolve, but resection (removal) of bowel is usually not necessary. The abnormality (obstruction, twist, entrapment, etc.) is simply reduced and intestinal patency re-established. Prognosis for uncomplicated surgery is typically good.

In some cases the blood vessels supplying the intestinal wall also become obstructed. Consequently, affected segment(s) of intestine might not receive adequate amounts of oxygen and nutrients normally delivered by the bloodstream. This condition is called *vascular compromise*. During vascular compromise the intestine may lose its ability to perform normal critical functions, such as removing toxins that accumulate in the intestinal tissues.

It is the job of the intestinal mucosa (lining) to protect the body from a substance called *endotoxin* produced by intestinal bacteria. This important job may become altered with changes in blood flow. Consequently, the body absorbs these toxins into the blood stream, creating a situation called *endotoxemia*. Endotoxemia is the *primary killer* of horses with colic. It can cause shock, organ damage, laminitis, and vascular anomalies. Therefore, compromised or "dead" bowel should be resected/removed to prevent further absorption of endotoxins into the body. Removal of dead bowel and re-attachment of viable ends (termed "resection and anastomosis") constitutes *complicated* surgery. Prognosis is usually worse for horses undergoing complicated colic surgery due to the potentially lethal effects of endotoxemia.

Fortunately, great strides have been made in colic research and surgical technique within the last 20 years. New diagnostic and surgical equipment are being developed on a regular basis. New teaching tools (such as The Glass Horse—see *Resources*, p. 368) have helped veterinary students understand the anatomy and nature behind many types of colic. The percentage of horses surviving colic episodes (even severe) increases each year.

Rehabilitating a Horse from Colic Surgery

by Bob Grisel, DVM

A WEEK-BY-WEEK PLAN

The following plan for bringing a horse back to work after colic surgery is presented as a road map. You should work with your veterinarian to design a rehabilitation program that will address the specific needs of your horse.

Stall Rest

Horses must be restricted to a stall as the incision line experiences a tremendous amount of tension due to its location on the bottom of the belly and the weight of the abdominal contents directly above. This tension greatly increases with activity. Any enclosure that would allow the horse to trot (even for a step) is not recommended.

Hand-Walking

We generally recommend hand-walking the day following surgery unless the horse is unable to walk safely due to other medical conditions. Consult with your veterinarian to plan a post-op hand-walking schedule designed specifically for your horse.

Weekly Schedule

Weeks 1 and 2: 10 to 15 minutes, twice daily
Weeks 3 and 4: 20 to 30 minutes, twice daily
Weeks 5 and after: Unlimited hand-walking is permitted

Q&A

Does hand-walking mean ambling along or walking briskly?
It is not critical how fast the horse walks, as long as he doesn't do anything beyond a walk (such as a trot). Horses can stop to briefly graze, but this should not be counted as time spent "walking" (see p. 18).

If my horse won't walk quietly, what can I do?

Initially, sedatives and/or tranquilizers are very effective for keeping horses calm during hand-walking. Administration in the muscle (rather than intravenously) results in a longer-acting effect and a slower recovery. Acepromazine (a tranquilizer commonly known as "Ace"), is probably the best medication for this purpose, but should not be administered to intact males (stallions or colts) due to the potential for paraphimosis (permanent dropping of the penis). Xylazine, a sedative, is also effective when administered in the muscle (see *Resources*, p. 365).

Can I longe my horse until he quiets down?

No. The circling pattern, coupled with the freedom horses are extended while on the end of a longe line means that excitable horses may be at a higher risk for injury when being longed. Bucking and kicking (a common occurrence during longeing) also impose a challenge to the incision line.

Should I also hand-graze my horse?

Ideally, horses should be hand-grazed for at least 30 minutes, twice each day, *in addition* to the time spent hand-walking. Grass is extremely easy for most horses to digest and functions as a natural laxative. It requires minimal acid production from the stomach for digestion and breaks down easily in the gastrointestinal (GI) tract. It is unlikely to be a cause of gastrointestinal impaction, even if motility is decreased. The greater the water content in the grass, the better.

What should I do during the winter or if I board at a barn without grassy areas?

The next best thing to grass for a horse recovering from colic surgery is a bland, broad-leaf hay. Examples include fescue, timothy, rye, orchard grass, and oat hay. Alfalfa is also good, although it has a higher energy-content, which may be counterproductive when a horse is restricted to a stall. Thin-leaf grass hays, such as Bermuda and Tift 44 are not recommended due to their predisposition to cause impactions postoperatively.

Things to Watch For

- Some postoperative *edema* (swelling) associated with the incision is normal and should dissipate within a couple of weeks. However, any increased *incisional heat, drainage, swelling,* and/or *discomfort* might indicate infection or compromise of the closure. A veterinary consultation is recommended if any of these symptoms are noted.

- *Depression* and/or *lack of appetite* would also justify a call to your veterinarian.

- In addition to frequently observing the horse's activity and attitude, the owner should take the horse's rectal temperature once daily (preferably each morning at the same time of day) to pick up a problem before it becomes severe. The horse's normal temperature is between 99.5 and 100.9 degrees Fahrenheit. A temperature above 101.5 degrees warrants a call to your veterinarian.

- Sutures or staples should be removed anywhere from 14 to 21 days postoperatively.

Turnout: On Hold

We strongly recommend you do not turn a horse out until he has completed eight weeks of rehabilitation under saddle (see proposed schedule as follows). Your horse is not familiar with the concept of a "rehabilitation program" and does not consider the potential consequences of excessive activity! Remember, once you unsnap that lead rope, everything is up to him—and at the end of eight weeks, your horse will be fitter, more coordinated, and at a lower risk for injury. For now, hand-grazing is the safest choice for getting your horse outside his stall.

Work under Saddle

It is essential that you consult with your veterinarian before returning your horse to work under saddle.

WEEK 1   Walk on a loose rein for 10 to 15 minutes, working up to 20 minutes by the end of the first week. Walk straight lines on a level surface and avoid circles, walking up or down hills, bending or tight turns, and riding on trails.

Q&A

How often should I ride my horse this first week?
We recommend a minimum of five days a week and a horse can be ridden seven days a week, starting now. The *frequency* of exercise does not affect the integrity of the incision line or the horse's metabolic condition (blood pressure, heart rate, how the digestive system works). However, the *intensity* of exercise can certainly affect both of these. Therefore, exercise intensity should begin as very light and be increased in a gradual and deliberate fashion.

Do I need to be careful about girthing up?
Not from the standpoint of the surgery. Your horse may seem a little "girthy" initially because he will have become unaccustomed to it. This should resolve quickly.

If my horse is very excitable, what should I do?
Consult your vet about using acepromazine or xylazine (see p. 365).
   Caution: Any tranquilizer or sedative can slow down the smooth muscle in the bowel and overuse can restrict bowel movements—not something you want when a horse is recovering from colic surgery. If you are using a tranquilizer or sedative to quiet your horse, you must follow your vet's instructions to the letter.

Am I now allowed to longe my horse to quiet him down?
No. We recommend that longeing not be resumed until Week 4 (see p. 22).

Things to Watch For

- By this time, your horse should "feel great" from a metabolic stand-point. In other words, his appetite and attitude should have returned to normal and he should be alert and nickering to other horses. The horse may, however, feel tired and out of shape when resuming exercise.

WEEK 2 Your horse can now be ridden for up to 30 minutes, at least five days this week. Reintroduce trot work, beginning with five minutes only, and working up to 10 to 15 minutes in a 30-minute ride by the end of the week.

Q&A

Should I still ride on a loose rein?
Begin to implement a small amount of contact at this point. No hard-core collection yet, however.

What should I expect the first few days of trot to feel like?
Very clumsy—the horse is still out-of-shape and just getting used to moving again!

If my horse feels stiff, should I give him bute? Call the vet?
You can administer "bute" (see p. 365), if needed, but if at any point during your horse's rehabilitation, more than two grams per day is required to produce comfort, your veterinarian should be consulted.

Things to Watch For

- If the horse feels weak and/or tired, keep working at the same intensity until his fitness improves. Begin to advance again as soon as the horse feels better.

WEEK 3 Your horse should be ridden at least five days this week for up to 30 minutes, and you can now trot for *up to* 20 minutes out of the

30-minute ride. You may also begin trotting 20-meter circles, asking for changes of direction, and walking up and down small hills.

Q&A

How can I tell if I'm asking for too much at the trot?

The horse might exhibit excessive resistance (flinging his head, refusing to go forward, or bucking, for example) or fatigue. Following an extended period of rest, the distal patellar apparatus in the stifle of the horse is often weak. Consequently, the horse may develop a stilted or disjointed gait. Since resuming contact on the bit increases challenge to the patellar apparatus, it is not uncommon for unfit horses to show resistance as you begin to ride with more contact. This should resolve with increased fitness, but may take some time.

What's happening now in my horse's recovery?

At this point the incision should be healed and the hair almost completely regrown.

Things to Watch For

- If the horse feels weak or tired, keep working at the same intensity until fitness improves. Advance again as soon as he feels better.

WEEK 4 Your horse should be ridden a minimum of five days this week and be working comfortably at the trot for up to 30 minutes during a ride of 45 minutes to an hour. You can now begin to trot serpentines and smaller (10-meter) circles.

Things to Watch For

- If the horse feels weak or tired, keep working at the same intensity until fitness improves. Begin to advance again as soon as he feels better.

WEEKS 5 AND 6 Horses should be ridden at least five days each week. Rides can last up to 60 minutes. You can begin to trot up and down small hills and add simple lateral work, such as leg-yield or shoulder-in.

Q&A

What should my goals be?

At this point, the rider should begin implementing collection and a proper frame for the horse. As the horse regains fitness, this becomes easier.

Things to Watch For

- If the horse feels weak and/or tired, keep working at the same intensity until fitness improves. Begin to advance again as soon as the horse feels better.

WEEKS 7 AND 8 Your horse should continue to be ridden a minimum of five days per week. "Working" rides can last up to 60 minutes, and you are allowed unlimited walking under saddle.

Canter work can now be added. Start with five minutes of canter in each direction (10 minutes total) and increase to 10 minutes in each direction (20 minutes total) by the end of Week 8. Begin by cantering straight lines, then see how comfortable your horse is when turning. Don't push him at this point—if he is unable to easily hold the correct lead when turning, do a little more work on the straight.

The canter will probably feel very bumpy and disjointed. The rider shouldn't ask for collection as long as the canter feels "bad." As fitness improves, the canter will smooth out and you can begin to ask for more collection. As with the trot, increase collection gradually, as a collected gait takes more energy and fitness.

In Week 8, you may also add more advanced lateral work, such as the half-pass.

Things to Watch For

- If the horse feels weak or tired, keep working at the same intensity until fitness improves. Advance again as soon as the horse feels better.

WEEK 9 Your horse can now return to his normal training routine on the flat and resume jumping if he is on track as outlined already. Obviously, we recommend starting small and adding height slowly.

Turnout: At Last!

With approval from your veterinarian, your horse can now return to his regular turnout.

RECOVERY TIMELINE

Hand-Walking	
Weeks 1 and 2	Hand-walk 10 to 15 minutes, twice daily.
Weeks 3 and 4	Hand-walk 20 to 30 minutes, twice daily.
Work under Saddle	
Week 1	Ride 5 to 7 days, walking on a loose rein for 10 to 15 minutes, working up to 20 minutes by week's end. Walk on straight lines and level surfaces only. No longeing or riding on trails.
Week 2	Ride 5 to 7 days for up to 30 minutes. Introduce 5 minutes of trot and work up to 10 to 15 minutes by week's end.
Week 3	Ride 5 to 7 days for up to 30 minutes. Trot for up to 20 minutes, adding 20-meter circles, changes

of direction, and walking up and down small hills as your horse's capabilities dictate.

Week 4	Ride 5 to 7 days, trotting for up to 30 minutes in a 45- to 60-minute ride. Serpentines and 10-meter circles may be added.
Weeks 5 and 6	Ride 5 to 7 days for up to 60 minutes. Trotting up and down small hills and simple lateral work such as leg-yield and shoulder-in may now be added.
Week 7	Ride 5 to 7 days for up to 60 minutes, adding 5 minutes of canter in each direction.
Week 8	Ride 5 to 7 days for up to 60 minutes, increasing canter to 10 minutes in each direction. More advanced lateral work, such as half-pass, may be added.
Week 9	Return to usual training routine on the flat. Jumping may be resumed, increasing height gradually.

COLIC CASE STUDY I

KATE TAYLOR – Event Rider
SKOOV – New Zealand Thoroughbred

Dover, New Hampshire

Kate

"When I was six years old, I went to my brother's graduation from the University of New Hampshire (UNH). The commencement ceremonies were the same weekend as the UNH Horse Trials, and when I saw all of the trailers in the parking lot, I wandered off to discover the world of horses—something My Little Pony toys had satisfied until that day. By the time my parents found me, I had learned how to feed a treat and scheduled my first riding lesson!"

By nine, Kate was eventing and competing at Novice Level. At 15, and after completing just four Preliminary Level horse trials, she was chosen to ride on the Area 1, One-Star team at the North American Young Riders Championships. By the time she was in college, Kate and Skoov had an accomplished horse trials resume, including three Preliminary wins at the Green Mountain Horse Association Horse Trials in Vermont, the UNH Horse Trials, and the King Oak Farm Horse Trials in Massachusetts.

To pay for Skoov's expenses, Kate has "had at least one, if not two or three jobs for as long as I was legally able. I've mucked stalls, worked at the front desk of a hotel, renovated and painted apartments, and been a waitress." She credits "a strong sense of civic duty" for a job she held throughout college and during the year following her graduation—two terms as a state legislator in the New Hampshire House of Representatives.

Kate recently graduated from UNH with a Bachelor of Arts in Communications and is now balancing a job in retail management with Skoov's training and competition schedule.

Skavoovae aka "Skoov"

"When I was 14 years old, I was offered the horse of my lifetime. A friend in training with Vaughn Jefferies in New Zealand called to tell me he was selling a bunch of his young horses to help fund his way to the Olympics in Atlanta, and there was one gelding that would suit me perfectly. With only a VHS tape and a lot of trust, my parents purchased Skoov, a high-spirited, seven-year-old, 16.3-hand New Zealand Thoroughbred.

During Skoov's flight from New Zealand, the pilot had a heart attack and the plane made an emergency stop in Honolulu. By the time Skoov arrived in Los Angeles, he had missed his trailer transport. We found him another ride, but then he was stuck in a blizzard in Texas. When he finally got to New Hampshire, we found out he hated insects. New Hampshire has a lot of bugs. Skoov has since become so much more than the upper level horse I always dreamed of—he is my shoulder to cry on, my confidant, and best friend."

Home Facility

Hilltop Equestrian Center in Somersworth, New Hampshire, has nine large grass paddocks, two outdoor rings, a dressage ring, an indoor arena, and a cross-country course up to the Novice Level. It is home to 32 horses: a combination of boarders and lesson mounts.

The Colic

Kate was hosting a bachelorette party when she got the call that 15-year-old Skoov appeared to be in the first stages of colic. Leaving an apartment "full of margaritas and bridesmaids," she and the maid of honor ("Aimee's been my best friend since we were on our first ponies in D-rally") took off for the barn. After a dose of Banamine® (see p. 365) and being hand-walked, Skoov seemed to be better, so Kate headed back to check on her party, leaving her mother to watch over Skoov and call if anything changed.

In 30 minutes, the call came and Kate headed back to the barn. "I called the Rochester Equine Clinic emergency vet on the way back to the farm and she arrived shortly after Aimee and I did. Within five minutes of the vet's arrival, we had Skoov loaded on the trailer and were on our way to the clinic. I rode with him the whole way there. I was terrified."

Diagnosis and Prognosis

Skoov's large intestine was completely filled with gas, with decreased gut sounds in all quadrants and displacement of the pelvic flexure into the pelvic canal. "As colic surgeries go, this one was very straightforward. Fortunately, nothing was tangled, so all they had to do was squeeze out the gas and sew him up."

Four days later, while still under observation at the clinic, Skoov began to have fevers. The next day he showed signs of colic again. "When my mom called, I was at the wedding re-hearsal dinner, sitting under a big white tent. She told me there was a chance they might have to operate on Skoov again and I needed to be ready to make that decision. But the vet felt that his chance of recovery from a second surgery was not good, and I remember going outside and just crying and crying. Aimee was close behind me, telling me that he was a strong horse and that he would pull through this fine. Once again, I just had to trust those around me and have faith in my best friend, knowing Skoov was strong and that he would pull through. As it turned out, he didn't need surgery as they were able to treat him aggressively with fluids to get him rehydrated, and he responded perfectly."

"The vet felt that his chance of recovery from a second surgery was not good, and I remember going outside and just crying and crying."

Rehabilitation

Early Days

They brought Skoov home on August 29. He was on stall rest for the first month and turned out in a round pen during the second.

Kate faced juggling Skoov's rehabbing needs with being a full-time student, working at the local mall, sorority meetings, house-sitting, and her duties in the Legislature. To stay organized, she created a chart that was posted on Skoov's stall door. On the top, she wrote that he could be hand-walked two to three times daily. Underneath there was a place to write the date, who had walked him, and for how long. "This way, if someone had the time and saw Skoov needed to be walked they could. This system proved to be infinitely useful. Luckily, I am blessed with a horse of sound mind, and I trusted him, for the most part, to be hand-walked by other barn folk."

Recovering from Loss

A month after Skoov's surgery, Kate's other horse, Blue, had colic complications due to melanomas in his intestines. The prognosis was dim and there was very little hope of the 25-year-old gelding recovering and living comfortably ever again.

"After Blue was put down, I didn't really seem to care all that much about anything. I was run down, emotionally and physically exhausted, and had never felt as sad as I was feeling each day. I was scared, didn't know what to do, and I didn't have the will to get up and going. I finally sought out some counseling—I only had one appointment, but that was all I really needed. Talking with someone allowed me to see all that I still had in front of me. Once I got my feelings out, they became real and something I could change and make better. I was able to go through the layers of anger, regret, and sadness, to truly discover that beneath these were layers of hope and a future. If you can feel it, you can heal it. This only reaffirmed the strong person that I always knew I was. I knew it was time to get back on track again, and not to lose sight of this amazing horse, Skoov, I still had to rehabilitate."

Kate had previously rehabbed Skoov from a bowed tendon, so this experience "was not as scary as a first major injury can be." She credits a favorite quote from author Kurt Vonnegut with helping her along the way:

> Be careful whose advice you buy, but be patient with those who supply it. Advice is a form of nostalgia. Dispensing it is a way of fishing the past from the disposal, wiping it off, painting over the ugly parts and recycling it for more than it's worth.

"This is true in so many ways. The best information I received was from my vets, but I also received great advice from friends who had rehabilitated horses from major surgery. By helping others, what we have done wrong in the past is not a regret, but a tool. I know when I can share a past experience; it makes that experience, no matter how bad it seemed at the time, a little more valuable.

"I strictly followed the directions given to me by my vet and asked for guidance from at least two other horse owners (who I knew and respected) before I made any decisions concerning Skoov's feeding and care. I was walking on eggshells, and there is nothing at all wrong with that."

Back to Ridden Work

By the end of November, three months after the surgery, Kate was able to begin riding Skoov. "I had the day marked down to the hour." She focused on muscle development, starting at the walk, making sure Skoov was fully stretched out. Over the next three weeks they worked up to walking for 40 minutes, and when the weather and his attitude allowed, they would hack outside.

"I was focused on bringing him back better than before. I would let nothing stand in the way of my less-than-healthy horse making a full recovery. He, however, was a little more focused on getting out his new-

To stay organized, create a chart and post it on your horse's stall door. On the top, indicate how often your horse can be hand-walked, and below that leave a space for helpers to write the date, who walked him, and for how long.

found energy. There were days when I almost had heart failure because of how crazy he would be. Fellow boarders would joke and say I might as well cover him in bubble wrap for all the concerns I had about him. I knew I had to 'let him be a horse' sometimes, and as silly as that sounds, it was very difficult.

"I was focused on bringing Skoov back better than before. I would let nothing stand in the way of my less-than-healthy horse making a full recovery."

"Trying to bring a horse back to work in the middle of a freezing New Hampshire winter should be an Olympic sport of its own. Cooped up in the indoor was not where Skoov wished to be. There were days when he would leap up almost to the rafters, just because I applied my left leg. It was up to me to be creative, even if that meant just hacking around in the snow."

In mid-December, they began short periods of trot, working long and low, eventually establishing a connection. They began with five minutes and added five additional minutes each week until Skoov was trotting for 25 minutes in a 45-minute ride. In late February, three months after bringing him back to work, they added cantering to the program, slowly increasing the canter until doing eight minutes in their 45 minutes of work.

Return to Competition

The first week of April, they attended a local jumper show. "We had only jumped a handful of times since the surgery, but he was ready to go. We came home with three blue ribbons that day.

"Two weeks later, I took him to the beach for his first real gallop since his surgery. It was a phenomenal feeling, and at that point I knew he had made a full recovery. He no longer looked skinny and weak; his coat was sleek and bright. He was energetic and exuberant, dragging me across the water. He was caring for me once again, and the 'weight' was lifted off me, because now he was helping me carry it. I was brought to tears that day, because I had this amazing animal that was my heart and soul. Without even knowing it, he was my hero."

On April 17, exactly eight months after his surgery, Kate and Skoov competed at Training Level at the Flora Lea Horse Trials in New Jersey. They finished a very proud fourth.

Skoov's Recovery Timeline

August 17	Colic surgery.
August 24	Allowed hand-grazing for 10 to 15 minutes per day.
August 29	Returned home. Began hand-walking 2 to 3 times daily, working up to a total of 35 to 40 minutes per day.
November 24	Began walking under saddle, working up to 40 minutes over the next 3 weeks.
December 15	First ride at the trot. Added trot at 5 minutes per week until trotting for 25 minutes in a 45-minute ride.
February 22	First ride at the canter. Worked up to 8 minutes of canter in a 45-minute ride.
April 3	Competed at a local jumper show.
April 17	Returned to eventing competition.

Skoov Today

Since his recovery from colic surgery, Skoov and Kate have won the Green Mountain Horse Association Training Level Three Day Event and competed in the *Chronicle of the Horse's* Adult Team Championship. Now 19, Skoov is currently competing at Preliminary. "Skoov shows no signs of slowing down. He looks fabulous and every year he just gets better and better."

KATE'S TIPS

- Remember that setbacks will happen during rehab, and when they do, don't be upset or angry, just readjust your goals. You may no longer be able to ride at that fall event, but try to accept the disappointment and move on.

- Make new goals for rehab: hand-walk outside without any leaping around, ride bareback, achieve a "correct right bend." The more fun you make rehabilitating your horse, the faster it will go by, and more often than not, you will not only rehab the physical, but also the mental aspects of your relationship and partnership.

- Do not settle for less than the best—the best farm and daily care, and the best people caring for your horse when you are not there. You want to be at a barn you trust. Make yourself known. Many boarders like to keep to themselves and ride when no one else is around. The downside to this is when you need a favor, fewer people will be apt to jump up and do it, because they don't know who you are and how you like your horse to be cared for.

- Pass along what you've learned in rehabilitating your horse. Sharing your experiences—no matter how trying they may have been at the time—can be invaluable to others.

COLIC CASE STUDY 2

JUDY LONG – Endurance Rider
WARPAINT – Appaloosa

Hayward, California

Judy

"I was a horse crazy little girl who never had real riding lessons as a kid, but I loved to hang around barns and be around horses." By the time she was in her early thirties and working as a software engineer, her dreams of one day owning a horse seemed long past.

That was until the day her husband, Nick Warhol, rode his bicycle past a local ranch. "I saw the horses out running around and decided it was time Judy finally had a horse of her own. I was going to do it as a surprise, but my friend's mom, who had horses, told me no, that Judy had to buy into it." Judy wasn't sure she really wanted to get a horse at this stage in her life, but one look at Warpaint and her mind was made up.

Judy got into endurance competition "because it seemed like the only thing I could do with Warpaint. He was terrible on trail rides—he'd often jig, spin, leap sideways, or even rear when he was ridden with other horses. Warpaint wanted to be in front and he wanted to run, which is actually a good thing in an endurance horse. Our first endurance ride was quite an event as he tried to run the whole 50 miles!"

Endurance soon became a family affair. "I'd been an off-road motorcycle racer all my life," says Nick. "I knew nothing about horses, let alone that they had personalities. I got Judy Warpaint and figured that was it, but I fell in love with the stupid beast and had to have my own. I got my first horse, Rowan, a few months later, and that marked the end of life as I knew it. When I tried endurance, it was perfect. I don't need to ride anything else."

Nachi Sunshine aka "Warpaint"

A 15.1-hand Appaloosa gelding descended from a line of racing Appaloosas, "Warpaint was a wild, green, powerful, and difficult six-year-old when I bought him. He'd been through more than a few owners in his brief life—mostly because of his 'Appy-tude.' He'd been tried as a trail horse, but since he refused to walk quietly in a group, he was considered unrideable. The guy we bought him from had a couple of broken bones thanks to Warpaint."

On their very first ride, Judy and Warpaint parted company, and he ran several miles back to their trailer. She walked back to the staging area and found him happily eating from his hay bag. "I got back on. Warpaint narrowed his eyes and looked at me, as if to say, 'Oh, yeah?' I looked back at him and said, 'Yeah.' That pretty much summed up how our relationship would go in the future."

Over the next three years, Judy and Warpaint logged 1,200 American Endurance Ride Conference (AERC) endurance miles. They completed their first two 100-mile rides (including the Tevis Cup), finished the Death Valley Encounter 200-mile ride with the fifth overall fastest combined time, and completed the Big Creek 100-miler in fifth place.

Home Facility

Warpaint lived in a 12- by 24-foot, shed-row barn at a large boarding facility with more than 30 horses. The stable was located in Garin Regional Park, less than 15 minutes from Judy's home.

Boarders at the barn had easy access to some 20 miles of trails with hills. "We used these trails for local conditioning rides and then trailered on weekends to the area's best conditioning locations: Mount Diablo, Sunol Park, Point Reyes, Pescadero Park, and the East Bay Watershed."

The Colic

On May 30, Judy and Nick had just returned from a weekend ride when a phone call from a friend at the barn alerted them that Warpaint looked restless and uncomfortable. After a shot of Banamine® (see p. 365), his condition seemed to improve. But by early morning, he was in great distress.

"We put him in the trailer and he promptly lay down! After a stop at our vet, Dr. Bryan Umstead, arrangements were made for him to go immediately to the vet school at the University of California at Davis, about 75 miles away. It was a miserable trip. We had trailered Warpaint thousands of miles, yet not one mile as bad as this. Every traffic delay seemed like an eternity. Nick drove the big rig on the shoulder of the road to keep moving in heavy traffic. When we stopped for gas, I watched Warpaint's eyes through the trailer window and started to cry as I thought about what could possibly happen."

"When we stopped for gas, I watched Warpaint's eyes through the trailer window and started to cry as I thought about what could possibly happen."

At Davis, Warpaint was immediately prepped for surgery. Nick remembers "standing at the front end of the stock holding Warpaint's head up in my arms so he could keep breathing. It wasn't until Judy started whispering something in his ear that I lost it. Every time she would gently say his name, his eye would glance over at her and his lower lip would flap. Judy and I were standing there, holding up his head, tears streaming out of our eyes, while the hospital technicians swarmed over the horse. I'd never before experienced that kind of emotional misery. It was excruciating to see our strong, fiery, energetic, athletic animal in this weakened state. I kept picturing him flying around in the sand arena at home. The doctor tried his best to encourage us, telling us that Appys are such a stoic breed. If it had been another breed in this condition, he would have been on his back from the pain. That was nice to hear, but it didn't help a whole lot."

Diagnosis and Prognosis

The surgery found that enteroliths or "stones" were plugging Warpaint's colon. The prognosis for a full recovery was excellent. Three days after his operation, the couple was allowed to take Warpaint home. "He was about 150 pounds lighter, had staples holding his 20-inch incision closed, and his belly was quite swollen. But he hopped right into the trailer as usual and gave us a dirty look when he realized that his feeder had been removed. That's our boy! It's funny how good that trailer felt with his weight in it."

Rehabilitation

Early Days

The first two weeks were a challenge for Judy, as Warpaint had to be confined in a stall. "This proved to be interesting, since he had never been in one for more than a couple of days. We had to be sure he was not pacing or jumping around, but as long as he had food, he was happy. We came up to the barn several times a day and at night to give him a snack, make sure he was okay, and inspect the now-healing incision in his stomach."

After another two weeks, Warpaint was able to be hand-walked. "We figured he would be his usual fire-breathing self, but he was actually very good about walking around in a halter." Judy started with a five-minute walk on level ground, then extended that time by a few minutes a day over the next six weeks. Eventually, they were walking for 30 minutes, "but still not on the trails, since he gets a little crazy once he puts those hooves outside the fence."

Back to Ridden Work

Eight weeks after surgery, Judy began walking Warpaint under saddle. "I really thought he might launch me the first time I got on, but much to my surprise, he was actually very good." They began walking for 30 minutes in the arena and gradually extended the time to a full hour over the next three weeks.

"Warpaint was back to his old ways, strong as ever, and showing no signs of his ordeal with the exception of the Frankenstein scar on his belly."

By the last week of August, 11 weeks after surgery, they were walking for an hour in the arena and Judy began adding a few minutes of trot, slowly increasing the time until they were working for an hour mostly at a trot. "We didn't do much cantering, since Warpaint really believes that the canter is a cue for him to take off at a dead run!"

In mid-September, the pair returned to the trail. "Warpaint was back to his old ways, strong as ever, and showing no signs of his ordeal with the exception of the Frankenstein scar on his belly." They began by walking up and down slight hills and doing some trots of about a mile. Since Warpaint was doing so well, they soon began trotting longer distances, increasing the distance by a couple of miles per ride. Judy also began to increase the hill work to strengthen his cardiovascular system. She kept slowly extending the distances and effort and after three more months, Warpaint was deemed ready to return to work as a competitive endurance horse. Or so they thought.

Setback

"At the Death Valley Encounter ride over the Christmas holiday, Warpaint developed a little cut in the coronary band on his left front hoof. It looked like a little scrape, but it turned out to be a quarter crack that extended from the middle of the hoof up into the coronary band. We took him to our vet and heard the bad news. It would take a long time to heal and a very long time to grow out. When a horse is put under anesthesia for surgery, it's very stressful to many of his internal systems. In his case it caused a weak spot to develop in his feet that just needed time to grow all the way out."

It may not have been an issue at all for another horse, but a small imbalance in his shoeing and the repetitive concussion of the Death Valley ride had taken its toll on Warpaint's still compromised feet. It took almost a year of very careful shoeing and very light work for this injury to heal. Warpaint could go for walks, but the endurance trail would have to wait.

Return to Competition

Warpaint's first ride back after the long recovery period was the prestigious "Race of Champions" 100-mile ride in Utah. "Warpaint really stood out in the crowd, being the lone Appaloosa among all the talented Arabian horses. We were having a good ride until about halfway, when he lost a shoe and came up a little footsore and had to be 'pulled.' But after that, we were back in business."

Warpaint went on to complete 3,000 more AERC endurance miles. During his career, he had only 10 "pulls" in 83 rides. He finished three out of five attempts at the Tevis Cup, and Judy and Warpaint were the first ever horse-and-rider team to complete 1,000 miles (during six rides) at the Death Valley Encounter.

Warpaint Today

Warpaint was retired at age 20 after completing 4,145 AERC endurance miles. He now lives with his barn buddies on a five-acre pasture. "We still ride him as often as we can, but usually by himself, so he won't think every ride is a race. Some men never change! We are really proud to have him be a part of our lives, and I like his legacy—he was known throughout the West as 'Warpaint, the Wonder Appaloosa of Endurance.'"

WARPAINT'S RECOVERY TIMELINE

May 30	Colic surgery.
June 15	Began hand-walking with 5 minutes daily, working up to 30 minutes a day over the next 6 weeks.
August 5	Began walking under saddle, beginning with 30 minutes and working up to 1 hour.
August 26	First ride at the trot. Began with 5 minutes of trot and worked up to rides of 1 hour, mostly at the trot.
September 16	Returned to riding on trails: working up and down slight hills and trotting longer distances.
December 25	Returned to competition.

JUDY AND NICK'S TIPS

- Pay attention to any changes in your horse's behavior. Subtle things like backing-up in his stall and shifting back and forth on his feet can mean something is very wrong.

- Even if everyone tells you, "It's nothing, don't worry," trust your instincts. No one knows your horse like you do.

- If you're feeling insecure in the saddle when you start your horse back to work, try riding in an Australian stock saddle. It's like riding with a seat belt.

- Postpone your horse's return to competition if there is any chance of hoof problems resulting from the surgery. Looking back, we should have waited at least six months after Warpaint finished his rehabilitation.

Warpaint
by Julie Suhr

(Julie Suhr has completed 22 Tevis Cups. At age 80, she competed in her twenty-third.)

All the bays, the grays, and the chestnuts stand in the vet line quietly. And then there is Warpaint.

All the bays, the grays, and the chestnuts bunch together as the ride starts. And then there is Warpaint.

The bays, the grays, and the chestnuts crowd each other on the trail, relying on the herd instinct of togetherness for safety. And then there is Warpaint.

He needs only his rider for, you see, Warpaint has always known he could take care of himself. After all, you could not put a spotted beauty such as he in the middle of the pack. So he just chose to be in front—even if his rider preferred another position. Who can't recall seeing the spotted beauty off by himself, pulling on the reins, asking for his head, begging Judy to go faster.

I think desert rides were his favorite. Always in the distance, a speck on the horizon, a solitary horse and rider, performing out of the sheer thrill of the challenge of the open trail ahead, the spotted rump always a dead giveaway as to their identity.

Judy's first horse, sharing the trails for over 13 years, a battle of wills at times, but a constant love affair, each benefiting from the companionship of the other, though always dueling for dominance.

There was never any doubt as to who was having the most fun. It wasn't the bays, the grays, or the chestnuts. It was always Warpaint.

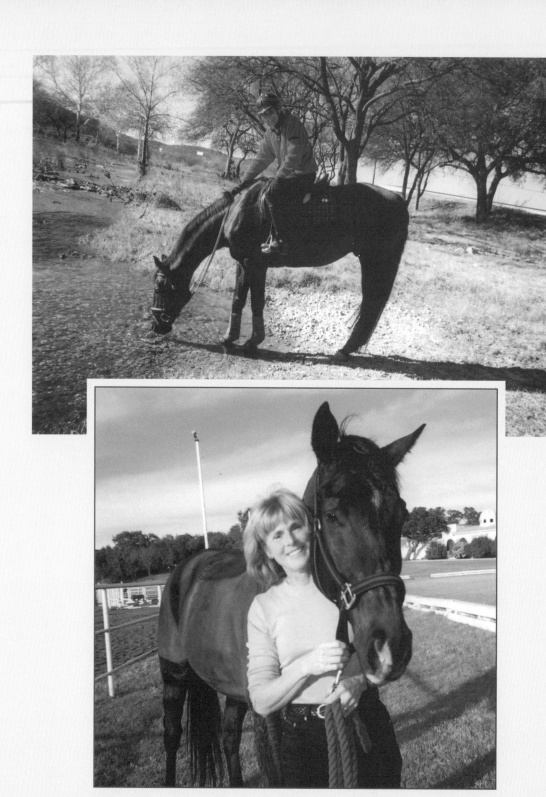

COLIC CASE STUDY 3

LINDY ARCHAMBAULT — Event Rider
NICK — Irish Thoroughbred

San Antonio, Texas

Lindy

"Riding is in my blood. My grandfather had a string of polo ponies and my uncle was Master of the Genesee Valley Hunt in upstate New York. I've ridden since I was seven, but didn't own my first horse until I was 32.

Lindy evented on and off for 15 years up to Training Level and trained five horses to First Level dressage and Training Level eventing. "I also taught riding for two years at the Fort Sam Houston Riding Stables in San Antonio and supervised a children's horsemanship camp. I'm a wife, mother, and grandmother who is lucky to be at a place in my life where I can devote a lot of time to my riding."

Irish Blessing aka "Nick"

A 16.1 Irish Thoroughbred that was untrained until the age of eight, "Nick was saddle broken when I got him but that was about it. We don't know where he was for six of those years—maybe a yard ornament. He was clueless about everything."

Lindy had heard about Nick from her trainers. "When I walked into his stall, he came over to me and nuzzled me as if to say, 'What took you so long to find me?' My friends say that he was a gift from my mother who passed away six years before. When we turned him out in the round pen and I saw him move, I knew he was the horse for me. I've always wanted a horse that would be competitive in the dressage phase of a horse trial but could never afford a horse of that caliber. Nick had perfect tempo,

Home Facility

Nick is boarded at a large, 50-stall barn in San Antonio. Boarders are a mix of eventers, hunters, dressage, and Western pleasure horses. There is an 800-meter galloping track with a hayfield in the middle and a smaller field with a water jump and a railroad-tie zig-zag jump.

"It isn't a very quiet place to ride—lots of people and the road in front of the barn is busy with motorcycles and ATVs going past. The farm owners also have several hundred head of exotic animals, including elk, gazelle, goats, and deer. When the grass in their fields grows really tall, all we can see are the tops of antlers and movement in the grass. The horses go nuts. If you're the unfortunate one to ride by first, unaware of the elk hiding in the grass…well, you know. We pass the word very quickly around the barn."

but when I rode him, I realized that he had no idea how to balance a rider let alone himself. We had a lot of work to do."

The Colic

"The day Nick colicked, late in July, he trotted out of his stall and into his run when I went to get him. When I was tacking him up, he didn't want to take the bit—all behavior that was out of the ordinary. Looking back, I should have sensed something was wrong, but since we'd only been together a short time, I didn't understand what he was trying to tell me—that he was already sick. I rode for almost 45 minutes before he showed obvious signs of being ill. I learned a big lesson that day. Horses communicate in many different ways; when you lead your horse out of the stall to tack him up, he'll tell you how he feels. Watch and 'listen' to him.

"Fortunately, my vet was at the barn and he made arrangements for us to go immediately to Retama Equine Hospital. I was so upset I couldn't get my trailer hitched up. A friend, who had driven over for a lesson, threw her horse in an empty stall, helped me with the trailer and rode with me to the clinic. That is true friendship…but now we look back and wonder why we didn't just take *her* trailer, which had been ready to go."

Diagnosis and Prognosis

"The prognosis was grave. We found out later that Nick had accidentally been fed moldy hay and become ill with gas colic. He must have then rolled and twisted his colon." After the vets at Retama examined Nick, they recommended euthanizing him.

"I remember sitting in front of his stall, seeing him suffering and thinking I should let him go. But my husband, in his infinite wisdom, said we had to give him a chance and that we should go ahead with the surgery. As it turned out, they only had to flip his colon back in place and Nick came through the surgery with flying colors."

At the time of the surgery on July 31, Lindy had owned the (now) almost nine-year-old Nick for just three months.

Rehabilitation

Early Days

Aside from hand-walking 20 to 30 minutes a day, Nick was confined to his stall for the first month. During the second month, he was allowed to go out into the small 12- by 20-foot run attached to his stall.

"Because our barn is so busy, with horses everywhere, hand-walking was often very difficult. I was worried that if I couldn't keep him quiet, he might rip his stitches out. One day, a boarder was grazing a horse in the field when I was nearby with Nick. Suddenly, her horse spooked, broke away from her, and galloped straight at Nick, who reared, bucked, and every other thing you can imagine, even a beautiful passage! I couldn't get control of him and a groom had to walk Nick back to the barn for me. He was fine, but it was a close call."

"The hardest part of rehab was knowing the best way to start that first day."

Back to Ridden Work

In early October, Lindy was given the go-ahead to begin walking Nick under saddle. "I think the hardest part of rehab was knowing the best way to start that first day. I made the decision to get on him in the indoor arena and picked a quiet part of the day praying that birds wouldn't decide to scramble on the roof or that one of the other boarders wouldn't come in to longe her bucking bronco. The first day went well as being out of shape kept Nick from any unusual antics. Luckily for me, there were no other distractions.

"I tried to plan our walks in the indoor arena for the early afternoon, when the morning lessons were done and the kids were still in school. Most of the time it worked out until the guys hauled a truck of hay by or decided to 'weed-eat' along the outside of the closed walls. If I ran into a lesson, I would stay out of the way. If I found myself with a wild horse and rider, I would leave the ring and walk outside to a quieter area."

"I tried to plan our walks in the indoor arena for the early afternoon, when the morning lessons were done and the kids were still in school."

When Lindy began trotting Nick in mid-October, "he felt like a piece of spaghetti. He still had a lot of spring, but he was pretty strung out and unbalanced." Over the next four weeks, they progressively built up his trot time, beginning with three minutes and working up to three sets of three-minute trots in a 20- to 30-minute ride. "We worked outside on the galloping track as much as possible, trotting by ourselves and sometimes with friends, always hoping the cows were not hiding by the fence line. Nick really enjoyed it when we could be with other horses.

"I rode Nick five days a week (not consecutively) and monitored his mood each day. Nick's moods are very easy to check—he never fails to tell you in some way that he's uncomfortable. We only had one setback during his rehab: the evening he had a very strained look on his face after a ride. I came to the conclusion that it was gas, so we gave him a shot of Banamine® and he was fine in 10 minutes. I now always keep Banamine paste on hand for those gassy times (see p. 356)."

While Nick was generally on his best behavior throughout his rehabilitation, there are always times when even the most mannerly of horses just can't help themselves.

"One evening, I was riding by myself. Nick was already a little cranky, as it was feeding time. As we came around the corner by the track, the elk were coming through the mist. Nick proceeded to trot and canter sideways down the field. I didn't know his body could go in that many directions, nor did he! A friend of mine saw him go by and couldn't believe it was Nick. I dismounted, but took him back to the outdoor arena. I remounted and proceeded to work for 10 more minutes. He got the message and quieted down very quickly."

Lindy began cantering Nick in mid-November (three-and-a-half months after surgery), gradually increasing his time at the canter in three- to five-minute increments. "Again, I always looked to Nick to tell me how he felt. If he acted sore after a ride, or his legs were swollen, then we would go back to riding straight lines on the track. I still follow this rule in my everyday riding."

Before Nick's surgery, Lindy had only longed him over fences a few times. In mid-December, she began trotting him over some small, simple gymnastics and also included trot poles on Nick's dressage days. "Once Nick was steady and confident with the gymnastics, we tried one fence at a time at a trot. We didn't canter fences for another month and then started schooling some of the cross-country fences on the property.

"When I bought Nick, he was just beginning to learn how to work and very suspicious about his new life. But nursing and grooming Nick every day while he was recovering created a bond between us that has really helped in his training. I trust him, and he trusts me to see him through new situations."

Return to Competition

Nick competed in his first dressage schooling show in February, seven months after surgery. At the end of May, he and Lindy competed successfully at the Meadow Creek Schooling Horse Trials.

Nick Today

"My daughter and her husband moved back to San Antonio so he could begin his medical residency, and Nick has become a family horse: my

"Nursing and grooming Nick every day while he was recovering created a bond between us that has really helped in his training. I trust him and he trusts me to see him through new situations."

daughter is learning dressage on Nick and my granddaughter is learning to post on him. He is a saint and loves them both."

Nick and Lindy are currently competing at Beginner Novice and schooling Novice Level. Two-and-a-half years after Nick's surgery, the pair earned third place honors in the Central Texas Eventing Association year-end rankings for Beginner Novice.

"Nick is my dear friend and so very loving. He is the best horse I've ever had. He is truly my Irish treasure."

NICK'S RECOVERY TIMELINE

July 31	Colic surgery.
August 10	Returned home. Began hand-walking 20 to 30 minutes per day.
October 2	Began walking under saddle for 20 minutes per day.
October 15	First ride at the trot, beginning with 3 minutes of trot and working up to 3 sets of 3-minute trots in a 20- to 30-minute ride.
November 15	First ride at the canter. Increased in 3- to 5- minute increments.
December 15	Began trotting small gymnastics.
January 15	Began cantering fences and schooling small cross-country obstacles.

February	Competed in dressage schooling show.
May 28	Returned to competition.

LINDY'S TIPS

- Monitoring your horse's progress means not only checking how he's doing physically but mentally as well. Make certain he's *mentally* willing to work each day. If horses are cranky and unwilling it is often a sign of physical discomfort, not disobedience. When you lead your horse out of his stall or paddock to tack him up, he'll tell you how he feels. Watch and "listen" to him.

- Never underestimate the support you can get from your non-horsey mate. My husband, David, is a very good problem solver and a fair and objective partner. When I was searching for answers with my emotional right brain, he would find the answer with a left-brain approach. When I wanted to give up on Nick, he was the one who wanted to give him a chance. David knew it was the right thing to do.

- Riding is not like putting a quarter in the slot of the hobby horse in front of K-Mart. When the ride is over you cannot just walk away. Owning a horse is a commitment just like a marriage. We owe these beautiful, proud animals the best care that we can give them. Their gentle spirit keeps them working and working for us. Aren't we lucky?

COLIC CASE STUDY 4

MICHELLE FERRERI – Hunter Rider
HASTINGS – Thoroughbred/Trakehner

Voorhees, New Jersey

Michelle

Michelle began riding at 11 at Camp Kiniya in Vermont. "I just loved the feel of riding, and when I came home, I began taking weekly lessons at an eventing barn in the area. When I was in sixth grade, I moved to another barn, which did more hunter/jumpers and began leasing my first horse. At our first show we did Beginner Rider and Pleasure classes—we were champion, and from that point on, I was hooked!"

By high school, Michelle was competing Hastings in the Children's Hunters at A, B, and C shows in New Jersey, Pennsylvania, and New York. At Lehigh University, she was a member of both the ski and equestrian teams, as well as continuing to compete Hastings. They showed in the Adult Amateur Hunters during her freshmen and sophomore years and in the Amateur Owner Hunters her junior and senior years. "It was tough to juggle everything, but I'm the type of person who needs lots of things going on. The more stuff, the easier it is for me to juggle it."

First Impression aka "Hastings"

The spring before her senior year in high school, the horse Michelle then owned "began to hate jumping and everyone agreed he had to go. Our first choice was to lease a horse, but horses of the quality we wanted were so expensive! It was agreed we would look to buy.

"I tried, no exaggeration, at least 25 horses that summer. I remember the first time I saw Hastings at a sale barn in northern New Jersey—he was standing on the cross-ties with white polos on. I immediately said to my trainer, 'I love that one; I want to ride him.' We took him to a show while he was on trial, and when we won a class in the Children's Over Fences, that just sealed the deal."

Michelle named the seven-year-old, 16.2-hand, chestnut Thoroughbred/Trakehner "First Impression" "because I fell in love with him the second I saw him. When we first got him, it was obvious he had not had a lot of human interaction. He didn't even know how to eat apples, so my mom would cut them up in small pieces for him. But after a few months, his personality really began to blossom."

The Colic

At the end of May, nine months after Michelle and Hastings began their partnership, they trailered to a week-long A show in central Pennsylvania. "When we look back on that trip, we realize that the show stressed him out more than usual, with a long trailer ride and hay he did not like and would not eat."

Home Facility

Michelle boarded Hastings at hunter barn in southern New Jersey, some 20 minutes from her home. The barn had approximately 30 horses, the majority of which regularly showed. The facility included two sand rings, an outdoor grass ring, and an indoor arena. Boarders also had access to 40 acres of trails.

Three days after their return, just as she was leaving high school for the day, Michelle got a call from the barn that Hastings was down in his stall. "By the time the vet got there, he was having trouble walking and appeared to be drunk. The vet examined him and declared he might have Equine Protozoal Myeloencephalitis (EPM) or some other mysterious neurological disease. She drew blood, did a rectal exam, gave him Banamine and left. She didn't think it was colic. Unfortunately, he was getting worse with each passing minute."

After more telephone conversations with the vet and the barn owner, who disagreed with the diagnosis, Michelle made the decision to trailer

Hastings to the Mid-Atlantic Equine Hospital.

"The 90-minute trip at breakneck speed was traumatic with Hastings getting lower and lower in the trailer. I fought with the barn owner and my mother because I wanted to ride in the trailer with him. I honestly thought he would go down before we got there. They both assured me that there was nothing I could do in the trailer so I rode up front in the truck, holding my breath every time I felt the trailer shift. Thank God, he stayed on his feet."

Diagnosis and Prognosis

Once at Mid-Atlantic, Hastings was taken immediately to a treatment room. "Yes, it was colic. He had a displaced colon and would need immediate surgery."

Hastings' colic episode happened on Michelle's last day of high school and just one day before her senior prom. "I told all this to the vet and he agreed to let me see Hastings early the next morning before official visiting hours. At that point he was not allowed out of his stall, so I just went in and talked to him. They let me curry him a little bit because he was covered in dried sweat from the day before. Then I went home, got my hair done and somehow went to the prom. The next morning I made the 90-minute drive to see him, as I did every day until he came home a week-and-a-half later."

Rehabilitation

Early Days

The first week of June, Hastings, "much thinner and visibly weak, arrived home with much celebration and became an instant celebrity in the barn." A detailed schedule of care was set up and written on a chart that was hung on his stall door. The chart recorded his temperature (taken three times a day), hand-walking schedule, "poop-pile count," and feedings.

Although the vet techs and vet students had instructed Michelle on the follow-up care Hastings would need once he returned home, she

"The 90-minute trip at breakneck speed was traumatic with Hastings getting lower and lower in the trailer. I honestly thought he would go down before we got there."

was "overwhelmed by the responsibility. I was 18 and had never been involved in caring for a horse that had been critically ill. I remember telling my mom and my trainer, 'I don't care if I ever ride him again; I just want him to be okay.'"

Michelle was also determined that she would be Hastings' principal caregiver. "I wanted to make sure we were doing everything right. It wasn't that I didn't trust anyone, but I just wanted to do it myself. I went to the barn early in the morning, took his temperature, counted the number of piles of poop in his stall, hand-walked him, and then cold-hosed his incision for 15 minutes. Then I would go home, shower, and go to work. I was really lucky because I was working for my dad that summer. While he is the most non-horsey person in the world, working for him meant I could get to the barn twice a day. I would leave work around two or three, drive back to the barn, hand-walk again, let him graze a little bit and then cold-hose again for 15 minutes.

"I was 18 and had never been involved in caring for a horse that had been critically ill. I remember telling my mom and my trainer, 'I don't care if I ever ride him again, I just want him to be okay.'"

"Hastings was actually really good about the hand-walking. Every once in a while a truck or something loud would drive by and he would jump a bit, but I always kept a chain over his nose just in case. Even though he tried to kick the vet every time he came to check on him, he stood like a statue when I cold-hosed his incision and was really good about letting me touch it. Without even realizing the significance of it, Hastings was now allowing me to take care of him. He had become dependent on me and he was a different horse."

Back to Ridden Work

The second week of July, seven weeks after his surgery, Michelle began walking Hastings under saddle. With guidance from her trainer, she laid out a specific schedule for Hastings' rehab. "Other than bringing Hastings back from a mild leg injury when I first got him, I had no experience with rehabbing a horse, so I was determined to be very cautious and very careful to not push him.

"Our first ride was great. Hastings was a complete angel and acted as if he had not skipped a beat since May. I had learned from Hastings' prior leg injury how important it is not to wander around aimlessly at the walk, so we 'power-walked.' That meant walking very *forward*, basically to the point where Hastings was walking fast enough he was almost trotting. We started out walking for 10 minutes in the indoor and eventually moved to the outside arena. I based my routine on what he could handle. If I saw he was getting tired, we would stop."

Michelle added five minutes of trot to their walk program during the third week of July and gradually increased it "by a few minutes" each time she rode. Late in July, Hastings was allowed to return to his usual turnout schedule. "We gave him a tranquilizer to make sure he didn't do anything crazy. He somehow managed to let out some bucks, but they were in slow motion. Almost like he was saying 'I am going to buck now.'"

Because she had planned on spending much of her summer getting ready for college, Michelle "hadn't set any high goals for the show season. But Hastings' injury did mean I wasn't able to do a few shows that I had been looking forward to, like the Lake Placid Show in New York. I was lucky that I did get to show my friend Cindi's horse, Montana. And because we weren't showing, I could really enjoy just spending time with Hastings and bonding with him."

By the beginning of August, Hastings was cantering—beginning with a canter around the arena in each direction—and Michelle could sense he was anxious to jump again. "When we began jumping in the middle of August, we started by trotting little cross-rails, then we would canter one jump and walk. We slowly worked up to cantering two jumps in a row. We did very little to start. I'd do one or two jumps and if he was good, I'd stop. It was amazing. And it made me realize how lucky I was to have my horse back. I only jumped a full course once or maybe twice before we went to our first horse show."

"I'd do one or two jumps and if he was good, I'd stop. It was amazing. And it made me realize how lucky I was to have my horse back."

Return to Competition

Just before Michelle headed off to college at the end of August, she decided to take Hastings to a large charity show at the Monmouth County Horse Park, about an hour from the farm. "I wouldn't recommend anyone doing it without first checking with their vet, but he had been jumping well and I really wanted to show him one time before I went to college. I entered him in the 2'6" division and he was champion out of 30 horses.

"We decided that when the new show year started in December, we would have a professional rider compete Hastings in the First Year Green Hunters, a professional division with jumps at 3'6". Hastings went on to qualify for and win a fifth place ribbon at the Washington International Horse Show. The next year I competed him in the Amateur Owner division and qualified for the Zone 2 Finals in Harrisburg, Pennsylvania, where I got ribbons on him. My Hastings was back!"

Hastings Today

"After his year in the Amateur Owner division, I decided he had more than done his job and I dropped him down to the 3' Adult Amateur division, where he still competes today, at the age of 16. Hastings and I are also now back home in New Jersey. He boards at a private farm 25 minutes from my home, and after clerking for a New Jersey Superior Court Judge, I am now a practicing attorney."

HASTINGS' RECOVERY TIMELINE

May 20	Colic surgery.
June 3	Returned home. Mornings: checked temperature, hand-walked for 15 minutes and cold-hosed incision for 15 minutes. Evenings: hand-walked for 15 minutes and cold-hosed incision for 15 minutes.

July 9	Began walking under saddle for 10 minutes a day.
July 16	First ride at the trot, beginning with 5 minutes and gradually increasing by "a few minutes" each ride.
August 4	First ride at the canter, beginning with one time around the arena in each direction.
August 21	Began jumping small cross-rails.
August 28	Returned to competition after clearance from the veterinarian.

MICHELLE'S TIPS

- Let your horse tell you when he's ready. After spending so much time with Hastings while he was recovering, we learned how to really read each other. I could always tell when he was getting tired or something was beyond his fitness level.

- Be patient. Honestly, it really isn't hard. Be willing to wait as long as it takes to make certain your horse has fully recovered.

- Hang a chart on the stall door where you can record your horse's temperature, hand-walking schedule, "poop-pile" count, and feedings.

- It's important not to wander around aimlessly when you are back walking under saddle. "Power-walk"!

Lisa Byk – Dressage Rider
Sass – Holsteiner/Thoroughbred

Howell, Michigan

Lisa

"The first photograph of me on a horse was taken when I was six months old. My aunt is holding the lead rope of one of her Arabians and my father is balancing me on the mare's back. It's one of those photos that you look back on now and wonder...what were the adults thinking?

"My aunts and uncles bred, sold, and showed Arabians and half-Arabians and I was always involved with horses, although I didn't start showing until I was 15." When Lisa did begin to compete, her show schedule included classes in everything from 4-H hunt seat equitation and Western pleasure to saddleseat equitation and First Level dressage. She began concentrating on dressage her freshman year in college.

Lisa is a single mother to three horses, three barn cats, and a dog. She works part-time as a receptionist for a local animal hospital and for the *Livingston County Daily Press & Argus* doing graphic design work.

Valboa's Mercedes aka "Sass"

A 16-hand Holsteiner/Thoroughbred mare, Sass was bred by Lisa's trainer, Valerie Mortier. "Because her previous owner had been intimidated by Sass, I bought a five-year-old that didn't cross-tie, didn't longe very well, didn't trailer well, and didn't have much respect for the people handling her.

"But what Sass did have was the willingness to learn and just be loved by somebody. One day, during the first week I was getting to know her,

Sass buried her head in my stomach and closed her eyes. That was when I knew she was ready to give me her heart and be owned by somebody who would love her right back."

In their nine years together, Lisa and Sass went from Training Level to Third Level, earning their United States Dressage Federation (USDF) bronze medal and were named the American Warmblood Society's Adult Amateur Horse of the Year.

The Colic

Sass had undergone colic surgery two years prior when she was 10—"no torsion, no impaction, and no resection, and her return to work had been uneventful. But because of that colic, I was always very watchful. And all through the pregnancy with Chevy, Sass had on and off gas colic episodes, which also continued post-foaling.

"On September 15, Sass became restless, unable to get comfortable. She'd lie down and stay still, get up and walk around, paw at the ground, then lie down and roll. I knew immediately that this colic was worse than the previous post-foaling ones. I'm not sure if Chevy was helpful or not, but each time Sass went to lie down, he would run at her and jump on her to get her back up on her feet."

Lisa and her veterinarian made the decision to trailer Sass to Michigan State University (MSU) and leave four-month-old Chevy behind for an unexpected weaning. "Fortunately, I had spent the last two months working up to weaning day by separating Sass and Chevy while I began riding Sass again. Chevy was used to being by himself in the stall—but only for a few hours every day.

"We gave both Sass and Chevy a very mild sedative for the separation and brought Parfait, my other mare, inside the barn and put her in the stall directly across from Chevy. This was definitely not the way I had

Home Facility

Sass was stabled at Lisa's home, a five-acre farm with a grass riding arena. The farm was also home to Lisa's 18-year-old Arabian mare, Parfait, and Sass' Holsteiner colt, Chevelle ("Chevy").

"I knew immediately that this colic was worse than the previous ones."

planned the final weaning process, and I was absolutely terrified about leaving Chevy at home with no one to keep a watchful eye on him until friends could check on him some four hours later."

Diagnosis and Prognosis

Within an hour of their arrival, Sass was operated on for a bowel torsion, impaction and a gas pocket. During the four days she was hospitalized, Lisa made the 40-minute drive to MSU each morning. "I really believe that this helped her recovery. We went for short walks and Sass was allowed to eat a little bit of the grass growing in a patch near the parking lot. The vet students who were sitting outside on their breaks were always very nice to us and even came up to Sass to offer their sympathy."

Rehabilitation

Early Days

When Sass was released, Lisa made certain she had contact information for the surgeons so she could follow-up with e-mails on Sass' progress. "They were great about answering my questions on how to revamp Sass' diet—switching her to Equine Senior, which is lower in starches and easier to digest; adding powdered milk for more calcium; aloe vera to help with any problems with stomach acid; and starting her on a biotin supplement. They also gave me a schedule that laid out how much hand-grazing I could allow on our hand-walks and how much and what kind of hay (very little alfalfa) Sass could have. I also sent digital photos of how the incision line was healing.

"The only thing that really took a toll on me during Sass' recovery was how stressed she was being confined to her stall."

"The only thing that really took a toll on me during Sass' recovery was how stressed she was being confined to her stall. The whole time I owned Sass, she was not a huge fan of stalls. When she wanted out, she'd rear. I can't tell you the number of water buckets she wrecked when her front feet landed in them. During her first surgery recovery, it was a real challenge to keep her quiet in a stall for 30 days with hand-walking two or three times a day. This time, to make it even more difficult, Sass was focused on getting back outside to be with her colt. And Chevy, who was now with Parfait in the pasture furthest from the barn, knew exactly when Sass arrived back home and started screaming for her."

To keep Sass as calm as possible, Lisa made certain that she always had hay in front of her and kept the barn radio on 24 hours a day. "The radio prevented Sass from hearing Chevy calling for her, and after about two days she finally settled down. We actually made it through the first two weeks with only a few rearing incidents and minor panic attacks."

When Sass' staples were removed 10 days after surgery, Lisa, with the consent of MSU's Dr. Paul Robinson and her own vet, Dr. Rob Renton, began turning Sass out in her grass dressage arena while she cleaned stalls. "Someone was always there to make sure all she did was graze quietly, and even as little as 10 or 15 minutes of turnout made her a much easier patient to work with and also helped increase her water intake. There were times when she would just refuse to drink any water, but when put back into her stall from her short turnout period, she'd suck down the entire bucket.

"During the first hand-walk with Sass, she was actually quite well-behaved. Even though Chevy called for her, she remained calm and only called back once or twice. She was more interested in trying to drag me around to get to the best grazing area. As long as she was eating, she was in heaven!"

But despite the daily hand-walks and time spent grazing in the dressage arena, Sass was "becoming extremely claustrophobic and mentally, she was fried from being confined to a stall. Thirty days after surgery, it was decided (with the consent of her vets) that for Sass' safety and well-being and the safety of anyone working with her, she should have unlimited access to the 12- by 24-foot paddock connected to her stall. It would take us another three months of slowly reintroducing her to stalls to get her to relax again in them. By this time, Chevy was well attached to Parfait and Sass was accustomed to being pastured by herself. So things worked out well."

Back to Ridden Work

On Halloween, 45 days after the surgery, Lisa hauled Sass to her trainer's barn, Valboa Farms, to begin work under saddle. Since the facility had an indoor arena, she also decided that Sass should board at Valboa for the winter so her rehab work could be consistent.

"For the first week at Valerie's, Sass got to just settle in with her pasturemates. The following weekend, I got on and walked her around the indoor arena. Even though the first ride wasn't anything special, it felt great to just be on my mare again. My friends laughed at me because I spent most of that first ride lying on Sass' neck hugging her with a huge smile on my face.

"Over the next few weeks I began using ground poles—three or four poles laid either in a straight line or on a very large circle—to work on Sass' walk and liven up the hours we spent walking in the arena. And since Valerie's indoor has a stereo system, I could listen to music, something that really helped the time pass. I was also able to try out pieces I thought might work when Sass and I returned to doing musical freestyles, and that gave me something to look forward to during the hours and hours of walking."

Use ground poles—three or four poles laid either in a straight line or on a very large circle—to work on the quality of the walk and liven up the hours spent walking in the arena.

Because of Sass's pregnancy, foaling, and colic surgery, she had been off regular work for almost a year. This meant that Lisa would be reconditioning as well as rehabilitating her mare. "But we had all winter to work before the show season was upon us. If everything took a little while longer, that was fine. We just took it slowly."

After six weeks of walking under saddle, Lisa began adding trot work, beginning with five minutes and increasing the trot work in five-minute increments. Two weeks later, they added five minutes of canter work, gradually increasing it till they were cantering for 15 minutes. Lateral work waited until January, four months after surgery. "When we started lateral movements we did shoulder-in and leg-yield. Then we worked slowly toward haunches-in and half-pass. Everything went quite well and the only bumps we hit were strength-related. Then, I'd just back off and ask for a little less."

Return to Competition

In June, nine months after surgery, Sass and Lisa returned to the show ring. "For the first season back we just competed at First and Second Level because Sass wasn't quite ready for the strength that was required at Third Level. Our big accomplishment that first season back was winning the Second Level Adult Amateur Championship at the July dressage show at Lamplight in Illinois. By the next year, we were back to showing Third Level.

"It's amazing how something like this changes a person. Prior to the second surgery my goals always revolved around showing and going as far as I could with Sass. Now, I focused more on Sass' well-being. I no longer wanted to ride multiple tests a day and go for that championship. My goals were to get through the test and be pleased with how I rode and how my mare performed. I wanted to leave the show that last day with a horse that wasn't worn out or stressed from a long show. Because of the change in my priorities, Sass was concentrating on working *with* me rather than anticipating which movement was coming up next in the test. She was waiting for me to ask her for every movement—with the exception of flying changes. She loved doing these and she seemed to think she knew more about them than I did!

"The things that Sass taught me will be carried onto other horses for the rest of my life. She taught me that yes, winning is fun, but what's really special is doing well with a horse that wants to please you and constantly gives you 110 percent."

Sass

Lisa lost Sass to Potomac Horse Fever two years after her second colic surgery. "We were at a show when she went off her feed and water. Her temperature spiked up as well. I immediately hauled her home and after the diagnosis of Potomac Horse Fever was made, we trailered her up to MSU and gave her supportive care for 48 hours before making the difficult decision to release her from her pain. It was my final gift to Sass. Our partnership started with Sass nestling her head in my stomach. And that's the way it came to an end, with Sass putting her head in my lap and closing her eyes.

"Sass' legacy now lives on through her son, Chevy, who will soon be four years old. He's inherited a lot of Sass' traits and is proving that he loves having a job like his mother did. The future will definitely be interesting with him around."

SASS' RECOVERY TIMELINE

September 15	Colic surgery.
September 19	Returned home. Began hand-walking 2 to 3 times a day, working up to 30 minutes.
November 3	Began walking under saddle, working up to 45 minutes over 6 weeks.
December 15	First ride at the trot, starting with 5 minutes of trot and increasing in 5-minute increments until trotting for 35 minutes.
January 1	First ride at the canter, starting with 5 minutes of canter and increasing in 5-minute increments until cantering for 20 minutes.

January 15	Lateral work added.

June	Returned to competition.

Lisa's Tips

- Keep in touch with the equine surgeon. Get the contact information at the veterinary hospital while signing the discharge papers and before you load the horse up. It's important to continue that relationship even after you get your horse back home after surgery.

- Consider using massage and chiropractic. To help Sass out post-surgery, I had her massaged every few weeks. I also started her back on a chiropractic program. This ended up being a great combination and it was really key in getting Sass back to a competitive level again.

- When others offer to help...take it! Don't be afraid to ask others for a hand. It's difficult to hold your own mentally and physically the first 30 days. You need to be able to give yourself a break every now and then to continue staying strong for your horse.

- If you have any doubts about how you horse's incision is healing, take pictures with a digital camera and e-mail them to your vet.

- Keeping a radio on in the barn can help a horse feel a little less lonely when his friends are turned out and he has been left behind.

Chapter 3

Ligament and Tendon Injuries

Before I began writing *Back to Work*, my knowledge of equine ligament and tendon injuries was largely limited to what I had read in various horse magazines and absorbed over the years from general reference books. As I started my research for this chapter I hoped to gather enough information to construct an overview of the more commonly experienced injuries of the internal structures of the horse's leg that would be both current and accessible to the lay reader. But it soon became apparent that while there was a myriad of information available, it was difficult to find a source that could clearly explain a superficial digital flexor tendon injury, or proximal suspensory desmitis. Thankfully, I discovered Dr. Nancy Loving's *All Horse Systems Go: The Horse Owner's Full-Color Veterinary Care and Conditioning Resource for Modern Performance, Sport and Pleasure Horses* (see *Resources*, p. 372). In her chapter devoted to tendons and ligaments, Dr. Loving had already managed to write precisely what I hoped to eventually compile, and it only made sense to excerpt a section of her excellent text and reprint it here.

In the pages following, I've included eight ligament injury case studies (pp. 94–170) and then six tendon injury stories (pp. 176–234).

INTRODUCTION

by Nancy S. Loving, DVM
(excerpt from *All Horse Systems Go*)

The Difference between Tendons and Ligaments

Tendons connect muscles to bones. Like a system of levers and pulleys, muscles contract, transmitting their force through the tendons to the bones. With each muscular movement, connecting tendons move the bones to propel a horse along the ground. In design, tendons withstand loading of a horse's mass on his skeletal system by dissipating concussion and strain. Tendons must be strong yet retain sufficient elasticity to deform and return to their resting shape and length. An example of a major tendon in the lower leg is the *superficial digital flexor tendon* (SDFT) that runs along the very back of the cannon bone, connecting the superficial flexor muscle of the forearm to the bones of the pastern.

Ligaments, while of similar fibrous composition as tendons, are less elastic. Their function is to attach bones to each other across a joint. Ligaments stabilize the joints from overstretching, overflexing, or twisting. An important ligament to an athletic horse is the *suspensory ligament,* which originates just below the bottom of the carpus joint (knee) or the hock. It runs as a pair down each side of the cannon bone to the back of the *sesamoid bones* of the fetlock joint where they then branch out along each side of the pastern. The suspensory ligaments take a considerable amount of punishment during downhill travel, over jumps, and during sudden stops and turns. Other important ligaments, the *collateral ligaments*, are located alongside joints, helping to hold them in place by limiting side to side movement. Collateral ligaments may be injured by abnormal rotation of a joint from a misstep.

Predisposing Factors to Soft Tissue Injury

Most tendon or ligament injuries occur during exercise involving an intense activity and/or as a horse performs a movement with a leg not quite square beneath him. Each time a horse sets his foot down, tendons are loaded and stretched. This is normal, as they stretch and rebound to their original configuration. If soft tissues are asked to perform beyond their developed strength during a particularly rigorous exercise, or if a horse's muscles are fatigued, failure can result.

A tendon is comprised of many fibers arranged parallel to one another. Like a rubber band that is stretched too far, a tendon and its fibers may similarly overstretch and fail to return to original length. Or, tendon fibers may tear or rupture. This results in a *bowed* tendon. Ligament doesn't have nearly the elastic stretch of a tendon, and is more easily stretched and torn. A sudden twisting force on a joint may result in ligamentous injury. Injury to a tendon is called *tendonitis*, while to a ligament it is referred to as *desmitis*.

A traumatic blow from an opposite foot, a kick, or contact with a stationary object like a rock or tree also creates soft-tissue injury that must

Since **Dr. Nancy Loving** graduated from Colorado State University Veterinary School in 1985, she has practiced equine medicine and surgery exclusively, currently at her own Loving Equine Clinic in Boulder, Colorado. She has been involved in the endurance world as an FEI-sanctioned veterinarian and as a team vet for the United States Equestrian Federation (USEF) national endurance squad, bringing to these pursuits her knowledge gleaned from many miles and years spent in the saddle training and competing her own endurance horses.

Dr. Loving regularly writes for *The Horse* and *Horse Illustrated* magazines and is the author of three books (see *Resources,* p. 372).

be treated as a stress-related failure. A wound or laceration can irritate tissues surrounding tendons or may disrupt tendon fibers. Constriction of soft tissues and surrounding circulation by an incorrectly applied bandage also has the potential to create significant tendon or ligamentous injury.

Not all soft-tissue injuries occur during a single event. Sometimes damage results from cumulative overuse, ultimately leading to failure. Repeated stretching of a tendon with each footfall may damage surrounding tissues that supply nutrients to the tendon tissues. With intensive exercise, such as galloping, the interior portions of the tendons heat up and may be subject to thermal injury. In either case, with time, progressive degeneration may transform a simmering problem into a recognizable injury.

A previously injured tendon or ligament is more at risk for reinjury since these soft tissue structures "heal" with scar tissue instead of replacement with normal fiber architecture. Sometimes the tissues thicken, and occasionally may calcify. Elasticity is less than optimal so fibers are more prone to disruption from stretching.

Injury-Prone Areas

There are a multitude of tendons and ligaments throughout a horse's body, but discussed below are those that most commonly incur injury in an athletic horse.

Cannon Bone Region

Superficial Digital Flexor Tendon

One of the most commonly injured soft tissue structures of the athletic horse is the *superficial digital flexor tendon* (SDFT). Significant strain to this tendon results in a bowed appearance, giving it the name *bowed tendon*. Injury occurs when the SDFT is placed under excess tension, especially as the fetlock is at its maximum drop just before a horse's foot leaves the ground. The danger of injury increases if a foot "sticks" and cannot lift off the ground yet the horse's body continues to propel forward. The SDFT is at greatest risk of strain because its point of rotation is farthest from the fetlock joint than other tendinous structures, so it receives the greatest strain. Many SDFT injuries occur at the point where the superficial digital flexor has the smallest cross-sectional area, which is in the middle of the cannon bone area. As the tendon's cross-sectional area decreases, it becomes stiffer and less elastic. In addition, there is an increased force per unit area on this narrower segment of the tendon.

Inferior Check Ligament

The accessory ligament of the deep digital flexor tendon is also referred to as the *inferior check ligament*, or IFCL. Injury to this ligament usually occurs in older horses as a result of athletic strain, most often developing on a front limb. In an acute injury, there is pain and swelling just above the midpoint of the cannon bone. A horse in pain may tip his heel off the ground and stand with the fetlock slightly flexed. Ultrasound exam defines the extent of injury, and examines surrounding structures, like the superficial and deep digital flexor tendons, that might also be affected.

This is a difficult injury to resolve, with successful return to athletic function noted in only 43 to 75 percent of those treated with three months of box stall rest, anti-inflammatory medications, and controlled walking rehabilitation over another three-month period. Recurrence is likely with this injury. One recommendation that has been made for chronic or recurrent cases is to cut the IFCL by a surgery referred to as an *inferior check desmotomy*. A more guarded outlook must be taken when there is concurrent injury to the superficial and/or deep flexor tendons, as well.

Proximal Suspensory Ligament

Injury to the uppermost third of the suspensory ligament is known as *proximal suspensory desmitis*, and can develop on a front or rear limb. Horses with straight hocks, or those engaged in activities (jumping, cutting, reining, calf roping, polo, or trail events with downhill trot or canter) that require hyperextension of the fetlock are most at risk. Use of the longe line is incriminated in creating proximal suspensory injury as well as fostering reoccurrence. Heel wedges also increase the risk of this injury, as does a long-toe low-heel (LTLH) hoof configuration.

Initially, when a horse suffers a front limb suspensory injury, he may demonstrate discomfort by shortening the stride. This can be an insidious lameness problem that starts out as a seemingly mild problem and responds to rest and confinement, only to reoccur following any exercise.

In a rear limb, lameness is worse when the affected hind is on the outside of a circle, or when a horse is exercised on a soft or deep surface. When a rear limb is affected, the lameness doesn't usually respond to rest, and instead continues to worsen. Some horses demonstrate discomfort by reluctance to go forward when asked; there is often a noticeable reduction in hind limb impulsion. Lameness also worsens when a rider "sits" on the weight-bearing diagonal of the affected limb.

Digital pressure over an injured proximal suspensory ligament does not always elicit a pain reaction from a horse. The normally sharp margins to a ligament may feel rounded along with a stiffer feel to an affected ligament. Radiographic exam is necessary to identify if there is a concurrent fracture of the outermost portion of the cannon bone or an *avulsion* (tearing away) fracture that sometimes accompany a suspensory injury. Definitive diagnosis depends upon a diagnostic nerve block to infuse anesthetic locally in the area of concern, coupled with a thorough ultrasound exam.

Proximal suspensory desmitis is a difficult problem to manage. Affected forelimbs reoccur 20 percent of the time, while hind leg proximal suspensory desmitis reoccurs 65 percent of the time. Application of shock wave therapy (ESWT) along with conventional anti-inflammatory therapy and controlled exercise has yielded a greater success rate for continued return to athletic function (see p. 366).

Curb

Curb refers to inflammation or tearing of the *plantar tarsal ligament* at the back outside aspect of the hock. It is easily confused with an overly developed splint bone. Also, inflammation of a rear limb superficial flexor tendon is sometimes confused as a curb because of close proximity of the tendon to the plantar tarsal ligament. Sickle-hocked conformation increases the propensity to develop inflammation of the plantar tarsal ligament. It may also occur as a result of a horse's rear limb slipping as he pushes up a steep hill or as a result of rapid sprint acceleration.

Fetlock Region

Low Bow

If the *deep digital flexor tendon* (DDFT) is injured, a *low bow* results. Tendon injuries in the fetlock area or below have a poorer prognosis than injuries higher on the limb. Because of the digital sheath over the tendon in this area, more connective tissue develops beneath the skin (subcutaneous) in the healing process. This tissue restricts gliding of the tendon through the sheath.

Volar Anular Ligament Injury

The *volar anular ligament* (VAL), a non-elastic band of dense connective tissue, runs horizontally across the back of the fetlock, and may be involved in a low bow. The volar anular ligament does not stretch as the deep digital flexor tendon swells; then the ligament binds down the inflamed tendon. This unrelenting pressure reduces blood flow to the tendon over time. Fiber death, reduction in gliding motion, and development of adhesions bind the two structures together as a result of reduced blood flow. The ligament constricts, resulting in a visible depression over the back of the fetlock, with a pronounced bulge above and/or below, near the digital tendon sheath.

Immediate surgical intervention to release the constricting ligament allows a more favorable prognosis for a horse to return to function. If adhesions are allowed to progress too long before surgery, they "glue" the structures together, permanently restricting the tendon and causing a mechanical lameness.

Degenerative Suspensory Desmitis

Some horse breeds, such as Peruvian Pasos, Paso Finos, and Andalusians, experience notable degeneration of the branches of the suspensory apparatus for reasons unrelated to trauma or injury. A high degree of breed-related incidence implicates a possible genetic component, and current information suggests that this is part of a progressive systemic disease of connective tissue containing abnormally elevated levels of proteoglycans. Older horses of any breed, especially broodmares, may suffer the same condition. The problem typically appears in the hind limbs. The fetlocks sink as suspensory support progressively declines. There is often associated stiffness or lameness related to suspensory and/or fetlock pain. Nothing can be done other than to keep a horse comfortable on soft ground, or bedding to prevent abrasions of the fetlock. Attempts can be made to support the fetlock and pastern joints by extending the heel branches of the shoes, or using elongated egg bar shoes.[*]

REHABILITATING A
LIGAMENT OR TENDON INJURY

by Barb Crabbe, DVM

A WEEK-BY-WEEK PLAN

This plan is designed to function as a road map for riders rehabilitating a horse from a suspensory ligament or tendon injury. Working with your own veterinarian, you can use this map to customize a rehabilitation program that will address the specific needs of your horse and his injury.

---

[*] From "Strong Tendons and Ligaments." *All Horse Systems Go: The Horse Owner's Full-Color Veterinary Care and Conditioning Resource for Modern Performance, Sport and Pleasure Horses* (North Pomfret, Vermont: Trafalgar Square, 2006) 181–8.

As you will see, the plan is based on "controlled exercise," which has become the gold standard for bringing horses back to work. We now know that movement (controlled exercise) causes "good stresses" to occur across damaged tissue and encourages correct fiber alignment as the injury heals. The plan begins with daily hand-walking as soon as possible after the injury has been diagnosed.

Check your horse's leg each and every day, before and after you exercise him—whether it is simply hand-grazing or work under saddle. Any lameness (and that includes being "just a little bit off") or unusual heat in the leg is a sign that something may be wrong. Never hesitate to call your veterinarian if you sense something is not going well for your horse.

Stall Rest

It's essential that a horse be confined to a stall, a stall/run, or a size-restricted paddock (generally no larger than 14 by 24 feet) until your veterinarian says it is okay to return him to his regular paddock and turnout schedule. One leaping/bucking/galloping episode may be all it takes for him to reinjure himself.

Q&A

What if my horse is hard to handle because he's been confined to his stall—what should I do?

If your horse becomes hard to handle during the time he's confined to a stall, talk to your veterinarian about the possibility of sedating him. We often recommend acepromazine (see p. 365), which is a safe and inexpensive medication that can be given orally (or injected if the owner is comfortable). Herbal "calming" supplements such as Valerian, tryptophan, or B vitamins are other alternatives (see p. 277).

You might also consider investing in a stall "toy"—the best are those that deliver a small food treat when horses manipulate them. Pasture Pal™ is a good one that mimics grazing behavior (see *Resources*, p. 367).

Dr. Barb Crabbe is a graduate of University of California—Davis School of Veterinary Medicine. She completed an internship in large animal medicine and surgery at Washington State University and did graduate work on biomechanics at UC—Davis, where she studied patterns of locomotion in exercising horses. She is currently in private practice in Portland, Oregon.

Dr. Crabbe is a contributing editor to *Horse & Rider* magazine and a frequent contributor to and member of the advisory board for *Dressage Today*. A graduate with distinction from the United States Dressage Federation (USDF) "L" judges program, she serves on the Oregon Dressage Society's Board of Directors.

An avid dressage rider and competitor, she and Darwin, her Oldenberg gelding, recently earned their USDF silver medal.

Hand-Walking

A horse should be hand-walked at least once a day. If you can manage it two times or have friends who can pitch-in and help, that's great, but don't feel guilty if dealing with a job or family means you can only get to the barn once a day.

Weekly Schedule

At least once daily:

    Week 1: 10 minutes

    Week 2: 15 minutes

    Week 3: 20 minutes

    Week 4: 25 minutes

    Week 5: 30 minutes

    Week 6: 35 minutes

    Week 7: 40 minutes

    Week 8: 45 minutes

Q&A

Does walking mean strolling or walking at a brisk pace?
Walking means "marching" not ambling along or stopping to let your horse graze.

Does the footing matter? Can you walk on a driveway or hard ground?
Footing does matter. It should be solid, consistent, even, and level. Avoid walking on deep or soft ground, and in deep sand.

My horse is generally much better behaved under saddle than when he's being hand-walked. Is it possible to ride my horse at the walk through the hand-walking section of his rehab? Any other suggestions?
If you're comfortable with your riding skills and find it easier to keep your horse under control when you're riding than when you're on the ground, discuss this option with your veterinarian.

Ponying is another option if your horse can be kept straight, not dancing sideways next to you (see Riding in Pairs, p. 287).

Walking under Saddle

Caution: Consult your veterinarian before beginning to walk your horse under saddle.

The horse should be ridden a minimum of five days a week and remain confined to a small stall, stall/run, or turned out in a size-restricted paddock.

Weekly Schedule

Walking once daily, at least five days a week:

Week 1: 30 minutes
Week 2: 35 minutes
Week 3: 40 minutes
Week 4: 45 minutes

Q&A

What should I do if I'm afraid my horse will act up and possibly hurt himself, or me, the first few times we ride?

If you're concerned about his behavior, consult your veterinarian about the possibility of mildly sedating him for the first few rides.

If he's more relaxed in the company of other horses, ask a friend or two to ride with you. Consider working in a confined space such as an indoor arena or an outdoor arena with fencing. And most importantly, wear your helmet every time you ride!

Should I ride my horse on a long rein or can I ask him to come into a frame?

It can be either. Stretching is also an option.

Should the walking be primarily on straight lines?

Yes, especially in the early stages. Riding the short ends of an arena is okay as long as there's not a deep track and you can keep your horse balanced. This means you *must* be able to keep him from bending or leaning sideways in a way that puts too much weight on his injured leg—not an easy task! If he's unbalanced, you take the chance he might reinjure himself.

May I do easy lateral work such as a leg-yielding?

No, not initially. I know everyone wants to do lateral work to break up the monotony, but it's very stressful on the soft tissues and risks reinjury. I don't recommend lateral work until the horse is cantering.

What about circles?

Big circles (20 meters or larger) are allowed *if*—and only if—your horse can stay truly balanced.

Can I walk up and down small hills?

In my experience, it's best to avoid hills until your horse is working at the canter.

I don't have access to an indoor arena, so what can I do about days that are "washouts" because of rain or snow? How do I stay on track with the program if weather doesn't permit me to ride regularly?

Buy rain gear and warm clothes! Find someone to help you who doesn't mind the cold or rain.

If you're lucky enough to live near a facility that has a horse treadmill, or even better, an underwater treadmill or pool where you can "swim" your horse, consider adding these high-tech options to your rehab program (see Swimming, p. 304).

At the end of four weeks of walking under saddle, you should be able to incorporate trot work into your rehab schedule.

Trotting under Saddle

Caution: Consult your veterinarian before adding trot work to your horse's program.

Your horse should be ridden a minimum of five days a week, while turnout remains limited with the horse confined to a stall, a stall/run, or a size-restricted paddock. Depending on the severity of your horse's injury and his progression in the healing process, trot work can be added in increments of two to five minutes per week. Work with your veterinarian to customize a program for your horse.

Weekly Schedule

Once daily, at least five times a week, add trot work to 30 minutes of walking as follows:

Week 1: 2 minutes
Week 2: 4 minutes
Week 3: 6 minutes
Week 4: 8 minutes
Week 5: 10 minutes
Week 6: 15 minutes.
Week 7: 20 minutes

Week 8: 25 minutes
Week 9: 30 minutes

A horse trotting for 30 minutes can begin work on 20-meter circles as well as the longe line. If working your horse on the longe line, make certain the work is controlled—absolutely no bucking, bolting, or cantering.

Q&A

How should I expect my horse to feel when we begin trotting?
Most likely, he'll feel "stiff" or even like you're "riding a wet noodle." All of this is to be expected. If you have any doubts at all about how he feels or something simply doesn't seem right, call your veterinarian.

When can I begin trotting my horse in a frame?
Riding on a long rein or with contact is fine.

Should I begin by trotting on straight lines?
Yes.

My only place to work is an arena. At what point may I trot through the corners?
If your corners are at least 20 meters wide, you can trot through them at the beginning of the trot program, but *only* if you can keep your horse balanced (see p. 84).

When may I add circles or begin working my horse on the longe line?
Trotting circles puts additional stress on legs. Working on circles and the longe line should wait until your horse is trotting soundly for 30 minutes and you have the okay from your veterinarian.

Is there anything I can't do at the trot?
No walking or trotting up and down hills, lateral work, serpentines,

figure eights, or circles. All these should wait until your horse is working solidly at the canter.

What are the signs that I may have asked too much of my horse?
Lameness, excessive heat, or swelling—if any of these occur, call your veterinarian.

Once a horse is trotting for 30 minutes, he should be able to beginning cantering.

Cantering under Saddle

Caution: Consult your veterinarian before adding canter work to your horse's program.

A horse should be ridden a minimum of five days a week, while turnout remains limited to a stall, a stall/run, or a size-restricted paddock.

Weekly Schedule
During daily rides of 45 minutes to an hour, at least five days a week, add:
   Week 1: 5 minutes of canter on straight lines only
   Week 2: 10 minutes of canter on straight lines only
   Weeks 3–8: Continue to increase work at the canter by 5 minutes per week. It should take about one to two months to get back to full work once canter work begins.

Q&A
Should I begin by cantering on straight lines only?
Yes, the same as with the trot.

When may I begin to canter a 20-meter circle?
It depends on the injury, but generally after several weeks of steadily improving work at the canter. Guidelines for the canter aren't quite as specific as for work at the other gaits—at some point common sense has to come into play.

When can I add lateral work, serpentines, figure-eights, and other more advanced work?

Again, common sense should prevail, so usually after several weeks. Most of the actual rehab from a suspensory ligament or tendon injury takes place at the trot because of the symmetry of the repetitive motion. Once you start adding canter, followed by lateral work, the injury should, theoretically, be "healed."

ACTIVE REHABILITATION OF SUSPENSORY LIGAMENT INJURIES

by Richard B. Markell, DVM

New diagnostics such as nuclear scintigraphy, high resolution digital radiography, and magnetic resource imaging (MRI), and new treatment options (see *Resources*, p. 365) now allow more than 80 percent of horses diagnosed with suspensory ligament injuries to return to their previous level of work. (Branch suspensory lesions have a slightly lower percentage of return.)

While these optimum therapies rarely accelerate the time your horse will need to spend in rehab (there is a genetic limitation on the speed of cellular recovery, and ligaments take from three to 12 months to heal) they can significantly improve the *quality* of healing. And if a ligament injury heals with a better fiber pattern, more elasticity, less fibrosis, and fewer adhesions, the chances of re-occurrence are lessened.

In addition to new diagnostics and therapies, significant advances have been made in our understanding of how horses should be rehabilitated. While horses once suffered through six months of incarceration in box stalls—and too rarely returned to full work—current research has shown us that ligaments must undergo stress in order to heal well. *Active rehabilitation* or "controlled exercise" is now the norm for bringing horses back to work. Carefully planned "ramping-up" of exercise will provide much needed stress on tissues. This stress will in turn stimulate healing without overloading and reinjuring delicate, newly repaired tissue.

But despite all these advances, strict hands-on attention must still be paid to all aspects of your horse's recovery and rehabilitation. Close and accurate monitoring of the process will afford your horse the best recovery possible.

Get to Know Your Horse's Injury

It's critical that you know how the injury feels in size and "density." Is it squishy or hard? Is it painful when you squeeze it? Is there heat? Where does the swelling start and end on the leg? Get a feel and assessment of the "good leg" so you can compare it to the injured one.

"Getting to know" your horse's injury can be as important in monitoring your horse's progress as a $100,000 3-D digital ultrasound machine. Knowing the injury means you will be alert to early warning signs (swelling, heat, or pain) that mean you are going too quickly or doing too much. This careful observation may intercept a reinjury and mean you have to take only "one step backward," rather than returning to square one or, even worse, causing greater injury.

Dr. **Richard Markell** has been a Fédération Equestre Internationale (FEI) veterinarian since 1990 and is accredited in show jumping and dressage. He was the Treating Veterinarian at three World Cup show jumping finals, a World Cup dressage final, and the 2004 Olympic selection trial. Dr. Markell has also served as a consultant to many riders on the United States Equestrian Team, as well as numerous other Olympic equestrian teams from around the world.

Dr. Markell's practice, Ranch & Coast Equine Practice in Rancho Santa Fe, California, is limited to equine sports medicine, working exclusively with hunters, jumpers, and dressage horses.

Do Not Overuse Ice, Wrapping, or Medication

These may cover up signs of overwork during the rehabilitation phase. Let the injury and your horse "talk to you" and tell you if you've been doing too much walking or trotting. If the injury becomes swollen and hot the day after you increase your horse's work, it's likely saying, "Hey, that's too much! Time to slow down."

Remember…No Two Horses Heal at the Same Rate

The length of your horse's rehabilitation will be determined by the degree of his original injury and the speed of healing. Just like people, some horses heal faster than others, so resist the temptation to compare your horse's progress with another. Follow the rehabilitation schedule you and your veterinarian have designed specifically for your horse to give him the best possible chance for a full recovery.

OLD-FASHIONED ATTENTION TO TODAY'S TENDON INJURIES

by Cooper Williams, VMD

With controlled exercise and new treatment options (see p. 365), horses are now not only returning to work and competition after a tendon injury, but returning with tendons that have healed more thoroughly and with tissue that is as strong and flexible as prior to the injury.

But while many of these new therapies and exercise plans are hi-tech, your horse's rehabilitation still requires old-fashioned attention to detail and daily monitoring of his progress.

Control

An "uncontrolled" horse risks reinjury or a setback in his recovery time. So until an ultrasound shows a significant level of healing, you must not allow your horse to do anything over which you do not have control. This means:

- Confining your horse to a stall or size-restricted turnout until your veterinarian clears him for unrestricted turnout.

- To the best of your ability, not allowing him to buck, bolt, or do airs above the ground when he's being hand-walked or ridden.

- If you're doing rehab at the walk, absolutely no trotting—even a few strides "just to see how he's doing." If you're in the trotting portion of the rehab program, that means no cantering. *Controlled exercise* means just that—you have control over what your horse does and for how long.

That said, we all know that most horses will, at some point in their rehab, do something "uncontrolled." If you think you'll have difficulty keeping your horse calm, consider the following:

- Discuss sedation options with your veterinarian.

- If your horse is quieter being ridden than when being hand-walked,

Dr. Cooper Williams grew up on the Eastern Shore of Maryland, playing polo with his father, who trained polo ponies. Williams played professionally while studying at the University of Pennsylvania School of Veterinary Medicine and even found time to coach the polo team at nearby Valley Forge Military Academy. After graduation, he interned at the Delaware Equine Center. He then moved south to be on staff at the Maryland Equine Center before starting his own practice.

His practice in Hampstead, Maryland, specializes in sports medicine and lameness in performance horses. Williams has designed controlled-exercise rehabilitation programs for hundreds of horses—from event, endurance, and dressage competitors to timber racers and steeplechasers.

talk with your veterinarian about doing the hand-walking portion of his rehab under saddle.

- Hand-walk your horse after he's eaten; he may be quieter and easier to handle.

- Be sensible about where you work your horse. Don't walk him past mares in heat or take him for a hack in an open field if you think you might have a difficult time keeping him under control.

- If your horse does get loose and take off for an uncontrolled romp, check his leg for heat and swelling, and if necessary, call your veterinarian immediately.

Turnout

While it's difficult to see your horse confined for month after month, tendons *must* regain fiber density and flexibility before a horse can safely be returned to unrestricted turnout. Except under the most extraordinary circumstances, a horse should remain in a stall or size-restricted turnout throughout his rehabilitation.

- If your horse will remain quiet in a size-restricted turnout, discuss options such as round-pen panels or a Port-A-Paddock™ with your veterinarian (see *Resources*, p. 367).

- Remember, a horse should never be returned to unrestricted turnout without clearance from your veterinarian.

Consistency

Hand-walking or riding your horse two or three days week is simply not enough to get the job done. A horse should be hand-walked or ridden a *minimum* of five days a week. This consistency will not only improve the healing process but a regular work schedule should make your horse less rambunctious.

If bad weather or a family emergency means that your horse must have some time off from his rehabilitation program, simply keep him at the previous level of work for a week or two and then resume his normal progressive rehab schedule.

Examining the Injured Leg

You should examine your horse's leg every day; before and after you hand-walk or ride:

1 Pick up the leg and hold it in a relaxed position—do not grip.
2 Using slow, even pressure, palpate along the tendon. If your horse has an involuntary reaction such as jerking his leg away, use light pressure for the first pass and then gradually increase the pressure.
3 Make seven or eight passes along the leg. If your horse reacts to continued palpation or you feel any heat or swelling, contact your veterinarian.

The importance of regular follow-up ultrasounds cannot be overstated. Do not progress in your horse's rehab program (i.e. move on from hand-walking to walking under saddle, walking to trotting, or trotting to cantering) without an ultrasound to confirm progress in your horse's healing and subsequent clearance from your veterinarian.

LIGAMENT INJURY CASE STUDY I

Fay Watchorn – Dressage Rider
Darius – Selle Francais

Salt Lake City, Utah/Phoenix, Arizona

Torn Right Hind Suspensory, Adhesions, and Blind Splints

Fay

"I was born with the horse gene but didn't discover its whereabouts until I was 10 years old and a family trip from Toronto to the sand hills of Nebraska awakened my love for horses. My cousin Don put me on a cow horse and off into the hills we rode. Something spooked my horse and he bolted, at which point I promptly fell off. Upon our return home, I begged my mom for riding lessons so that would never happen again. I didn't know about the saying 'seven falls makes a rider' (and then some!)"

As Fay's love for riding grew, she moved from pony-leasing to horse ownership. As a teenager, her main focus was show jumping. After graduation from high school, she took a 10-year hiatus from riding while she attended nursing school, moved to Utah, married and started a family.

When she was 36, Fay bought a Thoroughbred mare and took up dressage. "After a few years, I bred her to a Warmblood and over the next six years she produced three huge colts. The first born, Tovee, was my dressage prospect and the other two I later jumped and sometimes evented. Tovee and I showed our way up to Fourth Level before he passed away from colic at 11 years old."

Fay is married and the mother of two grown daughters, the oldest of whom has "inherited the horse gene."

Darius

A 17.2-hand Selle Francais gelding, he was imported from France three years prior to Fay purchasing him as an 11-year-old. "I found him just outside of my hometown of Toronto and felt an immediate connection the first time I saw him—someone was leading Darius up an aisleway in the barn and he turned and looked me right in the eye. The next day, as the trainer was taking him into the indoor arena to ride him for us, Darius stopped, swung his head around and once again, looked straight at me. I felt as if he was looking at me and no one else."

The pair has shown successfully from Third Level to Prix St. Georges, and in their first year-and-a-half together earned their United States Dressage Federation (USDF) silver medal.

At the time of the injury, Darius was 13.

Home Facility

Fay splits her time between Salt Lake City in the summer and Phoenix in the winter months. "I own horse property in Salt Lake and have access to 500 acres of equestrian park through my back gate. In Phoenix, I board at a facility in North Scottsdale with 12- by 16-foot stalls, several riding rings, and a 20-acre field with a riding track around the perimeter."

The Injury

"Darius and I were working hard toward the regional championships to be held in Phoenix the first week in November. Two weeks before that show, I was in the ring ready to start my lesson and when I picked up the trot, my coach saw what I was feeling—Darius was lame on his right hind."

Diagnosis and Prognosis

"Over the course of the next few days and after ruling out different areas of possible injury in the leg, a tear in the suspensory was diagnosed via ultrasound. We had no idea how or why it happened. The vet said it would be six to nine months before I could put him back in full work. I calculated in my mind it would probably be a year before we were in the show ring again and there was no way of knowing if he could tolerate showing Prix St. Georges again. I felt absolutely deflated."

Rehabilitation

Early Days

The vet prescribed two months of stall rest and a follow-up ultrasound in January. "It wasn't much consolation, but I kept thinking that if he had to be laid up any time of the year, at least it was November and December. That's always a slow time when I give my horses some time off and concentrate on the holidays and family.

"But I found it very hard to see him stall-bound knowing he didn't understand why. I felt so sorry for Darius that every time I groomed him in the cross-ties, I'd feed him treats. This made *me* feel better. Of course, this led to him pawing every time I walked away. Now I only give treats in his stall and the pawing has stopped."

The ultrasound in January showed little improvement and in February, Fay contacted Dr. Ross Rich of Cave Creek Equine to get a second opinion and ask about the possibility of stem cell therapy (see p. 365).

"Dr. Rich also had some very exciting news—he had recently installed a magnetic resonance imaging (MRI) machine. With my nursing background I was aware of what this meant—before injecting stem cells into the tear, he could do a MRI on the injured area and check for the possibility of two issues: Did Darius have adhesions where the suspensory is attached to the cannon bone, and did he have blind splints poking into the suspensory? As it turned out, he had both. On February 9, Darius had surgery to release the adhesions and shave off the splints. After the incision was closed the stem cells were injected into the tear using a digital ultrasound for guidance.

"I was sent home with a printout that included the diagnosis with an explanation of the surgery, a hand-walking schedule for the next six

"The vet said it would be six to nine months before I could put him back in full work. I felt absolutely deflated."

weeks, and instructions about bandaging, anti-inflammatory therapy, and suture removal. Since my memory isn't what it used to be I found these two pages very helpful."

Darius continued to stay in his 12- by 16-foot stall and was hand-walked five to 10 minutes a day for the first two weeks. During the next four weeks, his hand-walking was gradually increased to 30 minutes a day. Once Darius hit the 20-minute mark, Fay split the time and did half in the morning and half in the afternoon.

(Unlike many riders whose horses can't be ridden, loss of fitness was not an issue for Fay. She stayed fit by training for an upcoming triathlon in April where she'd swim for a mile, bike 26 miles, and run six miles.)

Back to Ridden Work

On March 26, Darius had his six-week vet check and the ultrasound showed significant healing. Fay was now allowed to get on his back for 30-minute walks in the outdoor arena and around the manure track that circled a 20-acre field.

Keep Your Hat On

One thing Fay never rode without was her helmet—with the exception of one day early on in Darius' walking program. "We were walking up a long lane beside one of the paddocks and a mare came running toward the fence. Of course, all the other mares wanted to see what was going on and they came galloping up to join her. Darius threw his tail in the air and started piaffing. I spun him around in circles to distract him and did a quick dismount. Of course, I was terrified that these tight circles might have reinjured him.

"Thankfully, Darius was fine. And I really learned a lesson that day. So many people assume that the walk is the safest gait. But if you're on a horse that is used to being fit and is coming back from a layoff, the walk's the most unpredictable gait. A horse may buck, rear, or bolt—at a walk anything can happen—always wear your helmet."

"I wanted to make certain that the first day I rode him under saddle would be a safe one for both of us, so I decided that some acepromazine would be in order (see p. 365). Well, Darius turned out to be a real light-weight when it came to tranquilizers — he could hardly walk. It was like trying to ride a stumbling drunk. Everyone at the barn had a good giggle. The next day I didn't give him anything and he was fine."

The second ultrasound on May 6, 12 weeks post-op, showed the tear had healed and Fay was allowed to introduce five minutes of trot. "I found the track around the big field a great place to start trotting. At the beginning, I wore a watch and timed it, but I soon got to a point where I knew how many times around the track I needed to trot. Darius was very hap-py to be back trotting and I let him move forward on a loose rein. I was lucky that he was a horse that was very amenable to that, and he never felt like he wanted to take off and buck and run.

"Every week I trotted him for my trainer, and she would look to see if his trot was getting better—not as short behind, stepping up and through. Having a ground person with ex-perience and a good eye who can watch your horse on a regular basis is invaluable. Sometimes there was slight improvement that she could see but I might not feel. It was so important that I knew we were progressing forward each week."

On May 14, Fay and her husband moved Darius back to Salt Lake City. "My comeback with Darius would now have to take place in a very large indoor arena, as we had put our farm up for sale."

By the end of May, Darius was doing 20 minutes of trot work six days a week. "I was still riding him on a long rein, and he felt more forward than he ever had—he didn't have those splints or adhesions troubling him anymore. If we hadn't done the MRI, Darius would have a healed suspensory tear but his other problems would have been undiagnosed and still plaguing us. Now, I had what felt like a new horse. His whole

Schedule weekly "trots" with your trainer. She can look to see if your horse's trot is getting better—not as short behind, stepping up and through. Sometimes there may be a slight improvement that she can see but you might not feel.

work ethic was more forward and he was much more willing to carry himself. Everyone commented on how different he looked and moved."

During the first week of June, Fay added five minutes of canter to Darius' 20 minutes of trot work. "I continued in this manner, adding another five minutes of canter each week."

While Fay had rehabbed horses before from suspensory tears and splints, she felt that the structure of the controlled-exercise program "made me feel as if I actually had some influence over the process. It was logical, it was step by step, and I knew exactly what I had to do that day. Because I had an 'itinerary' to follow, I wasn't always second-guessing myself and wondering 'am I doing too much?' or 'maybe I'm not doing enough?' This was by far the most positive experience I've had rehabbing a horse."

One unexpected bonus reaped from the months of slowly bringing Darius back to work were the now comfortable and well-broken-in dressage boots that had been a fiftieth birthday present from her husband. "Everyone knows how excruciatingly painful it is to break in new boots. This time, all I was doing for weeks and weeks was walking and posting trot, so there was no grimacing in pain as I sat the trot and the stiff new boots dug into the back of my knees. By the time Darius was able to be worked at the canter, my boots felt like I'd ridden in them for years."

While the bond between Fay and Darius had always been a strong one, the months of rehabilitation brought a new dimension to their relationship. "Now, when he sees my truck drive into the barn, he starts whinnying, and not too long ago, I returned from two weeks of vacation and he just danced around in his stall when he saw me. He's become much more dependent on me—I've never had a horse that's been this close to me."

Return to Competition

Seven months after his surgery, Fay and Darius won the Region 6 Adult Amateur Prix St. Georges Championship.

Darius Today

Now 16, Darius is schooling Intermediaire I. "He is truly a whole new horse physically. Before his injury, I had always thought he would max out at Prix St. Georges. Now, I wonder just how far we can go together."

DARIUS' RECOVERY TIMELINE

February 9	MRI (magnetic resonance imaging) performed.
February 11	Surgery and stem cell injection. Returned home. Began hand-walking 5 to 10 minutes a day.
March 1	Hand-walking gradually increased to 30 minutes a day over next 25 days.
March 26	Began walking under saddle for 30 minutes.
April 16	First ride at the trot. Began with 5 minutes and gradually increased to 20 minutes of trot over the next 5 weeks.
June 1	First ride at the canter. Began with 5 minutes of canter and added 5 minutes each week for next 4 weeks.
July 27	Returned to competition.

FAY'S TIPS

- A controlled-exercise program from your veterinarian will give you an "itinerary" to follow. Because it's step by step and tells you exactly what needs to be done on any given day, there's no more second-guessing— "am I doing too much or maybe not enough?"

- If you carry mortality insurance on your horse, I suggest also having major surgical insurance. I pay $250 a year and it covered my $8,000 bill from start to finish.

- A horse is an athlete, and when coming back from an injury, we have to take it slowly. I asked Darius to do some hard work but only for very short periods. I was happy to wait until he was strong enough to sustain our usual workout.

- Remember that the horse isn't the only one losing fitness. Unless you have other horses to ride, find an alternative way to keep yourself in training.

- Have a ground person with an experienced eye watch your horse move throughout his rehabilitation. Not only can they spot a potential problem, they may be able to see a slight improvement you might not be able to feel.

LIGAMENT INJURY CASE STUDY 2

KARIN OCCHIALINI – Endurance Rider
ZORBA – Arabian

Granite Bay, California

Torn Right Front Suspensory

Karin

On hiatus from her job as an operating room nurse, Karin found herself working in real estate with a group of women who rode endurance and called themselves the "Jolly Girls." Karin had ridden briefly as a child—"a friend owned a 20-year-old horse that we would ride double and bareback in the hills of Southern California"—but 30 years had passed since she'd last been on a horse. When one of the Jolly Girls asked if Karin would be interested in riding Heidi, her 16-year-old Arabian-cross, she didn't hesitate. "Heidi was steady and safe, but still had a few tricks left in her. One ride and I was hooked."

"When I told my husband, Pete, I wanted to buy a horse and take riding lessons, he was right there with me. We started lessons together and the search for the right horses for us commenced. When I expressed some uncertainty as to the breed I wanted, a friend, who owned an Arab asked me if I wanted a sedan or a sports car. I replied, 'a sports car, of course!' Her answer? Buy an Arab!

"So at 43 years of age, Pete and I bought our first horses. Both were gray Arabian geldings just turning seven—Zorba and Donald. Zorba was a steady, dependable ride as a youngster and each passing year found him stronger and more energetic than the last.

"Our social life now revolves around our horses with horse camping and endurance our main focus between April and November. While we are mostly middle-to-back-of-the-pack riders; we have 'top tenned' in a few rides. Our proudest moment was when Pete and Donald received the coveted 'Best Condition' award for the 1997 Gold Country 50 Mile Endurance Ride in Georgetown, California. Endurance riding for us is about having a good time and bringing our horses to the finish line safe and sound."

Zorba

14.3 hands and, at the time of injury, 15 years old, Zorba had completed the Tevis Cup three times—twice with Karin and once with her husband, Pete—and competed in numerous 50-mile endurance rides. Other than a splint injury, he had remained sound. "He's a fun ride with lots of energy and an easygoing personality. He can get fired up at the start of a ride, but quickly settles into a working trot. We have always felt safe on his back, even in the dark night of the Tevis."

Home Facility

At the time of the injury, Zorba, Donald, and two other horses lived at home with Karin and Pete in a neighborhood of equestrian properties and were turned out daily on a two-acre pasture. The majority of their conditioning work was done on the Tevis trail that runs from Auburn, California, to the canyons around the town of Foresthill. "There is riding closer to us, but the terrain is flat and lacks hill work. Little did we know how invaluable this flat land would be during the rehabilitation work that was in our future."

The Injury

In early July, Zorba was three days from competing in his fourth Tevis Cup when Karin walked out to the pasture and, as she usually did before a major ride, began watching Zorba for any signs of lameness or injury. "Riders of Tevis often joke—I think!—that horses should be kept in padded stalls the last few weeks before the ride. Zorba was trotting around and appeared sound, but when he stopped and I looked at his legs, I thought I could see a slight filling in his right front.

"When I palpated the leg, I had to really concentrate, but something was definitely there. At first, I was in denial and began calling friends to get opinions on what to do. Someone suggested that since it was so slight and without lameness, we could take him to the start and let the vets check him. If he trotted out sound then I should go ahead and ride and see what happened. For a brief moment this sounded reasonable, but common sense prevailed. We wouldn't do a 50-miler if we had doubts, why would we ask Zorba to tackle one of the most difficult 100s in the US?"

"I was imagining a 'lock up' of a few weeks and then slowly riding him until his leg healed— what naiveté!"

When their vet, Dr. Bob Morgan, palpated, trotted, and then longed Zorba, he felt it was suspicious enough to warrant an ultrasound. "Off we went to see Dr. Carol Gillis, the 'ultrasound guru' for our area. Upon examination, she diagnosed a slight tear in the right front suspensory ligament. Thank goodness calmer heads prevailed and we had not taken him on Tevis…'slight' may have easily become severe."

Rehabilitation

Early Days

Dr. Gillis prescribed a course of controlled exercise that Karin calls the "Full Monty" of rehabilitation programs. "I was imagining a 'lock up' of a few weeks and then slowly riding him until his leg healed—what naiveté! Oh, if it were only that simple! The program we religiously followed was an intense one."

Zorba began his rehabilitation immediately upon his return home. He was to be hand-walked for 15 minutes, twice a day. "In all honesty, I usually couldn't manage two times a day. I'd returned to nursing and was on the road by 5:30 A.M. Pete's commute to work began at 6:00 A.M., so the morning walk was usually not an option.

"I religiously walked him once a day and on the days I could not, Pete handled the job. Most of the walking was done in our pasture, with the other three horses following after us in a straight line. What the neighbors thought, I cannot imagine! When we were allowed to increase the walking time in increments of five minutes up to 30 minutes, we ventured out into the neighborhood. I usually heard comments such as, 'I thought you were supposed to ride those animals.' And, of course, leaving the pasture prompted much calling back and forth between horses left behind and the one being exercised.

"As benign as walking seemed, it provided its own challenges. Zorba was in great condition and constantly tried to trot or run in front and around me and periodically would attempt an escape that tested the integrity of my shoulder ligaments and tendons. But he soon settled in and accepted the routine."

"Most of the walking was done in our pasture, with the other three horses following after us in a straight line. What the neighbors thought, I cannot imagine!"

Zorba was confined for the first 60 days in a 12- by 24-foot combination stall/paddock. Karin dreaded the thought of her horse being interned for that length of time and even thought of boarding him for that period "so I wouldn't have to look him in the eye when I went to the barn. Every time Zorba saw us, he would call and call, convinced that we had forgotten to turn him out with the others.

"Where I normally would have eased my conscience with more hay, weight gain was now an issue. We bought a hay net so he would spend more time with his morning hay. Carrots were cut into small pieces and whenever we went near, a piece or two was given. At night, all the horses were in their stalls, but the days were difficult because, of course, his best friend Donald felt no obligation to keep Zorba company."

While Karin was fortunate in having two other horses to ride—Lakota and Ali; both Arabians doing endurance—Zorba's rehabilitation became the top priority. "I didn't do much traveling to endurance rides; we stayed in the area and rode the many miles of local trails. But having Lakota and Ali did enable me to stay involved in riding and all its social aspects."

Back to Ridden Work

At Zorba's 60-day check-up in early September, Karin got the go-ahead to ride him under saddle and was also allowed to turn him out in a small, size-restricted paddock. "I loved being back in the saddle with Zorba. He was pretty frisky at the start and did his share of jigging, but within about five minutes, settled into his walk. He did seem to spook and shy more than usual, but after being at home for two months, I thought that was to be expected. My biggest concern was a shy that would land me on the ground and send him running home."

She began with 15 minutes and after every 10 rides, increased the time by five minutes until she was walking Zorba for a total of 40 minutes, five days a week. "The walks started in the neighborhood, but as the times got longer, Pete and I would trailer Zorba to a lake about 15 minutes away. Zorba became so used to Pete walking on foot in front of him, that on the days Pete couldn't accompany us, Zorba would try to follow other hikers that passed by."

"Zorba did seem to spook and shy more than usual, but after being at home for two months, I thought that was to be expected. My biggest concern was a shy that would land me on the ground and send him running home."

After 50 rides and approximately four months, Zorba returned for another clean ultrasound. In early November, he and Karin began a trotting program, starting with 15 minutes of walk and five minutes of trot. They added five minutes of trot every 10 rides until they were trotting for 45 minutes.

"Now all this sounds well and good if your career is walking and trotting horses or you have trails right outside your back gate. I had neither. The rainy season approached, my work schedule was longer, daylight savings ended and all this had an impact on our ride schedule. I rushed home from work to ensure Zorba's ride was done for that day and errands waited until after dinner. If it was dark, we'd walk round and round in our pasture with the barn lights illuminating the way. Then I'd go out on the street and trot on any soft surface I could find. Riding in my neighborhood was always a bit of a challenge—we don't have street lights, so I counted on lights from other barns and pastures to show us the way—and we often had to fend off 'monster' lawn mowers, fast cars, and charging dogs. And, of course, as we turned to head home, I had to cope with a horse trying to return three times faster than he left."

When Karin could no longer do the necessary amount of exercise in her neighborhood, she once again began trailering Zorba to the lake trails. "It would have been wonderful to have a buddy, someone rehabbing their horse at the same pace and distance as Zorba. But time and again, I was the only rider on the trails. Solitude is peaceful and rewarding up to a point, but at other times it can be just a long and boring exercise.

"The further into his rehab we went, the more I put every move Zorba made under a microscope. We had put in a lot of time and effort and I was afraid if he spun in his paddock or tripped while on the trail, I would be starting over from the beginning. Once, while Pete was riding him, Zorba spooked at something and sent Pete to the ground. When I returned home and was given the details of Pete's harrowing experience—he fell hard on his shoulder while trying to hold on to Zorba's reins—all I could think of was, 'How's the horse and is his leg okay?' Luckily, I verbalized concern for Pete and then casually asked about the horse."

In April, nine months after Zorba's injury, the time came for his last ultrasound. "What a nail-biter. But, hallelujah, we were given the all clear." Zorba was able to return to full turnout and the next few months were spent gradually increasing distances and pace.

"Surprisingly, most of the time Zorba and I spent together was rewarding and pleasurable. It's a wonderful opportunity to form a bond with your horse. One very real positive was that trailering was never an issue after we finished this program. There had been times in the past when Zorba decided that trailering to a ride was not on his calendar but after months hauling to the trails to rehab, he never gave us an ounce of trouble again."

Return to Competition

In July, Karin brought Zorba back to competition. "After a few 25-milers, he began doing 50-milers. While Zorba has successfully completed all his rides since his return to competition, we decided not to do any more 100-milers—he's proven everything he needs to."

Zorba Today

"Zorba is now 25 and still trotting down the trail at an energetic pace. He did 50-mile rides until he turned 21 and his last 30-mile ride at age 23. Today, we're happy to trail ride for pleasure and go on camping trips."

ZORBA'S RECOVERY TIMELINE

July 3	Injury diagnosed. Began hand-walking for 15 minutes a day for the first 30 days.
August 6	Continued hand-walking, increasing in 5-minute increments until walking for 30 minutes a day.
September 6	Began walking under saddle. Started with 15 minutes and increased by 5-minute increments every 10 rides until walking for 40 minutes.
November 8	First ride at the trot. Began with 15 minutes at the walk and 5 minutes at the trot and increased trot in 5-minute increments until trotting for 45 minutes.
July	Returned to competition.

Karin's Tips

- Gain an understanding of why rest and then gradual return to exercise is so important. What a temptation it is to give your horse a few weeks off and then get right back to ridden work! My feeling was that if I had the time and energy to condition this horse for endurance competition, then I had the time and energy to put into his rehab.

- It sounds obvious, but follow the vet's advice. What's the point of spending money for an ultrasound and diagnosis if you don't adhere to the advice given? One thought continually ran through my mind during this long process—if Zorba reinjured his suspensory, I would, at the very least, be comfortable knowing that it was not because I cheated on the rehabilitation. On the other hand, if I did take shortcuts, I would always question whether I was responsible for a second injury. When you successfully finish whatever program is prescribed, it will be with a true sense of satisfaction and accomplishment for you and your horse.

- You may be dead tired when you get home from a long day at work, but once you're on and riding, everything will be okay.

- Concentrate on how much you can see and enjoy at the walk—I saw all sorts of things that I'd missed when we were flying down a trail at faster gaits.

- A change of scene will be good for both you and your horse. Consider trailering to a nearby trail or arena with good footing and a level surface.

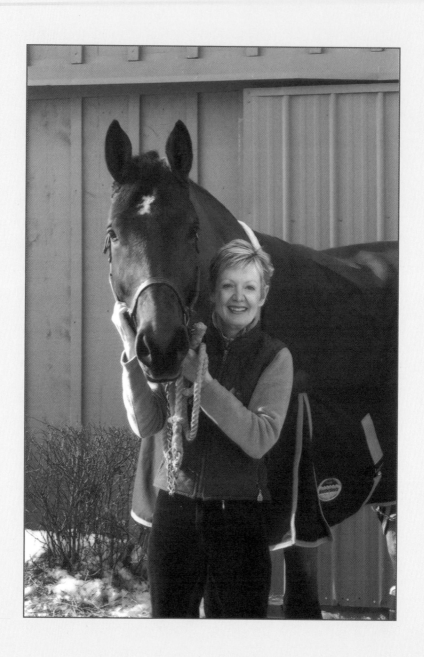

LIGAMENT INJURY CASE STUDY 3

PAT TROOST – Dressage Rider
MAC – Hanoverian

Oak Brook, Illinois

Torn Right Front Suspensory

Pat

"As a child, my whole week revolved around a Saturday riding lesson. The horses were school horses of 'non-aristocratic birth' and it was pretty much a 'follow-the-tail-in-front-of-you' lesson, but I was over-the-edge horse crazy and could not get enough of riding. I rode hunt seat through high school and then sadly had to give it up when I went to college.

"When my children were in elementary school I met two women who wanted to get back to riding as much as I did. After negotiating with our husbands, we started to horse shop. I don't remember much about how we found Gypsy other than there was an empty bathtub in the front yard of the establishment where she lived. She barely passed the vet check but was a kind horse and, at the time, suited our needs just fine.

"After several years of lessons on Gypsy, I knew I needed a horse in my life full-time. For a while I thought it would be at the cost of my sanity, as I was in graduate school, we were building a house, my kids had to be driven to their extracurricular activities, and I needed to get a meal on the table every night. I made several learn-the-hard-way purchases of inappropriate horses that needed exorcism rituals performed on them. Finally I found a wonderful little Quarter Horse that started my dressage career and then a lovely young Holsteiner that helped me further my dressage goals. I'd been riding for nine years when I purchased Mac."

Pat is married, a grandmother, and a clinical social worker in private practice.

Magnum Gold aka "Mac"

Pat bought the 17-hand Hanoverian when he was three and barely saddle broken. "I got a lead on a 'nice young horse in Canada,' so I phoned the breeder and arranged a trip to see him. The breeder said his farm was not far from the Toronto airport, but after three hours in the car I was beginning to suspect I was the victim of a kidnapping plot.

"I liked Mac the minute I saw him. He had an imperious, haughty look about him, and I felt like he was looking me over as much as I was looking him over. But I wanted to be sure he had a good mind so I asked the breeder if I could walk him along the road to see what he did when a car came by. After walking for what seemed like forever I realized cars didn't come down that road very often. Finally the breeder got into his car and drove it up and down the road. Sold!"

Pat and Mac were the Illinois Dressage and Combined Training Association First Level Champions the year before his injury.

The Injury

At the time of his suspensory injury, Mac, seven years old, had been battling an aggressive case of ulcers for several months. "The vet who did the scoping said he had never seen a horse with such terrible ulcers and this was after he had been on Gastro Guard® for two months. Then one day, just as the ulcers

Home Facility

Pat, like many riders in Chicago, boards her horse in Wisconsin and considers the hour and 20 minutes it takes her to get to the barn a fair trade off for having turnout and a good facility.

The barn where Mac boarded at the time of his injury has 40 stalls with grass pastures, two outdoor arenas and two indoor arenas. Mac's stall had a run-out attached, which was a bonus when he was on a restricted exercise plan. Boarders were primarily dressage riders with a sprinkling of pleasure riders and children taking Saturday lessons.

were seemingly under control, he came out of his stall stiff as a board. So back we went to the vet (who by now was booking trips to Hawaii every time we pulled into the driveway)."

Diagnosis and Prognosis

"At first, the vet thought he had arthritis in his fetlock. Then he said there was a slight chance of a suspensory tear. I didn't want to take any chances and told him I wanted the leg ultrasounded. Sure enough, it was a torn suspensory ligament in the right front.

"We have no idea how it happened. Mac was never lame on the leg, but looking back, his movements had not been as supple and full of suspension as usual. I was angry, disillusioned, and very sad."

Rehabilitation

Early Days

Pat and her vet decided on extracorporeal shock wave therapy (ESWT—see p. 366) and a program of controlled exercise, which would allow Mac to have time out of his stall each day. Mac's back-to-work schedule would be dictated not only by ultrasounds, but stomach scopes to monitor his ulcers.

"It was very difficult during the show season when all my friends headed off for shows and I stood in the driveway waving good-bye and wishing them luck."

"Emotionally, I dealt with his time off very poorly. I felt sorry for him and sorrier for me! It was very difficult during the show season when all my friends headed off for shows and I stood in the driveway waving good-bye and wishing them luck. I was also dealing with my mother's failing health so it was a very rough time. Riding was always an outlet for me and I had lost that most important diversion."

On May 6, the day he was diagnosed, Mac received his first shock wave treatment. Pat was instructed to keep him on stall rest (with access to his run-out) and immediately begin walking him. They were to begin with five minutes and gradually increase the time until Mac was walking for 30 minutes each day. She was also to cold-hose his leg for 20 minutes

after each walk and wrap the leg after applying DMSO and/or Traumeel®
Gel (see *Resources*, p. 365).

Back to Ridden Work

"Because I'm so light (105 pounds) and Mac is so big, the vet okayed
walking under saddle instead of hand-walking, which, considering Mac is
better behaved when I'm on his back, was a real blessing. Did I worry that
I'd made the right decision? I worried constantly! I practically held my
breath every step he took and wondered if that last step was *the* step that
would do us in. My uncertainty and worry was fueled by stories from fellow boarders who told me about horses they knew who'd torn a
suspensory and weren't right for years. But I'd done my research
about controlled-exercise recovery programs and I knew it was
the right decision for Mac."

*"Because I'm so light
(105 pounds) and Mac
is so big, the vet okayed
walking under saddle
instead of hand-walking,
which, considering Mac
is better behaved when
I'm on his back, was a
real blessing."*

Three weeks later, Mac had a second shock wave treatment
and Pat was instructed to continue his walking program. "Mac really liked getting out of his stall and enjoyed the attention. What
he didn't like was being confined to his stall and run-out area,
and I was terrified his ulcers would flare up again. We walked in
the arena for more controlled conditions but it was very hot and
very boring—just one foot in front of the other. Mac was very
well behaved, but he was also on small amounts of acepromazine to prevent any explosions."

When Pat took him back to the vet on June 10 for an ultrasound and
third shock wave treatment, she had his stomach scoped to check on
his ulcers. They were worse. "I consulted my vet and went online and
researched ulcers in horses. I called two universities and spoke to vets on
staff, but it was difficult to find two vets who agreed on the 'correct' treatment. I called the companies that make Gastrogard® and Neigh-Lox® and
explained my situation. Finally, the vets and I came up with a program
we thought would manage the ulcers while Mac was recovering from his
suspensory injury. It was a fairly complicated schedule and I was very

lucky to have a great barn manager, Phil May, who could not have been nicer, more understanding, or more helpful."

Since Mac's third ultrasound looked positive, Pat was given the go-ahead to add short straight-line trot sets to their 30 minutes of walking. They began with one set of three minutes of trot, working up over the next month to five sets (with two minutes of walk in between), trotting down the long sides of the arena and walking through the corners. "It's hard to describe what it felt like when 'The Day' arrived and we could begin trotting. Mostly I was terrified that with each step he would reinjure himself. At the beginning, it was hard to enjoy it because I was so scared.

"It's hard to describe what it felt like when 'The Day' arrived and we could begin trotting. Mostly I was terrified that with each step he would reinjure himself."

"In late June we decided to give Mac limited turnout in the round pen, in hopes that it would lessen some of the anxiety he was feeling from being kept in his stall and run-out. It was a fine line between protecting his leg and his stomach as treating one worsened the other. At first he walked quietly around, then he gave a few huge bucks and ran. I raced in to get him and took him out, fearing the worst. We tried the round pen several times, but he could never manage to remain quiet. At that point I arranged for him to go out alone in a grass paddock for at least half the day. The grass paddock was a risk as he could run, but the grass would be good for his stomach. There were a few times when he did take off but the barn help were great and they would run out and get him."

At the end of July, Pat was allowed to add corners to Mac's trot work. Over the next two weeks, they worked up to five sets of four minutes of trot. Pat continued to cold hose his leg for 20 minutes after each ride.

In August, after another positive ultrasound and a scope that showed Mac's ulcers were now under control, Pat was allowed to begin cantering him. One-minute canters on straight lines were increased by a minute every 10 days over the next month. Pat and Mac were now working at least 30 minutes a day with lots of "long and low" stretching work during their warm-ups.

By November, six months after Mac's injury, he was back in full work and beginning to school Second Level movements. Pat and Mac spent the winter attending clinics and preparing to show again in the spring.

Mac Today

"If someone had asked me if I would ever sell Mac, my answer would have been 'never.' But as it often does, fate intervened.

"The coach for the United States Paralympic Equestrian Team was visiting our barn and Mac caught his eye. One of his riders, Lynn Seidemann, a silver medalist at the 2004 Athens Paralympic Games, was looking for a new horse and he thought Mac would be perfect.

"His visit coincided with my growing realization that Mac would never make an upper level dressage horse; he did not have the will to do it, and I was certainly not going to force the issue. Mac wanted a life with much less stress.

"I invited Lynn to come to Chicago with her trainer. Mac was on his best behavior and didn't give a second look to Lynn's wheelchair. At the end of her three-day visit, Lynn told me she *had* to have him. It was one of the hardest decisions I've ever had to make, but in the end, I knew it would be a good life for Mac. A few weeks later, Mac left for his new home in Texas.

"I keep in touch with Lynn via e-mail and am grateful that she and Mac are getting along so well. Not a day goes by that I don't think of him."

MAC'S RECOVERY TIMELINE

May 6	Injury diagnosed. Began hand-walking and cold-hosing for 20 minutes each day.
May 28	Began walking under saddle, starting with 5 minutes and working up to 30 minutes.

June 10	First ride at the trot. Began with 1 set of 3 minutes (straight lines only) working up to 5 sets (with 2 minutes of walk between) over the next 4 weeks.
July 27	Began trotting through corners. Gradually increased to 5 sets of 4 minutes of trot.
August 27	First ride at the canter. Began with 1-minute canters (straight lines only) and increased by 1 minute every 10 days.
November	Back in full work.

PAT'S TIPS

- As a clinical social worker, I know the importance of therapy and medication when people are experiencing severe stress. To many riders, their horse is their best friend, and if that best friend becomes sick or injured it can often lead to a roller coaster of emotions. Don't hesitate to get help for yourself if you're experiencing any of the following symptoms: depressed moods, sleep or appetite disturbances, crying spells, feelings of hopelessness or worthlessness, or lack of motivation.

- Get horse-care help if you need it. I did 99.9 percent of the rehab work myself and looking back, that was crazy. The hour-plus drive to the barn was grueling under the best of circumstances, and at the beginning of rehab, it was often three hours of driving to simply walk Mac for 15 or 20 minutes. On the few occasions when I felt I could not go

→

another day or I'd lose my mind, I did have the good sense to pay my trainer's groom to walk him.

- Follow your instincts—you know your horse best. One vet told me for months that Mac did not have ulcers. And another vet would never have ultrasounded Mac's leg had I not insisted. Stick to your guns and listen to your gut.

CYNDI LORENZEN JACKSON
AND KAY LORENZEN – Dressage Riders
MAXINE – Tennessee Walking Horse/Quarter Horse

Phoenix, Arizona

Torn Right Front Suspensory

Cyndi and her mother, Kay

Cyndi and Kay have shared the ride on Maxine, a 15.1-hand Tennessee Walking Horse/Quarter Horse cross with a partially bitten-off right ear, for over 15 years. "We got Maxine from a local dude ranch when she was four and Cyndi was 12," remembers Kay. "We were looking for a horse for Cyndi to takes lessons on and when she saw Maxine it was love at first sight. We had never owned a horse and were very naive about the whole business of choosing a suitable horse for a beginner rider. Despite the fact that Maxine was too spooky to be used as a trail horse for ranch guests and had sent two cowboys to the hospital, we thought she'd be perfect!"

Growing up, Cyndi and Maxine tried everything from the hunter/jumper ring to barrel racing and team penning. Eventually, they evented at Training Level, but when Maxine started refusing jumps, Cyndi decided to concentrate solely on dressage, moving up to Third Level when she was 19 and Maxine was 11.

Four years later, the pair was competing at Prix St. Georges and Cyndi was training a growing clientele of horses and students.

At 15, Maxine began showing some weakness in her right hock and X-rays revealed a bone chip. Cyndi decided she'd give the ride on Maxine to her mother, who had been competing an off-the-track Thoroughbred at First Level. Kay and Maxine were competing at Second Level and planning the move up to Third Level when Kay was sidetracked by a hysterectomy. Cyndi once again began riding Maxine, and with her mother's encouragement, they began competing again.

Cyndi and Maxine had earned both bronze and silver medals from the United States Dressage Federation (USDF) and were competing at Intermediaire I at the time of Maxine's injury.

Home Facility

Maxine lives on Kay's two-acre property in a horse-friendly neighborhood surrounded by the city of Phoenix. There is a 20- by 80-meter lighted arena and a round pen. The property is irrigated and the horses have daily turnout in grass paddocks.

Maxine

"Her breeding and her diminutive size certainly made her an unlikely candidate for dressage," says Kay, "and over the years, many competitors have taken a look at Maxine and written her off. But Cyndi's skill as a rider and Maxine's willingness and heart made them an unstoppable combination."

The Injury

Warming up at a clinic given by a well-known German trainer, Cyndi felt "something not quite right up front." No one on the ground could spot anything amiss, so Cyndi proceeded into the arena. Voicing her concerns about Maxine, she was told by the trainer that "she was an older horse and she'd warm up out of it. But I knew this was something different and that she wouldn't simply work out of it." A confrontation followed, with Cyndi ultimately making the decision to dismount and trailer Maxine home.

Diagnosis and Prognosis

Two subsequent visits from the vet provided no answers. "It was so hard to keep test-riding her, hoping that something would show up that the vet could see. I felt really guilty." The difficulty, Cyndi discovered, was that she rode Maxine so "under" and Maxine took so much weight on her hind legs, that it lightened up her front end and the lameness was not apparent to anyone watching on the ground. On a third visit from the vet, Cyndi threw away the reins and allowed Maxine to fall on her forehand. It was only then that her vet was able to spot the lameness. An ultrasound at the beginning of January revealed a tear in the right front suspensory ligament. "Yes," says Cyndi, "the front. Just where my gut told me it was."

"It was so hard to keep test-riding her, hoping that something would show up that the vet could see. I felt really guilty."

Despite her age—Maxine was 18—Cyndi never thought about bringing the mare's career to an end. "Maxine was such a good friend and had such heart and loved her work so much that I didn't consider retiring her. We made a commitment to following the vet's directions to the letter so that we'd have the best chance at a full recovery. The only real concern we had was that Maxine had gotten so strong with her upper level dressage work and we didn't know how she would be affected by the muscle loss that would come with her being out of work for an extended period of time."

Rehabilitation

Early Days

Maxine moved into a 16- by 16-foot stall with an attached run of equal size and spent several hours a day in a separate 16- by 16-foot fenced grassy area that was located near the barn. "At the time of Maxine's injury, months of stall rest was the usual recommendation for horses with a suspensory injury," says Cyndi. "Today, we know how important it is to keep blood circulating to the injury and we would have started her on a controlled-exercise program immediately after her diagnosis."

Back to Ridden Work

In late May, Cyndi was given the okay to begin hand-walking Maxine. "I hand-walked her for a couple of days and then hopped on. Maxine likes being ridden better than being led, and she's so calm that everyone agreed this was the best choice."

Cyndi's first ride was bareback with a halter. "It was the most natural thing to do; very sentimental, as I'd ridden her bareback so much when she was younger." Their walks began with five minutes a day and increased to 30 minutes over the next five weeks. They often walked in the neighborhood, both on the streets and on the bridle paths that run behind the properties. "Since Maxine likes trail riding, I thought the change of scenery would be good for her. And our bridle paths can be pretty exciting, as the neighbors keep an amazing variety of animals—emus, ostriches, a longhorn steer, turkeys, pot-bellied pigs, miniature horses, and dogs galore. It's a good trail horse that can keep calm on these bridle paths!"

Making time for Maxine on top of 14-hour workdays was "often really hard for Cyndi," remembers her mother. "When you own your own business, you tend to ride everyone else's horses first and save your own for last. Very often, Cyndi was riding Maxine well after dark."

After five weeks of walking, "the first trot steps" says Kay, "were nail-biters. We watched her, and watched some more, looking for some sign that she was unsound on either of her front legs. She was even in front but really stiff behind. At 19, Maxine was an old lady and way overdue for hock injections. Once that was done, she went back to work and looked great." They started with two minutes of trot daily, then added a minute each day with Cyndi keeping Maxine on straight lines only.

Cyndi rode Maxine four to five times a week, and Kay rode one or two days. "With my long workdays," remembers Cyndi, "it was wonderful that someone who knew and loved Maxine could be there to pitch in." While Kay was thrilled to back on Maxine, she had her work cut out for her. "Maxine was hard to keep forward at that point, and I was afraid to push her too hard because I didn't want to stress the leg. But unless you

> Try trail riding—the change of scenery can be good for a rehabbing horse. And bridle paths can be pretty exciting, as neighbors can keep an amazing variety of animals—emus, ostriches, longhorn steer, turkeys, pot-bellied pigs, miniature horses and dogs galore.

kept her forward, she was really lazy and behind my leg. I had to find a balance that was healthy for her and not ask too much."

When Maxine was comfortable doing 20 minutes of trot work during a 40-minute ride, they added one minute of canter in each direction and increased it by one minute per day. When Maxine was doing 30 minutes of trot and canter in a 45-minute ride, Cyndi began to add lateral work. "I started with leg-yield, then added shoulder-in, haunches-in, and half-pass. I also started doing tempis (canter lead changes) again to keep her sharp and we constantly watched her for any unevenness in her strides."

That Maxine could come roaring back was no surprise to Kay. "She is all heart and always was. With her breeding, Maxine was not really meant to do dressage. But she learned fast, was patient with Cyndi growing up on her, and always acted little—but mighty."

"With my long workdays, it was wonderful that someone who knew and loved Maxine could be there to pitch in."

Maxine Today

While Maxine's lateral work and tempi changes were "as good as ever," Cyndi decided she would not return to upper level dressage. Maxine continued to give lessons to students learning tempi changes, shoulder-in, haunches-in, and half-pass and everyone assumed she would settle into a happy semi-retirement.

Then, Kay decided she and Maxine should "pick up where we had left off a couple years earlier." Maxine, now 21, is back in full work and she and Kay recently earned their USDF bronze medal. "Maxine's second bronze and my first," says Kay. "After this, who knows? Maxine is 'The World's Best Horse'!"

Maxine's Recovery Timeline

January 4	Diagnosis made.

May 25	Began walking under saddle. Started with 5 minutes a day and increasing to 30 minutes over 5 weeks.
June 30	First ride at the trot. Began with 2 minutes and added 1 minute per day until doing 20 minutes of trot in a 40-minute ride.
July 25	First ride at the canter. Began with 1 minute and increased in 1-minute increments.
August 14	Began simple lateral work, including leg-yield, haunches-in, shoulder-in, and half-pass.
January	Returned to competition at Third Level.

CYNDI AND KAY'S TIPS

- Trust your instincts. If something feels not quite right—even if no one can see it from the ground—*don't* give up until you find out what's wrong.

- Don't rush the exercise program. It's better to stay at the same number of minutes of work an extra day or two than to "up" the work when the horse isn't ready.

- Make sure the footing is not too deep once the trot and canter work begins.

→

- Use the time spent convalescing your horse to bond in a different way. Hand-walking can be pretty boring or it can be a time to notice little things about your horse, to talk or sing to him, stroke his neck while walking, or groom him just for grooming's sake.

SUSAN McNALLY — Event Rider
CODY — Irish Sport Horse

Boston, Massachusetts

Torn Right Hind Suspensory

Susan

Susan describes herself as a "not-very-brave adult amateur who aspires to Novice Level in eventing." She had a backyard horse as a kid—"he was of indiscriminate breeding, completely bombproof, and I thought he was incredible"—but had put her riding days behind her once she became an adult.

"It was too much of a commitment, too expensive, and too hard to find the right circumstances. There was no way to dabble in it, I knew. I work as an independent book packager for publishers and museums, coordinating the process of getting a manuscript through all the 'hoops' until it becomes an edited, designed, printed, and bound book. Deal with authors and a horse, too? And how could I ever fit riding into a freelancer's schedule and budget?"

But fit it in she did. At 39, she leased Jigger, a Connemara/Thoroughbred cross, and began competing him at Beginner Novice. When he retired eight years later, Susan knew it was "time for me to look for my first horse—a Novice/Training-Level packer."

Susan is single and works from home, with "a flexible schedule that has lent itself to many hours at the barn."

Coderus aka "Cody"

A 16.1-hand Irish Sport Horse, he was imported from Ireland and had competed at Preliminary with a young rider from Pennsylvania. "Cody jumped clean but slow, and his trainer thought he was better suited for the lower levels. He's wonderful under saddle and very cute, but he has horrible ground manners and is very territorial in his stall and turnout. I knew I could live with his manners—I was used to being bossed around by a Connemara!"

At the time of his injury, Cody was 10 years old and had been owned by Susan for just seven months.

The Injury

"In August, I started feeling an occasional funky step and some slight change in his movement. The vet found 'hock issues' and injected both hocks. Later that month, Cody and I had competed in our first ever event, Beginner Novice at the Millbrook Horse Trials in New York. Cody felt fine and I had a great time."

Diagnosis and Prognosis

"But by early September the intermittent lameness returned," remembers Susan. "The vet was called once again, and this time, Cody was diagnosed with tearing and inflammation in his right hind suspensory."

Rehabilitation

Early Days

Susan's vet recommended stall rest and restricted turnout in one of the barn's three small "hospital paddocks." In January, Susan got the go-ahead to walk him for 10 minutes a day under saddle. "This proved difficult during the cold temperatures and wind of a New England winter—riding him took courage! I had to steel myself to drive to the barn each afternoon and tack him up. Before I rode, I gave him acepromazine orally and this helped to calm his high spirits (see p. 365). Eventually Cody managed half-hour walks drug-free."

But after four months of walking 15 to 30 minutes a day, six days a week, Susan sensed that Cody was not making progress—a feeling that was confirmed by an ultrasound. "It indicated the suspensory was better, but not healing completely. Cody was not improving. More rest and more walking was prescribed.

"I worried constantly about him. I felt like his life was so compromised and I could see he was unhappy. I think I worried more about his current condition than what the future might hold. I was committed to Cody, but I also knew that if he had to be retired, I did not have the income to support another horse. If Cody could not return to work, my riding life would be over."

If you sense your horse is not making progress during rehab, arrange for your vet to do an ultrasound.

By April, Susan's concerns about Cody's progress intensified. "Although a field ultrasound now showed the injury to be 'healed,' I knew something was still wrong. Cody had lost muscle and mass and was all hips and angles." In early May, eight months after the initial diagnosis, Susan took Cody to Fairfield Equine Hospital in Connecticut for a hind-end bone scan and lameness evaluation.

"Dr. Rick Mitchell found some secondary inflammation in his sacro-iliac joint, but the injured right hind suspensory ligament was 'glowing' on the scan—it was obviously a long way from being healed."

Mitchell recommended an ACell injection to jump-start the healing of the ligament and fascia release surgery to allow the ligament to expand (see p. 365). "Another horse at our barn had the ACell treatment during the winter and was back competing in advanced combined driving events. I felt it was the last best hope for Cody's recovery.

"Dr. Mitchell was confident that Cody would recover, but he would need 180 days of rest and walking in hand. Even though the prognosis was good, it sounded like forever. I had reached my lowest point."

Two days after his surgery, Cody arrived home ready to start hand-walking for 15 minutes, twice a day. "This was not easy. As flexible as my work hours were, my job couldn't accommodate two trips to the barn every day. I decided to do the best I could and broke up the 15-minute sessions with 30 minutes of hand-grazing."

Back to Ridden Work

At the 60-day checkup and ultrasound in early July, Susan was given permission to walk Cody under saddle. "I thought it would be less scary now because it was late July and hot. But I forgot that Cody was finally feeling better. In mid-August he bolted and bucked, and I fell off. Only my confidence was truly bruised, but bruised nonetheless."

"My trainer and I would often share a ride—she would start him and I would finish him. She would work through the stiffness, and I would benefit from a more balanced horse."

On September 24 (one year to the day from the original ultrasound), Cody had his final checkup and ultrasound at Fairfield. Dr. Mitchell advised Susan that Cody could go back to work—but slowly. "In a 30-minute workout, we were to walk for 15 minutes, trot for five and finish with five minutes of walk. For the first two weeks, I was to cold-hose his leg for 20 minutes after every ride.

"Lisa Samoylenko, the barn owner and an eventing trainer, started him for me at the trot because my confidence was at its lowest ebb and Cody was not very focused on the job at hand—'checked out' was the description at the time. Lisa could hold him together and balance him, so Cody could gain strength. I could not. The good news was that with each ride, Cody seemed to be progressing.

"By the end of October, four weeks after adding trot work, we increased his trotting time to 10 minutes and added a bit of canter work along the long side of the arena with very easy slow transitions. I was still very anxious about riding Cody, so having Lisa ride him as well allowed me to build up my confidence. I could see that when Lisa rode him, Cody was really steady, quiet, and happy to have a job again. We would often share a ride—Lisa would start him and I would finish him. She would work through the stiffness, and I would benefit from a more balanced horse."

Setback

In mid-November, Cody reached a plateau—not getting worse, but no longer getting better. "When Sal Salvetti, an equine massage therapist, came for a regularly scheduled appointment, he found areas of discomfort in Cody's back and stiffness in the sacroiliac joint, something that had been hinted at in the hind-end bone scan back in May." Susan called Dr. Mitchell at Fairfield Equine; Dr. Mitchell thought Cody's halt in progress had to do with overall muscle weakness and possibly the inflamed sacroiliac joint and was not a problem with his suspensory.

"I then scheduled an appointment with Liz Maloney, a vet and chiropractor, to check out his back problem and double-check his suspensory. She watched Cody on the longe, felt his back, and to confirm, she 'blocked' the suspensory. You have never seen happier people watching an unsound horse. Whatever it was, the suspensory was fine—Cody moved exactly as he had before the block. Liz felt it was his right sacroiliac joint, and she recommended injecting it with flucort and Sarapin® (see p. 365).

"The injection in the joint did the trick and by December, almost six months after originally returning to ridden work, we were making real progress. Cody was now working six days per week: Lisa rode him twice a week, I had a weekly lesson, and Lisa would often stop by to watch my independent rides. By January, he was gaining both muscle and strength.

"Through the winter, Cody and I continued to work on his fitness and my confidence. We did lots of transitions, changes of rein, some lateral work, and to keep my confidence up, I planned my rides so I always had another rider for company and there was minimal chance of snow falling off the roof of the indoor. Lisa never gave up on Cody or me—even when it took me three months to finally sit his canter again in both directions! She encouraged and guided me and always made me laugh. I knew by March that Cody and I would actually make it, in large part because of Lisa's help and friendship."

Return to Competition

"In April, Lisa and I made a plan for Cody's return to competition. That spring, Lisa would take him Beginner Novice at the King Oak Farm Horse Trials in Massachusetts and the Green Mountain Horse Association Horse Trials in Vermont, and then Novice Level at Groton House Farm in Massachusetts. Cody was delighted to be out and cantered through most of his first dressage test at King Oak—even the judge was laughing. By his third event, Cody was truly back to his old self and still sound."

"Cody was delighted to be out and cantered through most of his first dressage test at King Oak—even the judge was laughing."

In September, 16 months after the ACell injection and surgery, Cody and Susan competed in the Beginner Novice division at the Green Mountain Horse Association Horse Trials in Vermont.

Cody Today

Susan and Cody continue to compete at Beginner Novice. "I've spent hours wondering whether I bought the right horse—and not because of the injury and recovery period. At some moments, Cody seems too athletic and strong for me, perhaps too much for someone at my level. I also fear that he might get hurt again—or hurt me. The uncertainties about my horse's condition and progress at times felt confusing and unnerving, but it gives me satisfaction to know that I tried to do the right things for Cody. And I feel incredible gratitude toward the friends and professionals who did their absolute best for Cody and me. The knowledge and encouragement of Lisa and Susie Symmes, a dressage trainer and our barn manager, was enormous and constant. I could not have done it without them.

"Susie had promised me that in the time it would take to bring him back to work, I would get to know Cody in a whole new—and much deeper—way. Now I know how much these words ring true. Despite everything, I'm glad I took the plunge and bought a horse, and I value what I've learned through dealing with Cody's injury. But most of all, I love him even more than I thought possible."

Cody's Recovery Timeline

May 24	ACell injection and fascial release surgery.
May 26	Returned home. Began hand-walking for 15 minutes, 2 times a day.
July 16	Began walking under saddle for 20 minutes, 2 times a day.
September 24	First ride at the trot. Began with 5 minutes of trot in a 30-minute ride and gradually increased to 10-minute sets over the next 4 weeks.
October 25	First ride at the canter.
March 25	Began jumping small gymnastics and cross-rails.
June	Returned to competition.

Susan's Tips

- Don't stop asking, "Why is my horse lame?" until you have an answer and your horse is making progress in his recovery.

- Never hesitate to get a second or even a third vet's opinion. If you're near a veterinary hospital or clinic with state-of-the-art equipment capable of taking bone scans or magnetic resonance imaging (MRI), take advantage of it.

→

• Use the recovery time to get back to the basics and improve your seat and position.

• If you have confidence problems when starting your horse back to work, talk honestly with your trainer. Don't be afraid to ask her to "share" the ride with you or work your horse for you several days a week until you feel confident taking over his rehab under saddle.

CAROL TRAVER – Jumper Rider
LILLY – Canadian Thoroughbred

Croton-on-Hudson, New York

Torn Left Front Suspensory

Carol

"My parents knew nothing about horses, but I convinced them to let me start taking once-weekly (all my parents could afford) riding lessons when I was about nine years old. At 16, I moved to a slightly more upscale barn for lessons and discovered that while I could pretty much ride anything with four legs, I lacked quite a bit in the 'polish' department."

Once Carol got her driver's license, she took a job at the Belmont racetrack in New York State walking "hots" and exercise riding. It wasn't long before she decided that life on the "backside" (in the stable area) wasn't for her. She graduated from Vassar, then Yale Law School, married, and was hired by a law firm in Manhattan. An ad in a local "penny-saver" advertising flyer announcing the opening of a new riding facility was all Carol needed to get her back in the saddle. "This time I started to learn how to really ride as opposed to just sticking on a horse."

After several years of hard work, Carol was ready to begin showing with a young Thoroughbred she leased from her trainer. But, before she could make it to her first show, she became pregnant with her son, Christopher. A year-and-a-half after Christopher was born, she finally made it into the ring on a Thoroughbred mare she had just purchased. Carol and Montego Bay (known as "Monte") went on to compete successfully for three years in the High Adult (3'6") jumper division.

Carol is a cofounder of Azimuth Interactive, Inc., which specializes in software and technical training products for the higher education and corporate markets. "Although my work life can be incredibly busy and hectic, I have the advantage of being my own boss, as well as having an understanding business partner, husband, and son, who all realize that horses help keep me sane and able to function at a high level in all the other aspects of my life."

Home Facility

Both Lilly and Monte were boarded at Riverstone, a 30-stall hunter/jumper facility in Garrison, 45 miles north of New York City. The barn has six large turnout paddocks, a 200- by 200-foot outdoor arena, a smaller outdoor ring, and an indoor arena attached to the barn.

Diamond in the Rough aka "Lilly"

Lilly is a 16.1-hand bay Canadian Thoroughbred mare that raced until she was six. She had been competing in 4' and 4'3" jumper classes before being purchased by Carol.

"I didn't immediately click with Lilly as I had with Monte. She has high withers, a long back, a hard mouth, and pulls like a freight train. She's very heavy on her forehand, and 'goes like a racehorse,' meaning that she leans into the bit and pulls down. I'm a relatively little person, and when I first got her, she would frequently pull me right out of the tack.

"Initially, Lilly was a bit standoffish. You could tell she was 'nice,' but that was about it. It was not until she hurt herself, and I began to spend a lot of one-on-one time with her, that we really got to know one other, and bonded. After that, as they say, 'the rest was history'—she was mine, and I was hers."

At the time of the injury, Lilly was 11 and she and Carol were competing in the High Adult (3'6") jumper division

The Injury

"Lilly came up lame after a rambunctious day out in her paddock. Since there didn't appear to be much heat or swelling, we decided to just wrap her in standing bandages and put her on stall rest for few days. When there was no improvement, we called the veterinarian, Dr. Richard Urban."

Diagnosis and Prognosis

"The ultrasound on January 18 showed a severely pulled ligament attached to the sesamoid that had aggravated an old upper suspensory problem." That evening, Carol e-mailed her friend and barn-mate Ann Cohen, whose horse, Mackie, had just been diagnosed with a torn suspensory (see Ligament Injury Case Study 7, p. 152).

> *Aargh. My head's spinning too much at the moment. It's so hard loving these animals and then they go and hurt themselves through no fault of their own, and if it weren't all so damn expensive, it wouldn't matter as much. I am on the razor's edge supporting both Monte and Lilly—my financial situation is like a deck of cards, robbing Peter to pay Paul, and just managing to keep my head above water, and the thought of trying to explain how it is that I am spending all this money that I basically don't have on two lame horses is beyond me. If I didn't have the money issues, I could perhaps be more philosophical. I just need to let my head clear for a bit. Perhaps when it does we can commiserate further.*

Rehabilitation

Early Days

For the first two months, Lilly was prescribed stall rest, with hand-walking once or twice a day for 20 minutes. Both her front legs were wrapped with standing bandages and LPC Tendonil linament was applied to her left leg underneath the wrap (see p. 365). Carol also treated her left leg for 20 minutes each day for the next eight weeks with Respond Systems, Inc., laser therapy (see p. 370).

"Lilly had another ultrasound at the end of February, five weeks after the fateful day in the paddock, at which point she was pronounced at about 50 percent. At that point, we started leaving her unwrapped at night, although the rest of the regimen—stall rest, hand-walking, Tendo-nil rub, and daily lasering remained the same.

"Ann and other friends at the barn helped tremendously by sending e-mails with supportive notes. Once I got past the initial stage of being devastated and feeling sorry for myself, I tried to focus on remaining positive. Since I did most of Lilly's hands-on care, that kept me occupied on a daily basis. I occasionally rode various friends' horses, or horses owned by Riverstone, although certainly not every day.

Once you get past the initial stage of being devastated and feeling sorry for yourself, try to focus on remaining positive.

"In terms of keeping myself in shape, hand-walking a hot, otherwise stall-bound Thoroughbred during three of the coldest months of the year without the help of tranquilizers was enough to keep me both on my toes and in shape!"

At the end of March, Lilly was again allowed turnout out in a size-restricted (20- by 20-foot) paddock.

Back to Ridden Work

By mid-April, about 12 weeks after the injury, Carol was able to start walking Lilly under tack in the indoor arena. A week later, Carol e-mailed Ann:

Went to the barn tonight. Go to Lilly's stall and start to pull her out. She took one step forward and it was immediately apparent that something is seriously wrong. She is dead lame in the left front. So lame she can barely put any weight on the foot. Not sure what it is. Kim thinks maybe from shoeing—I'm hoping abscess, although how she could get an abscess from standing in her stall is beyond me. Un-freaking-believable. This roller coaster is making me insane.

"As it turned out," remembers Carol, "it was an abscess that responded relatively quickly to soaking and some Banamine®, and I was able to resume riding at the walk in the indoor arena within a few days. We then picked up where we had left off and walked for several weeks.

"The major challenge that I had to deal with was trying to bring a very hot Thoroughbred back into work. My trainer gave her some acepromazine (see p. 365) before our first few rides and again once we started working in the outside arena the first week of May, but I didn't want to give her acepromazine for too long, because you can't really do any productive work—you can walk and perhaps trot a bit, but that's about it."

By the time Carol added trotting to the mix in early May, she sometimes had her hands full dealing with Lilly's high spirits. As she reported to Ann one evening during the first week of June:

> We started out by walking for about five minutes on a loose rein and then for 15 minutes in a frame, and then trotting two times around the ring in each direction, trotting through the corners one time each. Anyway, we were almost finished walking after the last trot, Lilly was still keyed up but was listening (or so I thought), and I was very relaxed when out of nowhere she stuck her head between her ankles, squealed, and took off bucking like the best rodeo horse in the business.
>
> At first I thought she was just acting out and I would be able to get her back really quickly, but she kept on building and bucking, heading for a line of jumps (we weren't going very straight). I lost my stirrups at the first or second buck since she was as round as a butterball. Luckily, she never got me in front of the saddle or I would have gone flying. I was finally able to pull her up. I stayed on for my eight seconds—I would have won a prize at a rodeo! After that, we walked around for about five more minutes, and

then I trotted her for about two or three strides in each
direction to make sure she was okay, and finally, I got off.
We poulticed her (there was no heat whatsoever in her
front legs but just wanted to play it safe).

"There were several more instances in which Lilly took off with me or started to buck," says Carol, "and I was always a bit fearful that I would not be able to get her back, or that she would toss me and then run around like a 'nut' and hurt herself again. But thankfully, she never did get totally away from me, and it all worked out in the end."

With the arrival of spring, Carol and Lilly had moved most of their work outside, interspersing their time in the ring with time out in the fields, walking and then later on in the recovery period, trotting up and down the slight rises on the Riverstone property.

Although Carol finally added cantering to the mix in the middle of June, 14 weeks into recovery, she now found Lilly had other soundness issues that needed to be addressed. "Lilly had come to me with some arthritis in her back, hocks, and stifles—not surprising, given she was 12 and had raced and done 4' jumpers in her past life—so in June we gave her a series of Legend® and Adequan®. That appeared to have a very beneficial effect, so I had her hocks, stifles, and back injected with hyaluronan in the beginning of July" (see p. 365).

The treatment was so successful that in August, Carol was able to begin jumping Lilly for the first time in eight months. As it happened, Ann jumped Mackie for the first time that same day. That evening Carol e-mailed her friend:

I am so happy for you. It is only fitting that we began this
odyssey together and are coming out of it on the same day.
I, too, am still glowing—everyone is wondering why I am
in such a good mood today. Had happy horse dreams last
night, too—you're right, it just makes everything better.

In September, Carol added monthly acupuncture and chiropractic treatments, and daily use of an electromagnetic blanket from Respond Systems, Inc.—the type with the electric coils, rather than standard magnets—to Lilly's regime (see p. 370).

I tried the magnetic blanket on Lilly for the first time today. I am totally flabbergasted. I still can't quite believe it. I had expected maybe no change, or perhaps a small improvement, at best. What I got was a significant—and I mean significant—improvement! She felt so good!!! It's really hard to describe. In fact, I daresay she felt as good as she has felt since we started back—smooth, fluid, just really good. I'm almost afraid to go back and try again tomorrow in case this is just a one-day wonder. I sure hope not. All I can say is that if this keeps up, that thing is worth every penny it costs.

Return to Competition

After Lilly returned to competition in October, almost 10 months after she injured herself, she and Carol competed successfully in the High Adult jumper division at "A" shows up and down the East Coast (including HITS in Ocala, Florida, and Saugerties, New York; the Vermont Summer Classic in Manchester, Vermont; the Hunter Farms Jumping Derby and Fall Classic in Princeton, New Jersey; and Old Salem Farm in North Salem, New York). "We won a number of classes and almost always got good ribbons in the Marshall & Sterling Adult Jumper Classics at shows."

Lilly Today

"She is now retired and living a happy life with her 'sister' Monte at Old Friends Farm in central Pennsylvania. My very last ride on her was a double-clear round in a Marshall & Sterling Classic—I couldn't ask for any more from her than what she had already given me; it was time."

LILLY'S RECOVERY TIMELINE

January 18	Diagnosis. Began hand-walking for 20 minutes once or twice a day.
April 14	Began walking under saddle.
May 4	First ride at the trot.
June 14	First ride at the canter.
August	Began jumping.
October	Returned to competition.

CAROL'S TIPS

- Trust your instincts, nobody knows your horse better than you. Just because someone can't "see" a problem from the ground doesn't mean that what you're feeling while riding your horse isn't real. The temptation is to look to others to validate your feeling (perhaps because you would rather that it not be true, or because you worry that you are being "neurotic") and to discard it if the person you look to doesn't agree. In almost every one of the situations that I have experienced, that "gut" feeling was correct.

- The electromagnetic blanket worked wonders for my horse. Although extremely expensive, this was one purchase that I would make again in

→

an instant. The two major manufacturers, Respond Systems, Inc., and Centurion, both have lease/option-to-buy programs, and if you can share the cost with friends, it makes it more affordable (see *Resources*, p. 370).

- Once you get past the devastated and feeling sorry for yourself stage, focus on remaining positive.

LIGAMENT INJURY CASE STUDY 7

ANN COHEN – Hunter Rider

MACKIE – Quarter Horse/Thoroughbred

New York, New York

Torn Left Front Suspensory

Ann

Ann started riding at eight years old, when her family moved from Manhattan to nearby Westchester County. "A house with a back-yard was a big change for this city girl and, as I told my father, 'all little girls who live in the country ride horses.'" She took weekly lessons and, much to her parents' surprise and dismay, didn't grow out of it in six months.

College and starting a career meant long stretches away from hors-es and it wasn't until Ann was 28 that she returned to riding regularly. At first, she showed leased horses in adult hunter and adult equitation classes at local rated shows in Westchester, Connecticut, and New Jersey. Occasionally, she rode Mackie, a friend's six-year-old mare. Mackie was for sale, but her price was out of Ann's reach.

When Mackie was sent to Connecticut to be tried by a potential buy-er, Ann found herself in tears. "My friend Carol said that if Mackie came back she was my destiny. But all I could think was that until that moment, I had no idea how much I had wanted this horse."

A few weeks later, Ann had dinner with Mackie's owner, who once again asked if she wanted to buy the horse as the potential buyers were dragging their feet. He offered Ann the option of putting down a deposit and paying the rest off over two years. She agreed, all the while assum-ing that the mare would be purchased by the people who had taken her on trial.

Home Facility

At the time of her injury, Mackie boarded at Riverstone, a 30-stall hunter/jumper facility in Garrison, 45 miles north of New York City. The barn has six large turnout paddocks, a 200- by 200-foot outdoor arena, a smaller outdoor ring, and an indoor arena attached to the barn.

Boarders are juniors and adults who show everything from ponies to Amateur Owner jumpers. While they show primarily in the Northeast, some go to Ocala, Florida, or Gulfport, Mississippi, in the winter. "It's a tight-knit group of incredibly fun, nice and supportive people."

"Two nights later, Mackie's owner phoned to tell me I had just bought a horse! Mackie had already been returned to her old stall at Riverstone and was there, unconcernedly eating her hay. At 37, I was a horse owner for the first time. I left work early the next day and headed to the barn and didn't even care that Mackie slobbered all over my silk pants and blouse."

Ann works in Manhattan as vice president of Bide-A-Wee, one of the oldest animal humane organizations in the country. Her focus is fundraising and marketing. She has co-written a book on human infectious diseases and epidemics, edited several others and "hopes someday to be able to make a living at it."

Got Milk (originally Fleetwood's McIntosh) aka "Mackie"

She was born Cold Spring, New York, just a few miles down the road from where she was boarded by Ann. Kim Perlman, Ann's trainer, met Mackie the day she was born and was the first person to ride her and teach her to jump.

"She's a 15.3-hand Quarter Horse/Thoroughbred cross; a pinto with unique symmetrical markings, so she stands out in a crowd," Ann says. "I'm just over five feet on a tall day, so she's the perfect size for me."

Mackie and Ann have shown successfully in the Adult Hunter divisions at shows from Ocala to HITS/Catskills, Old Salem Charity, Monmouth County, and the Vermont Summer Festival. Once, to help raise money for Lou Gehrig's disease research, she showed in the 2'9" jumpers at the Riverstone Jumper Classic—several of Ann's friends donated

$100 after seeing photographic evidence of Ann and Mackie jumping the liverpool.

The Injury

It didn't take a long time for Ann to learn that if horses can fulfill your dreams, they can also break your heart. Shortly before Christmas, Mackie came up lame on her left front leg.

Diagnosis and Prognosis

"When it didn't get better after a few days, we called the vet. He watched her jog and suspected it was a suspensory tear, which he confirmed with an ultrasound; she had a small hole down low on her left front suspensory. The only good news was that with this type of tear the chance of a full recovery was likely. In trying to figure out how it happened, our best guess was that she did it running around either out in a field or turned out in the indoor arena, although we will never know for sure."

It doesn't take long to learn that if horses can fulfill your dreams, they can also break your heart.

Rehabilitation

Early Days

Ann, in consultation with her vet, Dr. Rick Urban, and trainer, Kim Perlman, decided on 12 weeks of stall rest with Mackie being hand-walked for 20 minutes each day. They also used laser therapy on the ligament for 10 minutes a day and LPC Tendonil as a liniment (see *Resources*, p. 365). Other than during the laser treatments and application of the liniment, both of Mackie's front legs were kept wrapped for the entire 12-week period.

"I did research on the Internet, read whatever I could find—including a book on tendon and ligament injuries in horses—and talked extensively to other riders. It was great to hear about people who had been through similar experiences with their horses and were out there successfully competing again, but I was very careful about whom I talked to for comfort and hope, and whom I took advice from. Although there are some people who post on Internet bulletin boards who are extremely knowledgeable, it can be a dangerous place to look for advice since you often don't know anything about who is giving it. Bulletin boards are great as a support system, but for qualified advice, not so much help."

Mackie's 12 weeks off were spent in a 12- by 12-foot stall and, because the injury happened in December, she was hand-walked for 20 minutes each day in the indoor arena. When Ann couldn't get there, a groom did the hand-walking. "Emotionally, this was a very difficult time. I had waited 37 years to have a horse and this happened so soon after I got her. I was afraid she would never come back and never be able to jump again. It was very difficult to be at the barn three, sometimes four days a week hand-walking her while others rode. When there was another horse for me to ride, I jumped at the opportunity.

Do research on the Internet, read whatever you can find, and talk to other riders.

"In addition to hand-walking and the daily laser routine, I groomed and played with Mackie so that she wouldn't be horribly bored. When I was around, I opened her stall door and put up a web stall guard so she could look out. She's a very curious, social horse so I thought it was important to do this to prevent her from becoming restless and irritable."

Back to Ridden Work

At the end of March, 12 weeks after the injury was diagnosed, an ultrasound showed that the ligament had healed and Ann's vet laid out a plan for bringing Mackie back to work. "I'll remember the conversation we had for the rest of my life. The best advice he gave me was that horses can gain a lot of fitness from walking and that I shouldn't waste the walking time by letting Mackie wander around aimlessly—one of her favorite activities. I should let her warm up by wandering for a few minutes, and then I should put her in a frame, make her use her hind end, and really work at the walk.

"I was so excited to finally sit on my horse! Although my trainer could have ridden her first, he waited and let me do it. As a precaution, we gave her a small dose of acepromazine (see p. 365), so that she wouldn't hurt herself. Mackie was very quiet and walked around with her white nose practically in the dirt. I had tears in my eyes as we circled the indoor ring for 10 minutes. This was the first of a series of firsts. My trainer made sure that I was the first one to sit on her back, the first to trot her, the first to canter, and the first to jump."

After the first week, her walking time was increased to 20 minutes and Ann and Mackie continued walking for the next month. When they began trotting at the end of April, it was in the ring and the long sides only. Then they began using the whole arena—trotting once around each way and slowly increasing the amount of trot time in two-minute increments until they were trotting for 10 minutes in a 30-minute ride. Every time she trotted and Mackie was sound, Ann breathed a sigh of relief. "Mackie seemed happy to work, but every week it was possible that something could go wrong. My mood during this time swung from elation to paranoia on a regular basis."

"Mackie seemed happy to work, but every week it was possible that something could go wrong. My mood during this time swung from elation to paranoia on a regular basis."

Ann made incorporating Mackie's rehab into her busy life a high priority. She got to her office as early as possible during the week so she could leave early on Friday afternoons. When she could fit it in, she rode on Wednesday evenings as well. "I took the train out of the city (faster than driving at rush hour) and used the hour-plus train ride to work on writing and editing projects that were hard to concentrate on during a busy work day. My family, friends, and boyfriend understood that the horse was a priority and only occasionally gave me a hard time about it. Every Saturday and Sunday were spent at the barn with Mackie."

Mackie was ridden five days a week—three or four days by Ann and one or two days by Ann's trainer or one of the working students. "The most difficult part about working full-time and rehabbing Mackie was that I wanted to be there every day of the week. My friend Carol Traver, whose mare Lilly had a similar injury at the same time, was a great source of comfort (see Ligament Injury Case Study 6, p. 142). Carol lives close to the barn and was able to give me almost daily reports about exactly how Mackie was doing. We talked for hours about things we had heard and read, and our hopes and fears about whether our horses would come back. I'm not sure I could have gotten through it without her, since my non-horsey friends didn't understand and when they asked how she was, I knew they wanted the short answer!

"The problem of wanting to be at the barn with her and riding every day is an ongoing challenge. The way I look at it is that without the job I wouldn't be able to afford to have a horse, so the days away from her are a necessary evil. And I am extremely fortunate to have had such a great relationship with the people at the barn so I know they are always keeping an eye on her."

"The best thing that came out of this slow process was that Mackie and I built an incredibly strong bond."

By the first week of May, 16 weeks after the injury was diagnosed, Mackie and Ann made the move outside, walking on the dirt road that circled the outdoor ring and then working in the ring for 20 minutes. During that month, Mackie progressed to going on short trail rides, always ending with some trot work in the ring.

In May, Mackie was also allowed turnout in a small 16- by 18-foot paddock. "We gave her hay so she would stay calm and she was clearly happy to be able to move around without a person holding her or sitting on her back. We literally had to drag her back inside when her time was up."

After another ultrasound in mid-June, Ann began cantering Mackie, increasing her time at the canter in two-minute increments just as she had with their trot work. "There was one small setback around then, but it wasn't the ligament. Mackie was footsore for about a week, probably from stepping on a rock. When that went away, we moved her to a larger paddock. I really worried the first day she had room to run and buck. She was wild! She stood all the way up on her hind legs and stayed there for a few seconds, then took off bucking like a fiend. Kim, my trainer, said we had to let her do it and as usual he was right—she was no worse for wear.

"In mid-July, we were flatting around and Kim had us canter a pole on the ground. Mackie turned the corner, saw the pole, pricked her ears, arched her neck, and I'll venture to say, she smiled. We did that a couple of times, then Kim left the pole and put up a small vertical a stride after it. We cantered down to that and her ears were pricked so far forward I thought they'd fall off. She was quite proud of herself. We used a landing rail after the jump so she'd have something to think about other than galloping away. I shed a few happy tears that day.

"The best thing that came out of this slow process was that Mackie and I built an incredibly strong bond. She became very sensitive to me and I became very attuned to her. We 'learned each other' by spending so much non-riding time together. And, by bringing her back slowly and becoming very conscious of how she felt physically, I started to know when she felt right and when something was wrong. This experience also helped me develop a level of 'feel' that I don't think my riding ever had before. Mackie truly became my horse—or I became her person, which is certainly the way she sees it."

Return to Competition

The last week of August, eight months after the injury, Ann and Mackie attended their first show, competing in the 2' Schooling Hunter division.

"This experience helped me develop a level of feel that I don't think my riding ever had before."

Mackie Today

After Mackie's recovery, she and Ann started again in the 2' Schooling Hunter division and soon moved up to the 3' Adult Amateur hunters. The highlight of their show career came two years after the injury when they won ribbons in the Adult Amateur Hunter division in Ocala, Florida, and continued the year with top ribbons at HITS/Catskills and the Vermont Summer Festival.

Now age 13, Mackie has recently gone on to a successful new career—competing in Western pleasure classes with a longtime friend of Ann's.

MACKIE'S RECOVERY TIMELINE

December 22	Injury diagnosed. Began hand-walking for 20 minutes per day.
March 26	Began walking under saddle for 10 minutes, increasing to 20 minutes over the next 30 days.
April 26	First ride at the trot. Began by trotting down the long side of the arena then added trot in 2-minute increments until trotting for 10 minutes in a 30-minute ride.
June 14	First ride at the canter. Began with 2 minutes and then increased in 2-minute increments.
July 14	Began trotting ground poles and tiny verticals.
August 27	Returned to competition.

ANN'S TIPS

- Work with a veterinarian you know and trust, and don't be afraid to ask him or her questions every step of the way. Mackie's vet's advice was very helpful, not just when she hurt herself, but all the way through the rehabilitation process.

- There are many treatment options, more now than when Mackie went through her rehabilitation, so do some research and talk to your vet and your trainer about what will work best for your horse.

→

ANN'S TIPS CONT.

- Ask your vet about what to do to minimize the formation of scar tissue, which can impact your horse's ability to return to doing his job safely and well.

- Talk to your friends, post on Internet bulletin boards, do whatever you need to minimize your own stress, but only implement advice from qualified people, primarily those who know you and know your horse.

- In addition to hand-walking, spend time with your horse grooming or simply playing with him. While you're in the barn, open the stall door and put up a web stall guard so he can look around and socialize.

LIGAMENT INJURY CASE STUDY 8

Lucy Chaplin Trumbull – Endurance Rider
Mouse – Arabian

Sierra Foothills, California

Torn Right Front Suspensory

Lucy

Lucy started riding at age 12 while living in Holland and continued after moving to England as a teenager. At 32 and now living in California, she saw a photo of a coworker competing in the Tevis Cup and decided, "I want that!" Lucy began taking lessons, "at a *jumping* barn of all things—I am not a jumper by any stretch of the imagination!" One month later, she purchased Mouse.

A graphic artist, Lucy works for an engineering consultancy firm in Sacramento. "It's a 60-mile commute and I travel in with my husband, Patrick. Our work schedules don't always coincide, so we frequently end up waiting for each other to finish work. We often don't get home again until 12 or 13 hours later. Needless to say, that really cuts into my riding time."

Lucy has completed 500 American Endurance Ride Conference (AERC) endurance miles of 50s, and 100 AERC limited-distance miles of 25s and 30s. She is also the editor of the *Gold Country Endurance Riders Newsletter.*

Mouse

At the time Lucy purchased her, Mouse was a green, four-year old, 14.1-hand Arabian mare. "The reasoning behind this not terribly suitable choice was that I would have a horse with a clean slate. She wouldn't have any prior 'baggage' (yeah, right) and I'd be able to train her myself. The fact that I'd never trained a horse before was neither here nor there! The other 'plus' was that we wouldn't have to spend any money right away on saddles or a truck and trailer, because Mouse would require lots and lots of groundwork before we got to the riding stage.

"Of course, within a month, we acquired Provo (an Arabian gelding who had already completed one 50-mile ride), bought a saddle (which didn't fit, so we had to buy another), and a truck and a trailer, and we were off down the slippery slope of horse ownership."

At the time of the injury, Mouse was nine.

The Injury

"At the final trot-out of Mouse's first AERC 30-miler, the vet thought he could see something, but it wasn't enough to put a finger on. I figured she just needed more conditioning. Four months later, we did our second AERC 30-miler and this time the vet thought he could see something before we even started. But again, it wasn't enough to put a finger on. We completed that ride—Mouse behaving very cheerfully—and I put it down to her needing new shoes."

In September they did two Competitive Trail Rides—a two-day 50 and a fast 30-miler on a 105-degree day—without Mouse showing any signs of lameness. In late October, they attended the Lake Sonoma 50. At 30 miles there was a vet check and Lucy once again heard the dreaded "I see something" after the vet watched her trot out. A flexion test didn't make it any worse, so she opted to continue. Mouse was dead lame by the end of the ride.

Home Facility

Lucy and her husband own a five-acre property in the foothills outside Sacramento. Mouse lives at home with Provo, another Arabian, and Zini, an Arabian/Saddlebred mare. While Lucy doesn't have an arena, she does have easy access to miles of trails in the American River Canyon area. "These trails are mostly old, narrow, twisting, single-track gold mining trails with hundreds of feet of climbs in and out of the steep canyons and hundreds of feet of drop-offs, in some cases. They are fun, beautiful, and challenging for both horse and rider."

Diagnosis and Prognosis

An ultrasound determined that Mouse had a tear in her right front sus-pensory and moderate tendonitis in the superficial digital flexor tendon in the same leg.

"It was so sad that just as Mouse was starting to be in condition and 'get it' mentally, she was injured. Her endurance career had been so fleet-ing, it felt a bit like we'd been beaten before we ever got going properly."

Rehabilitation

Early Days

Lucy was directed to put Mouse on a course of "bute" (see p. 365) to reduce the inflammation in her leg and shoe her in egg bar shoes to give more support to the back of her heels. Additionally, Mouse was to wear ice boots for 20 minutes, two times daily, for three weeks.

"Mouse lived in a 12- by 18-foot turnout area for the whole of the winter. The set-up was lousy—every time it rained, all the water flowed directly into her paddock, turning it into a bog. So three times that win-ter I took my truck down into Sacramento and got a bed-load of Muck-Buster®—a local brand of cedar wood chips. I laid these down about two-feet deep and it would last another few weeks before she trampled them into the mud."

After Mouse's diagnosis, Lucy felt as if her life had been "turned into one long trudge, especially for the first few weeks when I was grinding bute pills into powder, filling electrolyte syringes with applesauce and bute, then trying to get most of it into Mouse's mouth, in the dark, with-out getting the goop in my hair or in her eye. As for icing her legs, forget the 20 minutes twice a day—I was lucky to manage once a day."

Dr. Carol Gillis also prescribed a course of controlled exercise for Mouse, a program with which Lucy was unfamiliar. "I posted something about Mouse's rehab on 'Ridecamp' at www.endurance.net, and I re-member one person 'slamming' me, asking why I was going to do all that hand-walking—that I should leave the horse alone in stall rest. But other people on the site had done the University of California—Davis rehab plan of controlled exercise and had very positive results to report."

After a week of stall rest, Lucy began the hand-walking. "I wasn't able to hand-walk her every day although I tried hard, and there were some nights when I was out there, quietly plodding along the lane at midnight with Mouse and my dog, Chili." Worried that the threesome might not be seen by drivers on a road without streetlights, she bought some reflective tape and made a set of "night safety clothes" for Mouse and Chili. Mouse had a reflective noseband on her halter and a set of leg wraps. In addition to Chili's reflective "coat," Lucy duct-taped a flashing bicycle light to her collar.

"My life had turned into one long trudge."

Lucy's biggest challenge was getting Mouse safely to the road to begin her walks. "We were told to stick to flat ground and I live on a steep hill. I'd walk her down the driveway taking tiny, tiny steps. Sometimes it would take us five minutes just to get off the property. Once down on the lane, it was relatively flat—at least when we were just going for 30 or 40 minutes. Further than that, and I was starting to hit hills, so I was worried about what would happen when we were supposed to add trotting to the regimen. Would I end up riding continuously up and down the same half-mile stretch of lane?

"I was supposed to hand-walk Mouse every day and increase the time walked by five minutes every two weeks. Looking back at my calendar, there were weeks when I was only able to walk her every other day. Because of that, I ended up limiting myself to upping the time every eight to 10 sessions. So, the less often I was able to hand-walk her, the longer it took for us to increase the workload. As a result, the rehab plan took much, much longer than it would have had I been able to do it every day, as prescribed. For instance, her first eight-week recheck didn't get done until the 12-week mark because I felt I was behind."

Shortly before Christmas, Mouse escaped from her pen. "She galloped down our 400-foot long driveway, galloped back up, then tore through the newly bulldozed hock-deep clay area we were leveling to build a barn. I was in floods of tears because I felt like I'd just wasted the last seven weeks and would have to start from scratch again—assuming she had reinjured her leg (or worse!) during her escapade. That was about the hardest, most stressful time of the whole rehab."

An ultrasound showed no further injury and confirmed that Mouse was healing nicely. "In the end, I think it helped me in a way, because I knew she wasn't quite as fragile as I'd assumed. After the 'Great Escape,' things actually calmed down a bit. I got to a more 'que sera, sera' state and because I was calm, Mouse settled down, too. I used our hand-walks to work on some holes I'd discovered in her training. We worked on gate opening and shutting, and I did a lot of this type of training with a clicker training/ reward system. This made our walks much more interesting, and the added benefit was that Mouse was a lot more attentive to me because there was food involved. I doubt I would have worked so conscientiously on this type of training without the aid of enforced hand-walking."

"I was in floods of tears because I felt like I'd just wasted the last seven weeks and would have to start from scratch again—assuming she hadn't badly reinjured her leg during her escapade."

Back to Ridden Work

On January 23, three months after the injury, Lucy got the go-ahead to start riding at the walk. The only complication: Provo was coming back from a bowed tendon and he also needed light, slow riding. "At that point, I was trying to ride both of them a total of 90 minutes a day. Again, I felt pretty good if I managed to ride them four times a week." By April, they were beginning a trot program that called for adding five minutes of trot every two weeks. "Mouse was feeling really good. So good, that in early May, while we were on a grazing break at one end of the lane, she spooked, bucked me off, fell down and split her lip, turned and galloped the half mile home without me."

Shortly after this incident, Lucy made the difficult decision to put Mouse's rehab on hold. "I was working full-time and preparing Provo for

Tevis. Mouse was now six months into her rehab program and everyone agreed that nothing would be compromised by turning her out until my life settled down. After all we'd been through, this was very tough. I had to tell myself that it couldn't be helped and that Mouse wasn't going backward, she was just 'on hold' for a while."

Mouse's return to work a year later was equally unexpected. Lucy was going to a fun ride and fundraiser and "decided to take Mouse along as an introduction to the idea that we might be starting work again. I figured I'd just let her soak up the bustle. After we arrived, I saddled her up and took her for hand-walk. On the way back, she was being so good and quiet that I decided to just get on her—and it was like I'd never left. She trudged along in her Mouse-like manner and I was thrilled to be up on her back again."

Shortly after, Lucy began Mouse on a second walking-under-saddle program, working up to one hour—"and maybe four miles"—over the next six weeks. To keep her third horse, Zini, going, she often ponied her off Mouse. "The three of us, plus Chili-dog, would go out on these fun and relaxing jaunts."

All went well until Mouse came up lame after a five-mile ride. "It was the same leg and I was convinced it must be the suspensory again, and I was sick with worry. But after a trip to the vet and a set of X-rays, it turned out that Mouse simply had sore feet."

Mouse's second rehab merged easily into Lucy's normal conditioning program of lots of long, slow distance. "I guess in my head, the rehab part never really comes to a specific conclusion, it just kind of segues into the standard getting her up and running again and back in condition, which is an ongoing thing. Distance riding requires a horse to be so strong. It's not just the fitness part—the cardiovascular stuff comes quickly—it's conditioning the tendons, ligaments, and bone that can literally take years to get really strong. You're never really done with it, you just keep adding to it like the layers of an onion. If you do too little homework, a

> Rehab never really comes to a specific conclusion—it just kind of segues into the standard getting your horse "up and running" again and back in condition, which is an ongoing thing.

horse can get injured if you let him do too much at a ride. On the other hand, if you do too much conditioning, the horse can also injure himself by plain overdoing it, so you're treading a tightrope to get it right."

Mouse Today

Mouse is now retired from her career as an endurance horse ("the vet told me her pasterns are too 'sproingy'"). She and Lucy are riding the trails around Lucy's home and investigating new career opportunities.

MOUSE'S RECOVERY TIMELINE

October 26	Injury diagnosed.
November 3	Began hand-walking for 5 minutes and increased by 5 minutes every 8 to 10 walk "sessions."
January 23	Began walking under saddle. Gradually increasing the time to 45-minutes.
April	First ride at the trot. Began trot with 5 minutes in a 45-minute ride and added 5 minutes every 2 weeks.
May 6	Rehab put on hold.
May—1 year later	Rehab resumed with 6 weeks of walking under saddle, then merged into a normal reconditioning schedule.

Lucy's Tips

- Never ride a horse that shows the slightest bit of lameness. It's too costly in time and money. I was recently watching the vetting at a 100-mile ride and every time a horse would come in that was even slightly off, I'd want to shout to them, "Stop now, while the horse isn't too broken!"

- Enjoy the time you get to spend together. Try not to make it into a chore. I saw so many beautiful full moons and starry skies that I never would have seen had I not been hand-walking at night.

- If you must ride or hand-walk after dark, you can create "night safety" gear for your horse by putting reflective tape on your halter or bridle and leg wraps. An LED (light emitting diode) headlamp from sporting goods retailers like REI can be worn by you or even attached to a dog's collar (see *Resources*, p. 367).

- If there are "holes" in your horse's training (like Mouse, with opening and closing gates) or other "issues" that need attention, incorporate clicker training in your rehab program (see *Resources*, p. 372).

Homework, High School, and Rehabbing Horses

Bringing a horse back to work is challenging under the best of circumstances, but imagine trying to manage your horse's rehab program when you can't drive yourself to the barn and have to schedule weeks of hand-walking around algebra homework and studying for history tests.

Meredith & Willy

"I think that teens can and should take responsibility for their horse's rehabilitation," says Meredith Baker of Columbia, Maryland. Meredith was planning to compete her seven-year-old Thoroughbred event horse,

Willy, at Novice Level when he was diagnosed with a tear in his left hind suspensory. A freshman in high school, Meredith was determined that she would not only have a role in making decisions about Willy's medical treatment, but that she would be the one to bring Willy back to work.

"I think if a teen who is a rider and owner doesn't step up and want to be at the vet appointments or spend deadly boring months doing nothing but walking and trotting, perhaps he or she shouldn't own a horse. It's not the ribbons and medals that prove you are a horseman, it's being there for your horse when he needs you. Riding is only an eighth of horse ownership, and that's really the bottom line."

When Willy was finally able to start back under saddle, Meredith never considered letting anyone else do the job. "The way I looked at it was that I was the one who did all the hand-walking in 30-degree temperatures and dealt with Willy freaking because he was fresh from being in a stall, so I wanted to be the one to ride him and bring him back from his injury. The feeling when you finally reach your goal is amazing.

I can't describe the incredible sense of achievement and joy when Willy and I finally jumped over that first fence—even though it was only 18 inches high!

MEREDITH'S TIPS

- If I could give one piece of advice to parents, it's try to schedule vet visits and ultrasounds around your teen's school schedule, or even let them miss an hour of school here and there for one or two appointments. It was very frustrating for me when things were being decided about Willy and I wasn't able to be there.

- As a young rider and horse owner, step up to the plate and be responsible for as much of the rehab as possible. It brings you a real sense of pride and you'll form an amazing bond with your horse. I thought that Willy and I had already bonded, but after walking and grooming him, and being his only source of entertainment for endless weeks, he's much more loving than he was before. Now he'll even walk up to me in the field—I used to have to chase him around before I could catch him.

- Rehabbing your horse teaches you lessons you can use in your non-horse life. I definitely learned patience during all those weeks of hand-walking! And, it really taught me about perseverance. Now, whenever Willy and I hit a roadblock in our training and the thought pops into my mind—"I could just sell him and find another horse that is more experienced"—I remind myself that I waited patiently while he was injured, so for Pete's sake, I can certainly get us past whatever comparatively trivial challenge we might be facing.

- Take it one day at a time. Instead of thinking about all the events you won't be able to compete in, concentrate on the fact that your horse is better today than he was yesterday, and that is something to be thankful for.

• Injuries give you a reality check. It definitely reminded me that nothing is for sure with horses. Everyday I go out and think, "I hope nothing is wrong with him today." But if there is, now I know we can roll with the punches!

Suzanne & Stoney

The summer before Suzanne Hardesty's freshman year in high school, she and Stoney, her 12-year-old Appaloosa/Arabian gelding, were competing at a horse trial in Illinois when Stoney caught his foot between the ground and the door of a temporary stall.

The vet on call came to the barn, looked at Stoney's leg and told Suzanne that the wound was superficial and her horse would be fine. "After he walked away, I turned to my dad and said, 'We need to get home to our vet, Dr. Monfort, *now*.' I knew what the vet said was wrong. I could tell by the look in Stoney's eyes that he was in unbearable pain and pleading with me for comfort and relief. And I was right—it turned out that Stoney had pulled a ligament in his hock, chipped his small pastern bone, and his hoof had pulled away at the coronary band."

Stoney and Suzanne returned home to Peoria, Illinois, and spent the next six months bringing Stoney back to work. "My vet wouldn't ever give me a time frame for when he was going to pronounce Stoney as 'better,' because he didn't want to discourage me. Once Stoney was sound again, Dr. Monfort told me that horses rarely recover from injuries like his, and if it hadn't been for my care, he would never have been able to return to work."

Suzanne and Stoney are once again competing successfully at Novice Level.

SUZANNE'S TIPS

- When an adult challenges the way you're handling your horse's medical treatment or rehab, it's okay to disagree. Being in Pony Club has taught me that it is okay to speak your mind as long as you're respectful. So learn the communication skills you need to calmly, rationally, and respectfully convey your thoughts and feelings to adults.

- Put your horse's downtime to good use. If you board at a barn, volunteer to help out. I groomed other horses, helped feed, and cleaned stalls. People offered me rides on their horses and my trainer let me ride her horse in two Pony Club rallies and a horse trial.

- Take it one day at a time and visualize competing again. Competition is my passion—I couldn't live without it. When thoughts of Stoney never recovering crossed my mind, I refused to let them get me down and focused on the small steps that helped me reach my ultimate goal of making Stoney a happy, healthy, competitive horse again.

- Never underestimate how much your non-horsey family is supporting you. I was so busy and caught up in taking care of Stoney, I didn't find the time or energy to shop for my brother Ted's birthday. I gave him a card and wrote how much I cared about him, what he meant to me, and let him know that I owed him one. He hugged me and said, "Thanks—it's okay." Ted and my family really understood what I was feeling and going through.

TENDON INJURY CASE STUDY I

JULIA WENDELL — Event Rider
REDMOND — Canadian Sport Horse

Upperco, Maryland

Bowed Right Front Tendon

Julia

"I grew up riding Quarter Horses, Arabians, and ponies in my back-yard in Pennsylvania. My grandfather bred and showed gaited Saddle Horses and my mother was a serious competitor of three- and five-gaited show horses. But by the time I came along, those classy horses were long gone and I rode the 'family' horses. I rode bareback more often than I was in a saddle and I never rode as an athlete until I was in my mid-thirties."

Diverted from horses altogether for about 15 years, Julia followed a career path as teacher, editor at a small literary press, poet, and mother of two now nearly grown children. It wasn't until she was 34 and took a lesson on a whim after her daughter, Caitlin, began taking riding lessons, that she rediscovered her childhood passion.

"I ended up making a serious career change at age 39, when my husband Barrett Warner (also a poet, who breeds and races Thoroughbreds) and I bought a ramshackle farm and started a boarding facility in northern Baltimore County. I completed my first Baby Novice event when I was 38 and my first Advanced horse trial at the ripe old age of 46!"

Julia's most recent books of poetry are *Scared Money Never Wins* and *Dark Track*.

Redmond

A 16.1-hand Canadian Sport Horse, Redmond was purchased by Julia as a six-year-old from 2004 Olympic Eventing Team member John Williams, who had competed him through Preliminary Level.

"What attracted me to Redmond? His cute pony ears? His eager expression? His fabulous, and I mean *fabulous* jump? Actually, it was because my first event horse, Huey, was having soundness problems and I bought Redmond with the hope he could get me through a One-Star—my goal at that time. I had no idea we would someday be competing at the Three-Star level. (Huey, now almost 18, is still running around Intermediate horse trials.)"

Three years before his tendon injury, Julia brought Redmond back to competition from a torn hind suspensory. At the time of the tendon injury, Redmond was 11.

Home Facility

Julia's 83-acre farm, which consisted of "a decrepit farmhouse, a falling-down barn, and not a board of visible fencing" when she purchased it, now has indoor and outdoor arenas where she hosts clinics and classes, and a cross-country schooling course that is open to local riders.

The Injury

"With Hurricane Ivan barreling up the northeast coastline toward the Millbrook Horse Trials in New York, the event organizers made the decision to run show jumping the same day as cross-country. I remember doubting my decision to continue, as Redmond has a tendency toward sore feet and he'd thrown both front shoes going clean around the Advanced cross-country course. But ambition got the better of me; finishing at Millbrook would mean we qualified for the Fair Hill International Three-Day Event, so I damned the torpedoes and decided to show jump. Redmond scooted around the show jumping course in his indomitable pony style and ended up one of a handful of clean rounds that day.

"I was able to skirt Ivan and get safely home but in the succeeding days, I thought I noticed an ever-so-slight change in the profile of Redmond's right front tendon. I watched the leg in silence, sure I was imagining the change and clearly not having learned anything from my previous wishful thinking when Redmond tore his suspensory.

"Two weeks after we returned from Millbrook, Barrett told me he'd noticed a 'blip' in Redmond's tendon. 'You see it too?' I asked, now mortified because I'd kept my dread and fear brewing inside instead of getting it out in the open and to the bottom of the problem."

Diagnosis and Prognosis

With her vet, Dr. Rachel Westerlund, on vacation, Julia turned to Dr. Cooper Williams, who immediately spotted a core lesion on the ultrasound. "In about 30 seconds, my aspirations for Fair Hill that year were dashed. I can only hope I have finally learned that when the rider has a hunch, she better listen to herself. If she thinks she notices a change, no matter how small, or feels a hitch, it's probably there."

Rehabilitation

Early Days

When Dr. Williams suggested treating the tendon with ACell (see p. 365) and a program of controlled exercise, Julia readily agreed. "It was an interesting choice to go this route, as I had chosen to let time do the healing of Redmond's suspensory. This round, we decided to interfere with the natural process and become more aggressive."

While the challenge of once again bringing Redmond back from an injury was daunting—"especially since he'd already spent a year off recuperating from the almost career-ending suspensory injury"—Julia found she was able to look back on the "positives" that came from that first experience. "Redmond was the first horse I'd bought with some competition mileage, having in the past brought my event horses along from nothing, so initially my relationship with Redmond was based more on the romance of the road—of horse trials in Vermont, Massachusetts, North Carolina, and all around Area II—and less on heart, or the day-to-day. But Redmond's suspensory rehab changed all that, as our relation-

"Redmond and I had a lot of serious and not-so-serious conversations together during those long days of hand-walking. He learned his times tables and I re-read War and Peace."

ship deepened to include the beauty of daily rehab care and the closeness that developed between us because of it. Redmond and I had a lot of serious and not-so-serious conversations together during those long days of hand-walking. He learned his times tables and I reread *War and Peace*."

Back to Ridden Work

During Redmond's rehab from his suspensory injury, he was confined to his stall for four months before Julia could even begin hand-walking him. "He went from 'Three-Day-fit' to just standing. This time, I began hand-walking him almost immediately and within a week after the injury was diagnosed, I was—on Dr. Williams' recommendation—walking Redmond under saddle. Redmond is a pretty sane guy and I figured I could handle riding him at the walk in our indoor arena. Only a couple of times did he spook and buck and carry on, but I was able to keep my seat. I guess I figured I had nothing to lose at this point and had faith in the program prescribed. I'm pretty good at following directions and have a history of having my faith in my vets—both Rachel Westerlund and Cooper Williams—rewarded by good outcomes."

"I was able to bend and stretch Redmond, but was instructed not to do any lateral work. So we worked seven days a week through the long winter on the quality of our working walk and trot, on stretching and loosening up his back, adding longer trot sets as we went."

Julia and Redmond began with five minutes of walking, increasing it until four weeks later, they were walking for 35 minutes each day. After another ultrasound the first week of October confirmed the tendon had made substantial progress, she began slowly adding trot work to her daily rides. "We began with three, one-minute trots interspersed throughout our walk work. After a month of these trot sets and another ultrasound that showed continued progress, we began three, two-minute trot sets. Before I knew it, three months had passed—as had Fair Hill. At that point, I was well beyond the disappointment, but I did note the day on my calendar.

"I was able to bend and stretch Redmond, but was instructed not to do any lateral work. So we worked seven days a week through the long winter on the quality of our working walk and trot, on stretching and loosening up his back, adding longer trot sets as we went. All this slow bending and stretching really paid off when it came to the quality of our dressage work.

"Because we were busier in our rehab program, the weeks and months passed more quickly the second time around. And Redmond seemed happier. He was always good about the walking and so on, but he never really comes alive until he's jumping and galloping. I had a sense that he was just waiting around for that to happen, almost as if he knew that he was hurt and that he had to go through all these steps, but that if he were patient he would eventually be able to do the things he loves again. Redmond's a really smart horse."

By January, five months after the injury, Julia and Redmond were cantering and by February, they were able to re-introduce lateral and collected work as well as "blessed turn-out. We gave him acepromazine (see p. 365) the first couple of times we turned him out in our smallest paddock but he was actually pretty okay about it—he certainly knew the drill by this time. And I think because he'd been under saddle the whole time, he never really lost his mind and manners, so turnout wasn't that big a deal when it happened.

"My neighbor and trainer, Gayle Molander, noted that Redmond's gaits, particularly his canter (which she had pre-viously described as 'lumpy') had really improved. The other good news was that Redmond never really lost much of his fitness in the time he was off. Sure, he gained a few in the belly, but he never got all that out of shape, because he was never really out of work."

In late February Julia took a break—with Redmond's rehab being continued by "my barn elf, Katee Yeiser"—to travel to Aiken, South Caro-lina, with her other event horses and "jump-start the season." When she returned home in early March, another ultrasound cleared her to begin jumping Redmond.

Have a ground person on hand when you jump to keep a careful eye on your horse: the way he is jump-ing, the soundness of his gaits, his form over fences, even the look in his eye, in case he gives any clues as to how he might be feeling that you might not pick up on from the saddle.

"While Dr. Williams had given us the okay to begin jumping, I decided to give Redmond more time. Counting back from the next Fair Hill in October, I wouldn't need to begin competing him until mid-July, so I felt I could put off jumping Redmond till the beginning of June."

Julia began by trotting fences, then cantered simple gymnastics and single fences—nothing over 3′. She also found it important to have a ground person on hand when she jumped. "I needed someone—in this case, Gayle—to keep a careful eye on Redmond: the way he was jumping, the soundness of his gaits, his form over fences, even the look in his eye, in case he gave us any clues as to how he might be feeling that I might not pick up on from the saddle. But nothing went awry, and I found that once I started jumping him again, his retraining program went smoothly and swiftly, and I could feel that for all intents and purposes, I'd gotten Redmond back."

Return to Competition

In July, 11 months after his diagnosis, Redmond competed in the Preliminary division at the Surefire Horse Trials in Virginia. Redmond returned for Surefire II and finished fourth in his Intermediate division, clean in both cross-country and show jumping. "He even showed himself to be quite the dressage pony, our 32 percent being the result of our focus on flatwork during his rehabilitation. The best news of all was that his legs looked better than ever. I was beaming!

"I've learned to appreciate and love the simple day-to-day interactions with my horse. Competition goals are now just that—goals."

"Redmond has now come back from two major injuries, either of which could have been career-ending. In dealing with those injuries, I've become much more flexible over the last few years, and I've learned to appreciate and love the simple day-to-day interactions with my horse. Competition goals are now just that—goals. It's true; it is hard for Redmond at the upper levels. He slaps the ground with his front end with a little too much concussive force on the flat and while jumping, plants both feet a little too hard before takeoff and landing. And because of his short-stridedness, he has to work a lot harder than most to go the upper level speeds and distances. But it's amazing what horses can come back from if they love their jobs enough to want to come back and if their owners take the time and follow a slow, progressive rehabilitation."

Redmond Today

One year after his injury, Redmond and Julia competed at the Fair Hill International Three-Day Event, going clear cross-country and having one of only seven clear show jumping rounds.

"As an amateur who never had any plan of running Intermediate, let alone a Three-Star, Redmond has helped me fulfill more competition dreams than I ever thought I had, and at this point he doesn't owe me another mile. But he wanted to come back and continue to do the job he loves so much to do. I learned a lot of things during Redmond's two rehabilitations, including that a year isn't such a long time, after all. Where there's a will, there's definitely a way—and when you've got the right horse, you go for it."

REDMOND'S RECOVERY TIMELINE

August 25	Injury diagnosed and ACell administered. Began hand-walking.
September 5	Cleared by vet to begin walking under saddle, beginning with 5 minutes and gradually increasing to 35 minutes over the next 4 weeks.
October 3	First ride at the trot. Began with 3 sets of 1-minute trots in 35 minutes of walk.
November 8	Increased trot work to 3 sets of 2-minute trots

	and gradually increased to 20 minutes of trot in a 35-minute ride.
January	First ride at the canter. Began with 1 minute of canter and gradually increased to 5 minutes over the next 4 weeks.
February	Added lateral work and collection to workouts.
June 3	Began jumping, starting by trotting fences, then cantering simple gymnastics and fences under 3'.
July	Returned to competition.

Julia's Tips

- Don't let ambition get the best of you—if you have any doubts about your horse's health, stop, analyze, and get to the bottom of any lurking medical issues. Trust your "hunches," and listen to yourself no matter how insignificant the problem may seem.

- Be serious about "time." Wear a cross-country stopwatch and set it so you can follow your vet's instructions to the second. Being "anal" about the process is what can make or break a horse's recovery.

- Put your horse's time off to good use. I spent countless hours reviewing old competition videos and learned that my overly-eager position tends to send Redmond at his jumps, rather than waiting for the jumps to come to us. I also saw that I tend to weight my right stirrup more than my left, which makes Redmond crooked and causes him to bulge right over his fences.

→

JULIA'S TIPS CONT.

- Don't begrudge the weeks you spend walking and trotting your horse. Going back to the basics will pay off once you get back in the dressage arena.

- When you begin jumping, enlist a knowledgeable friend to watch for things you may not be able to "feel" from the saddle—if your horse isn't straight or if his knees aren't equal and level over fences, it may be due to residual pain.

TENDON INJURY CASE STUDY 2

Jennifer Malott Kotylo — Dressage Rider
Raf — Thoroughbred/Warmblood

Chicago, Illinois

Torn Right Front Tendon

Jennifer

A former "B" Pony Clubber, she began riding dressage in her late teens—"my knees just couldn't handle a two-point any longer." She received her B.A. in Economics from the College of Wooster and her M.B.A. in Finance from Indiana University and then, "in pursuit of becoming a 'real adult,' I went out to conquer corporate America, all the while pining over the lack of horses in my life." Jennifer went to work in telecommunications and in her mid-twenties was able to start taking riding lessons after work. It wasn't long before she began leasing a series of horses and competing at Training and First Level dressage.

"But this was still not enough—the all-consuming desire to be around horses all the time that had been with me as a child was as powerful as ever." She became determined to transition her life from that of "real" adult to "happy" adult. At the time of Raf's injury, Jennifer was working full-time doing in-house public relations for Charlie Trotter's, one of Chicago's most famous restaurants. Today, she teaches and coaches dressage riders and eventers and is also a certified Core Dynamics Pilates teacher and Equilates™ instructor. Jennifer credits her time with Raf and especially his injury as helping her find her "true path to all things horsey."

A United States Dressage Federation (USDF) bronze and silver medalist, Jennifer is a past president of the Illinois Dressage and Combined Training Association.

Rafferty aka "Raf"

A 16.3-hand bay gelding of unknown origin that "looks like a Thoroughbred/Warmblood cross," Raf came into Jennifer's life when he was 13 years old and recovering from a series of tendon and lameness issues. He had been out of work, off and on, for several years.

"When I took him on lease, Raf was sound but terribly out of shape. I spent that first year rehabbing him—stretching him, straightening him, strengthening him—all the while falling head-over-heels in love with his generous heart and buoyant personality." When his owner decided to put him up for sale, Jennifer hesitated, but only briefly. "My heart said, 'Yes!' but my brain looked at his textbook over-at-the-knee conformation and said, 'Are you out of your mind?' Needless to say, my heart won the argument."

Home Facility

At the time of his injury, Raf was stabled at a large boarding/Arabian-training facility, with 60 stalls evenly divided between Arabians and boarders of various disciplines. There were large indoor and outdoor arenas and six sand paddocks.

The Injury

"The second week of June, off we went to a very soggy horse show where Raf was to make his Third Level debut. The show ring footing was fine. The warm-up ring footing was sloppy. Despite the mud, we came home with blue ribbons and scores in the mid 60s. All was right with the world, or so I thought.

"After a couple of days off, Raf was sound, but stiff in his back and a bit uneven in the reins. He took a few funny steps, but he had the propensity to do that, given his over-at-the-knee condition. I thought he was being lazy and needed to be pushed through this difficulty."

Diagnosis and Prognosis

Jennifer walked Raf back to the barn, untacked him, removed his polo wraps and went to rub down his tendons with isopropyl alcohol. It was then she noticed the steaming bump on his right digital flexor tendon. "My heart and my stomach both seized up. I packed his leg in ice and called the veterinarian. Palpation and ultrasound confirmed my fears; his tendon had a small tear."

Rehabilitation

Early Days

Jennifer began an immediate two-week course of icing, cold-hosing, and applying DMSO (see p. 365), and began hand-walking Raf, starting with 10 minutes and gradually working up to 20 to 30 minutes. In mid-July, to stave off boredom for both of them while Raf was on stall rest, Jennifer incorporated long lining into their 30 minutes of hand-walking. "The benefit of long lining was that I learned how to do something new and it helps a horse retain somewhat of a topline. In addition, I had Raf massaged on a weekly basis, so despite not having much tone, at least his muscles remained balanced and supple."

Because Jennifer lived and worked in downtown Chicago, travel time to her barn "was an hour-plus from our condo in the city and that assumed no traffic accidents, no pothole repairs, and no bad weather. Some days I spent over four hours on the road, just so that I could hand-walk Raf. There were definitely times that pulling off the road and bursting into tears of frustration seemed like a good idea."

While Jennifer had rehabbed horses before—"I've been around horses for a long time and unfortunately, they have a pesky way of finding trouble; if not my horse, then a friend's or colleague's"—her experience didn't make dealing with Raf's injury much easier. "I often woke up in the middle of the night, having had a nightmare about Raf. And I think I lived on antacids!

"Some days I spent over four hours on the road, just so that I could hand-walk Raf. There were definitely times that pulling off the road and bursting into tears of frustration seemed like a good idea."

"I'd leave work between five and six at night and get to the barn around seven. Fortunately, many of the folks I rode with also worked, so I was never lonely in the evenings. In fact, the barn was a hubbub of activity. On days I couldn't make it, my more-than-competent friend, Joan, was always there to help out. She would do everything I'd do for Raf—walk him, groom him. I don't know what I would have done without her.

"Before the weather got bad in October, my husband, Ken, would come out to the barn with me on the weekends. There was a little golf course, just down the road, so depending on how much time I needed, he would play either nine or 18 holes. Then we would stop at the little burger joint on the way home. That was our together time!"

If your horse is generally a good guy and usually doesn't have an attitude but begins to show resistance such as not picking up a lead, not bending, tail swishing, teeth grinding, bucking or bolting—he's probably hurting somewhere.

After the initial heat was out of the tendon—about two weeks after diagnosis—Jennifer asked her vet about alternative treatments, specifically about magnetic boots (see *Resources*, p. 370). His response was that while it couldn't hurt, he didn't feel it would be of any benefit. "But because I'm the type of person who needs to feel as if I'm doing something, not just waiting for nature to take her course, I bought a magnetic boot from a catalog. I had seen articles regarding magnetic therapy in various sports and health sources and the theory behind it was something that made intuitive sense to me.

"The first time I used it, I left it on Raf's leg for about 10 minutes. Over the next three months, I gradually left the boot on longer and longer, going from approximately 10 minutes to 90 minutes—always while Raf was in his stall. By mid-September, I could leave the boot on for 90 minutes with no sign of increased heat at the injury sight. I called my vet and announced that I thought Raf was healed and that I would like to have him ultrasounded.

"My vet thought I was insane, because given the nature of the first ultrasound, 'healing' should have been another month or so off. But to humor me, he brought out his machine and lo and behold, the tear was completely healed. Since that time, I've overheard this particular veterinarian recommend magnetic therapy to a number of his patients.

"First lesson learned—if your horse is generally a good guy and usually doesn't have an attitude, but begins to show resistance—such as not picking up a lead, not bending, tail swishing, teeth grinding, bucking, or bolting—he's probably hurting somewhere. He doesn't need to be lame, doesn't need to spike a temperature or be off his feed. His 'attitude' is his way of letting you know something isn't right.

"The second lesson I learned is to be creative with the stall-bound phase. If you think you are bored because you are not riding, think about how bored your horse must be! Play with long lining, learn the Parelli™ method, teach your horse tricks. In other words, keep his mind active even if his body has to remain inactive. Keep yourself active too; take this time to work on your body and mind. Go to the gym, catch up on those equine videos, or audit clinics.

Be open to alternative ideas. There are many protocols out there that are not "tested" by Western standards, but this doesn't mean they don't have merit.

"Third lesson learned—be open to alternative ideas. There are many protocols out there that are not 'tested' by Western standards, but this doesn't mean they don't have merit. It also doesn't mean that any one modality is a panacea. Sometimes Western medicine works, sometimes it doesn't. Sometimes Eastern medicine works and sometimes it doesn't. Sometimes Mother Nature works and sometimes it doesn't."

Back to Ridden Work

The first week of September, three months after the injury, Jennifer began walking Raf under saddle. "Luckily, Raf is a true gentleman, so walking him under saddle was not a life-threatening experience." She spent a month walking straight lines—beginning with 10 minutes and working up to 20 minutes over the next four weeks.

When they added trot work in early October, the sessions began with 10 minutes of walk, then a trot down the long side of the arena twice in each direction followed by another 10 minutes of walk. Over the next month, Jennifer gradually increased the time until Raf was trotting a total of 10 minutes in addition to 20 minutes of walk. During the second month of trot work, she added wide turns and large circles.

"The most important thing to remember when you start your trot work if your horse's tendon injury is on a front leg, is to keep your horse off his forehand. No 'long and low,' unless you can keep your horse balanced on his hindquarters—a difficult thing to do."

"I know it sounds funny, but in a way Raf's injury had a positive side. While I rehabbed him, I was forced to concentrate on the basics, and in the end, Raf became a much better upper level dressage horse."

Jennifer rode Raf for three months at the trot before adding the canter at the beginning of January. "With the canter stride, all of the horse's weight lands on one front leg, so when I did add canter, it was very collected and uphill and only on straight lines for the first month. I began with a canter down the long side—only once the first time—and gradually increased it to a whopping five minutes by the end of the month. The second month I added large circles and our rides now consisted of 10 to 15 minutes of walk, 15 to 20 of trot, and five minutes of canter."

Lateral work began in February with shallow leg-yields, shoulder-fore, and slight haunches-in. "I've never been one for drilling my horses in movements, so I didn't feel I was holding back, we just kept slowly building until one day we were doing Prix St. Georges movements.

"I know it sounds funny, but in a way Raf's injury had a positive side. While I rehabbed him, I was forced to concentrate on the basics, and in the end, Raf became a much better upper level dressage horse. He taught me to listen to the nuances of life, to be open to different ways of solving problems and to be aware and experience a whole range of emotions. Some of my friends called him an angel. And that he is. But to me, Raf was more of a teacher or a Buddha. He was a once-in-a-lifetime friend."

Return to Competition

"Raf returned to competition in late May, but it was approximately 15 months from the time of his injury to our Prix St. Georges debut."

Raf

Raf showed through Grand Prix without another tendon incident. During his "semi-retirement," he continued to be ridden three to four times a week—"once as a lesson horse, once as a trail horse, and twice a week for me to focus on me and make sure he stayed supple." Raf also performed several times a year at exhibitions and fund-raisers and even contributed his talents to the handicapped riding division of the North American Young Riders Championships.

At 23, Raf was put to sleep to relieve the pain associated with a quickly deteriorating case of laminitis. "I truly believe that his team of caregivers did the best they could," says Jennifer. "But it was his time to relinquish his body and let his soul be free to run and buck and roll again. Luckily, I know that his spirit will be a part of mine forever. I wouldn't be who I am without him."

RAF'S RECOVERY TIMELINE

June 10	Injury diagnosed. Began hand-walking for 10 minutes, gradually working up to 30 minutes per day.
July 14	Began incorporating long-lining at the walk into 30-minute hand-walking sessions. Began magnetic-boot treatment starting with 10-minute sessions and gradually increasing to 90 minutes over a 3-month period.
September 4	Began walking under saddle on straight lines only. Gradually increased the time from 10 minutes to 20 minutes over the next 4 weeks.

October 3	First ride at the trot. Began with 10 minutes of walk followed by a trot down each long side of the arena and then 10 minutes of walk. Gradually increased to 10 minutes of trot and 20 minutes of walk over 4 weeks.
November 3	Added wide turns and large circles at the trot.
January 7	First ride at the canter. Began with a canter down one long side of the arena and increased to 5 minutes of canter over the next 4 weeks.
February 10	Added large circles at the canter and lateral work—shallow leg-yields, shoulder-fore, and haunches-in.
May 26	Returned to competition.

JENNIFER'S TIPS

- Be aware of changes in your horse's attitude and try to discover the cause. Use every analytical tool you can to diagnose a problem—but don't discount your own "hunches."

- Be open to alternative therapy such as massage, chiropractic, and acupuncture, which can help your horse stay balanced and supple throughout his confinement.

- Know your horse's legs—every bump and every scar. Know where the blood vessels wrap around the tendons. Know how the legs heat up during work and how they cool down.

→

- Try not to blame yourself for your horse's injury. What is done, is done. Use your energy to help your horse heal, not to beat yourself up.

- If the tendon injury was on a front leg, it's essential to keep your horse off his forehand when you start back at the trot. No "long and low" unless you are certain you can keep your horse balanced on his hindquarters.

- Don't forget your non-horsey husband! Find something he'll enjoy doing (like my husband playing golf at a course near the barn) while you're spending those additional hours with your horse.

- When your horse returns to full work and/or competition after a tendon injury, avoid working him in even slightly deep or sloppy footing, limit schooling of medium or extended gaits, rub his legs with isopropyl alcohol after each schooling session, and consider adding acupuncture and chiropractic treatments to his regimen.

TENDON INJURY CASE STUDY 3

Nikki Husky – Equitation Rider
Buddy – Dutch Warmblood

Los Angeles, California

Torn Right Front Deep Digital Flexor Tendon and Strained Right Front Suspensory

Nikki

A "horse-crazy little kid," she begged her mother for riding lessons practically from the time she first learned to talk. "My mom was a horse crazy kid too. She did any chores she could around a neighbor's barn so she could ride—mostly bareback. She still rides bareback at least three days a week and takes us to the beach to ride, which no one else ever does, because she thinks it's really important to do other things with horses than just show them. My mom never showed a day in her life until we talked her into a class at the Santa Barbara National Show. And she won her equitation class!

"When I was five, my mom volunteered to exercise other people's horses, give shots, and pull manes in exchange for me having a horse to ride. Unfortunately, the only horses my mom was taking care of were either very young or very strong so I got bucked off a lot. My trainer, Meredith Bullock, finally told my mom, 'Get this kid a pony; it's not fair for her to have to ride all these giant horses.'

"Our budget was very low and my mom went everywhere trying crazy and ornery ponies until she finally found 'Bailey' (formally known as Seeing Is Believing). She hadn't been ridden in a year so she was very out of shape, but she was a beautiful mover and very sweet, and best of all, we could afford her. Bailey would eventually take me all the way to the

National Pony Finals (both in the Pony Medal and the Large Pony Hunters). And she became so fabulous that we were able to sell her to buy Buddy. The great end to this story is my mom bought Bailey back last year. She's now ridden by wonderful little girls and we get to see her every day."

Home Facility

Buddy is stabled at a 16-stall barn less than a mile from the Husky's home. Nikki's mother, Kevan Husky, manages the barn in exchange for free stabling for Buddy. There is a jumping arena, dressage arena, and adjoining trails.

Time to Believe aka "Buddy"

"My mom first saw Buddy, a 16-hand Dutch Warmblood gelding, go in a Special Jumper class at the Los Angeles Equestrian Center. I tried him and fell in love with him, but he was more money than we had planned to spend. In order to buy Buddy, my mom and I had to work extra hours grooming and trailering horses to shows—something I was perfectly willing to do!"

At the time of his injury, Buddy was eight years old. He and 14-year-old Nikki had just won the Interscholastic Medal Finals and qualified for all the upcoming major 3'6" Medal Finals. Nikki was looking forward to fulfilling a longtime dream and competing in the West Coast United States Equestrian Team (USET) Talent Search Jumping Finals.

The Injury

On September 8, the first day of the Pacific Coast Horseman's Association's 14-and-Under Medal Finals, Nikki and Buddy placed first out of 53 riders. "If the first day was like a dream then the second was a nightmare. As Buddy and I were warming up at around 7:00 A.M., I was certain something was wrong. He wasn't head-bobbing lame but there was definitely something there." Although no one could detect any swelling or heat, they immediately began icing Buddy's right front leg.

"Nikki made the decision to take our guy home," remembers her mother, Kevan. "I felt incredible pride in my daughter that day as there was not even the slightest hint of 'woe is me,' or 'life is not fair.' Instead there was a warm pat for her beloved friend as she wrapped him carefully and loaded him into our trailer. The few tears that fell were out of genuine concern for her horse as she repeated more than once 'I don't care about any of the Finals. I only care that Buddy will be okay.' This from a teenager, who had worked all year helping me trailer horses, pull manes, and exercise horses to earn money for the entry fees and trip expenses."

Diagnosis and Prognosis

The Huskys decided to trailer Buddy three hours north to the Alamo Pintado Equine Medical Center in Los Olivos, California, for a complete evaluation. "Nothing showed up in the X-rays or ultrasound, but Nikki was convinced she felt something and Buddy was definitely favoring the right front leg. So we probed further and ordered a bone scan. It was only then our fears were confirmed. Buddy had torn a small hole in his deep digital flexor tendon as well as straining his right front suspensory ligament. Thankfully, the prognosis was fairly optimistic as we caught the injury very early and laid Buddy up immediately."

"We probed further and ordered a bone scan. It was only then our fears were confirmed."

Rehabilitation

Early Days

The Huskys chose to treat Buddy with a bone marrow injection (BMI), a treatment pioneered at Alamo Pintado (see p. 365). Buddy was placed under general anesthesia, and bone marrow was then taken from his chest bone and injected at the site of the injury.

After surgery on September 22, Buddy remained at Alamo Pintado for two weeks and Nikki and Kevan made the six-hour round trip as frequently as possible to visit him. The decision was then made to move him to High Sky Farm, a nearby retirement and rehab facility in Los Olivos that was run by Moira Gill, a close friend of the family. "Buddy does not trailer all that calmly," says Kevan, "so we wanted him to remain as close as possible to the vet clinic. They could do regular check-ups on Buddy at Los Olivos without subjecting him to the long, six-hour-round-trip trailer ride."

Buddy was immediately put on a program of hand-walking, which was gradually increased over the next month until it reached 20 minutes, twice a day. He was ultrasounded at four weeks post-op and again a month later. Both times the ultrasounds showed Buddy's healing was on schedule.

"By November," remembers Nikki, "we were missing Buddy so much that we decided to find a place close to home where we could continue his rehab." Buddy was moved to Shadowbrook Stables in Moorpark, run by Jeni Brown, the trainer from whom the Husky's had purchased him.

"Homework was done in the car on the way to and from Moorpark—on the way home often with a flashlight aimed at the pages. Laundry was done between midnight and 1:00 A.M. and grocery shopping was frequently done at bizarre hours like 5:00 A.M."

At Shadowbrook, Buddy was put on a EuroXciser for 20 minutes every morning and 20 minutes each afternoon (see *Resources*, p. 367). Nikki and Kevan began to reorder their lives so the often hour-long trip to Moorpark could become part of their daily routine.

"Luckily, Nikki was the last of four kids and the only one left at home, otherwise I don't think it would have been possible. I'd drop Nikki at school in the morning and then go directly to the barn where I worked. I'd then have to get everything done for 16 horses before 2:00 P.M., when I'd pick up Nikki for the drive to Shadowbrook. Pam de Selliers, who owns the barn where I worked, was unbelievably supportive during the time Buddy was in rehab. She never complained that I was finishing my work as early as I could every day so that I was free to take Nikki to see Buddy.

"Nikki's father was very definite that if her grades started to suffer in any way, the trips to Moorpark would be curtailed. Nikki did her homework in the car on the way to and from Moorpark—on the way home often with a flashlight aimed at the pages. She also woke up many a morning at 5:00 A.M. to finish what work she had not managed to complete the night before. Laundry was definitely done between midnight and 1:00 A.M., and grocery shopping was frequently done at bizarre hours like 5:00 A.M. I think the toughest part of the whole rehab was that we could not have Buddy at home from the very beginning. But we felt it was important to keep him in a facility where he could use the EuroXciser and we would have access to an indoor arena. While an indoor might seem unnecessary in sunny southern California, the winter of Buddy's rehab was the wettest in memory. That indoor became indispensable."

In early January, three months after his surgery, Buddy returned to Alamo Pintado for another ultrasound, which confirmed his tendon was healing and that Nikki would now be allowed to continue Buddy's rehab under saddle.

Back to Ridden Work

In addition to Nikki's time riding, it was decided that Buddy would continue his EuroXciser routine. "It helped take a little edge off him before I rode and was really helping to build his muscles back up.

"I got a watch with a big face so I could tell exactly how any minutes we'd been riding. We started with two minutes of trot in each direction and over the next two months, built up to a routine of five minutes walk, four minutes of trot, five minutes walk, four minutes trot, and ended with five minutes of walk."

Get a watch with a big face so you can tell exactly how any minutes you've been riding.

Initially, Nikki and Buddy spent most of their time working alone in the indoor arena. In March, almost five months after Buddy's surgery, she began to ride Buddy in group flat lessons. "I would walk with the others to warm up and when we had trotted as much as he was allowed that day, I would just peel off and walk by myself. Then I'd put Buddy away and watch the rest of the lesson. You really can learn lots from watching lessons even if you can't ride in them.

"The first day I rode Buddy in a group lesson, I had to take a time-out after he let out a buck and excited another horse. We all held our breath for about a minute thinking Buddy might just have broken himself into pieces. But Buddy was just letting us know he felt terrific."

By the end of March, Nikki and Buddy were out of the indoor, riding around the perimeter of the property and along the paths that lead around the rings and then back to the barns. She often rode with friends Allison Van Sickle and Tara and Katee Hill. "Buddy always loves walking in groups. I can chat with my friends and he gets to hang out with his horsey friends at the same time. He's a real social guy.

"I was so lucky to have friends who understood how hard it was to have a horse laid up. They helped me just by being positive and talking about other things besides Buddy's injury. Tara has lost two horses, but she still has the best attitude in the whole world. She loves her horses so much and never blamed anyone for what had happened. I really admire her and want to act like she does, always keeping a really good outlook."

"I was so lucky to have friends who understood how hard it was to have a horse laid up. They helped me just by being positive and talking about other things besides Buddy's injury."

By the first of April, Buddy was working for a total of 30 minutes at the walk and trot. They then added canter to the mix and by the end of the month, they were doing a full 40 minutes of work. At the beginning of May, nine months after Buddy's injury, Nikki was given the okay to start over a few small fences.

"Buddy was thrilled and would get quite excited after the fences. I think he was probably wondering why we were having him jump such little fences. We could all tell he felt great."

Throughout May and June, Buddy continued work over low fences ("never over 3'") and Nikki added "trotting poles on the ground and playing the 'stride game'—you try and canter a different number of strides each time you go through the poles, lengthening or shortening to fit in a different number of strides each time." In July, 10 months after his injury, Buddy was brought back to the 3'6" ring.

Return to Competition

In September, Buddy and Nikki competed in the Maclay regionals at The

Oaks in San Juan Capistrano, California, and qualified for the ASPCA-Maclay National Championships at the Metropolitan Horse Show in New York City.

"I don't know to this day who was more excited to return to jumping, Buddy or Nikki," says Kevan. "Buddy returned stronger than ever, happy and carefree and sound to do the job he does so well. Carrying an incredibly lucky now 16-year-old over every jump in every big equitation class. The first time they jumped the open water again in a USET class, tears of joy ran down my face.

"I know we are definitely some of the lucky ones to have had such an excellent and full recovery, but I also know that an injury to any horse is a huge lesson in life. The scares, the sadness, the ups and downs all teach us ways of dealing with disappointment."

Buddy Today

That fall, a year after his injury, Nikki and Buddy competed at both national Medal Finals, the ASPCA-Maclay National Championship in Washington, DC, and the USEF/Pessoa National Hunter Seat Medal Finals in Harrisburg, Pennsylvania.

BUDDY'S RECOVERY TIMELINE

September 8	Injury occurred.
September 22	Bone marrow injection performed.
October 14	Moved from veterinary clinic to rehab facility and began hand-walking for 5 minutes, 2 times a day, increasing to 20 minutes, 2 times a day over the next 30 days.

November 3	Began walking on the EuroXciser for 20 minutes, 2 times a day.
January 7	First ride at the trot. Began with 2 minutes of trot and increasing over the next 60 days to 5 minutes of walk followed by 4 minutes of trot, 5 more minutes of walk, 4 more minutes of trot, and ending with 5 minutes of walk.
April 2	First ride at the canter.
May 4	Began work over small fences (under 3').
September	Returned to competition.

NIKKI'S TIPS

- Trust your judgment, even if you're "only" a teenager. Always speak up if you think something is wrong with your horse.

- I think more than anything this experience taught me patience and that is something that will help me forever! So often I just wanted Buddy to be fixed fast, but I knew we had to really wait and take things slowly to get the best results. No cutting corners or rushing him back to work.

- Throughout Buddy's rehab we poured over books, magazine articles, and the Internet. We read up as much as we could on his type of injury and kept in constant contact by fax and e-mail with Susan Erickson, the physical therapist at Alamo Pintado who had outlined his rehab program.

→

NIKKI'S TIPS CONT.

- While riding, use a watch with a face large enough that you can easily check the amount of time you've been walking or trotting.

- Add interest to your workouts—don't hesitate to join group lessons and do as much as your rehab program will allow.

AMY CROWNOVER – Event Rider
CHESTER – Thoroughbred

Nashville, Tennessee

Torn Right Hind Deep Digital Flexor Tendon

Amy

Amy grew up in Rhode Island "loving horses, but no one in my family shared my passion. I pestered my parents for lessons and finally, when I was seven, they agreed." She soon joined the local Pony Club and at 12 got her first horse—a mare of mixed parentage named Har-Money that she rode through high school and competed in hunter/jumper and dressage classes at local shows.

After college and a degree in chemical engineering, Amy was able to return to riding and began taking weekly lessons. "But they were almost like torture, as I desperately wanted to ride more often than one day a week." To gain more riding time, she began exercising an acquaintance's foxhunters, and seven years later bought Nubian Power ("Nubi"), a Thoroughbred mare. "After a season of foxhunting with Nubi, I met a woman at my son's playgroup who told me about eventing. When I found out eventing meant you could jump stone walls and logs in the woods without the chaos of dozens of other riders around you, I knew it was for me."

Amy is married with a son and daughter and works as a fund-raising consultant for non-profit organizations.

Chester Cheetah aka "Chester"

After seven years competing Nubi and moving from Beginner Novice to Training Level, "it became clear to everyone that Nubi hated the work involved in being an event horse. She was sold to a teenage hunter rider and went on to great success in a new career she loved.

"After Nubi was sold, I must have looked at a dozen horses. When I saw Chester, I immediately liked the way he moved and jumped—and he had what Jimmy Wofford refers to as 'the look of an eagle' in his eye." A 16.1-hand off-the-track chestnut Thoroughbred, he was bought by Amy as "probably a four-year-old. No one knows for certain as we can't read his tattoo. Rumor has it that he was blackballed from the track for bucking.

"Chester was still quite green, despite the fact that he had recently been run around a Training Level cross-country course by a very foolish trainer. He needed to go back to the very beginning and learn how to properly walk, trot, and canter."

Six months after Amy purchased Chester he was diagnosed with bastard strangles and given a slim chance of survival. With aggressive treatment and a patient and careful rehabilitation by Amy, Chester returned to work and a year later, competed in his first Beginner Novice event.

Home Facility

At the time of the injury, Chester boarded at a private barn 35 minutes from Amy's home. The barn, whose owner and boarders were all competitive event riders, was on 40 acres with 13 stalls, a sand dressage arena, jump field, and several cross-country jumps.

The Injury

Early in March, while schooling a cross-country course in preparation for an upcoming Training Level event, Amy remembers Chester having "an unusually expressive" reaction to jumping a coop set on the top of a bank. "He gave a huge buck coming back down the bank and although we jumped a few more fences, he didn't, in hindsight, feel quite right from that point on. When we returned home to the barn that evening, I went over his legs, but felt no heat or swelling and he appeared completely sound. I put it down to Chester's being tired."

Diagnosis and Prognosis

Later that month, Amy and several friends were trail riding and she remembers that while Chester "acted really ornery, I never felt anything that would indicate he was lame. But when he came in from his paddock that night, his back right leg had blown up." Amy's vet, Dr. Matt Povlovich, was called and she was instructed to poultice and pressure-wrap the leg and keep Chester confined to his stall. While the swelling did go down, by week's end he was lame at the trot. An ultrasound showed a 20 percent tear in his right hind deep digital flexor tendon.

Rehabilitation

Early Days

"After consulting with Dr. Scott Hopper at Rood & Riddle in Lexington, Kentucky, Dr. Povlovich recommended extracorporeal shock wave therapy (ESWT—see p. 366) as they didn't initially feel that Chester was a candidate for stem cell therapy."

Chester had his first EWST treatment on March 30, about three weeks after the cross-country school believed to have caused the injury. Amy was instructed to continue Chester's stall rest and hand-graze him—but only if he behaved and remained quiet. "Chester seemed to understand that he was in a stall 24/7 for a reason, perhaps because of all he went through with the bastard strangles. I have to imagine that he knew we were trying to help him deal with his injured leg."

Chester received a second treatment on April 13 and a third on the first of May. A follow-up ultrasound on May 23, two months after he injured himself, showed only modest improvement, and both Dr. Povlovich and Dr. Hopper agreed that the healing was not as significant as hoped for and Chester should be taken to Rood & Riddle for stem cell therapy.

"By now, I was feeling really riding deprived. Luckily, my friend,

"While Chester acted really ornery, I never felt anything that would indicate he was lame. But when he came in from his paddock that night, his back right leg had blown up."

Susan Kaestner, offered me the chance to ride Bodoni Bold ("Simon"), her Two-Star event horse that was returning to work after back problems. Needless to say, I was thrilled to be able to ride an upper level horse. I knew Simon would help me understand the technical questions that would be asked at Training Level and above—like how to jump scary coffins and big mean trakehners."

On June 13, Chester arrived in Lexington where he underwent annular ligament release surgery and stem cells were injected into his injured tendon (see p. 365). Five days later, he returned home with instructions that he must again remain confined to a stall for three more weeks and be allowed out only to hand-graze. During this time, the incision was to be covered with sterile gauze and his leg pressure-wrapped. A 10-day course of "bute" (see p. 365) was also prescribed.

"At this point Chester wasn't feeling sick; he thought he had recovered and he was ready to rock and roll. He bolted, spun around me in a tight circle, and would occasionally rear up and paw like Black Beauty. I was terrified that he would reinjure himself."

Amy began hand-walking Chester the second week of July, a month after the surgery, "but only for five minutes at a time, as he still had his stitches and I wanted to be extremely conservative at the beginning of his rehab program." He was also hand-grazed twice a day for up to 30 minutes by Eduardo Juarez, a barn staffer. "Eduardo loved to talk on his cell phone, and Chester was the perfect companion for this enterprise."

During the first week of August, Amy began increasing Chester's hand-walking by five minutes each week until he was walking for 15 minutes a day. "At this point, Chester wasn't feeling sick; he thought he had recovered and he was ready to rock and roll. He bolted, spun around me in a tight circle, and would occasionally rear up and paw like Black Beauty. I was terrified that he would reinjure himself."

Back to Ridden Work

"After two weeks spent trying everything we could think of to get Chester to walk quietly, it was decided that because he is always better behaved when ridden, the safest thing for him—and for me—was to do the remainder of his walking rehab under saddle." So now five months after his injury, Amy was back on board: they began with 15 minutes of walking under saddle and increased the time by five minutes every week.

Amy and Chester moved from walking in paddocks near the barn to the farm's extensive pastures, and they were occasionally accompanied by Amy's five-year-old daughter, Emma, riding bareback on S.S. Skipper—a retired One-Star event horse (whose career included a win at the Radnor Hunt in Pennsylvania) who was "a suitably sized 15 hands with a back as wide as a couch.

"Emma was just learning how to ride and Skipper was the perfect partner. I was thrilled not just for the company, but that my daughter loved horses and loved to ride." Emma, who has now moved on to "regular" riding lessons, credits Skipper with teaching her "not to look down when you're crossing a creek and how to get on and off by myself."

Over Labor Day weekend, Amy had the chance to compete her friend's horse, Simon, at Training Level in the Kentucky Classic at the Kentucky Horse Park. "Some things on cross-country were pretty scary, but being on a horse that had seen it all before meant I could tuck my anxiety in my back pocket. Riding Simon taught me so many lessons that I can now use with Chester—one of the most important was not to 'fuss'; to have a quiet seat and hands. Simon made certain I understood that *my* job was to make sure my aids were clear and concise. *His* job was to jump and I was to sit quietly and let him do it his way."

The first week of October, just short of four months since his surgery, a third ultrasound cleared Chester to begin trotting. "But he'd lost so much muscle that it was like trotting a wet noodle," says Amy. "Because of that, we began with just two minutes of straight-line trot and added two minutes each week. It was six weeks before we were trotting for 15 minutes."

Once they were up to 15 minutes of trot, Amy began extending

"He'd lost so much muscle that it was like trotting a wet noodle. Because of that, we began with just two minutes of straight-line trot and added two minutes each week. It was six weeks before we were trotting for 15 minutes."

Chester's trot time by dividing it into two blocks. "After warming up at the walk, we would trot for eight minutes, walk for five, and trot for another eight. Every week, I added two minutes of trot to each block until we were trotting for 15 to 16 minutes, walking for five, and trotting for another 15 or 16 minutes. We rarely worked in the arena, as riding in the fields gave me the space to make circles or serpentines as large as I needed.

"The thing that surprised me the most was that Chester had lost his 'go button.' Chester, who had always been happy to move off my leg, now needed spurs and a crop to get him going. After making certain it was nothing physical that was holding him back, we came to the conclusion that he was just plain-old bored stiff! I was bored, too, so I couldn't blame him. Life prior to his injury had been pretty full—jumping, lots of trail rides, going off to schooling shows and events. Hard as I tried, there just are not a lot of ways to add variety to 15 minutes of trotting."

A fourth ultrasound in mid-January—10 months after the injury and seven months after the stem cell surgery—cleared Chester to begin cantering, something Amy began "literally in yards, as he was still building back his muscle. I would trot, throw in a minute of canter, and trot again. I began with three, one-minute canters and increased them in one-minute increments." By the end of March, Amy was working Chester for up to 60 minutes, five days a week. Each ride consisted of a 10-minute warm-up at the walk, followed by three blocks that included eight minutes of trot, three minutes of canter, and five minutes of walk.

"Dr. Povlovich had cautioned me about the danger of letting Chester get fatigued; that the greatest risk of reinjury would be when his muscles were tired. So each day I pushed him just enough to make progress, always making sure I stopped if I sensed he was tiring. I probably tended to err on the side of doing too little, but the thought of a reinjury made me sick to my stomach.

"Even though we were now cantering, my concentration was still on the basics—making sure Chester was supple and balanced. We did lots of stretching 'long and low' and often trotted poles I laid out in grids in one of the fields. We also began taking bi-weekly dressage lessons and worked on getting Chester back in a Training Level frame."

After a final ultrasound on June 1, nearly a year after the stem cell surgery, Chester returned to work over fences. "I had used the exercises in Jimmy Wofford's *Gymnastics* for years, and when Chester was ready to start jumping again, I began with some low level gymnastics from the book and gradually built up to higher fences and more challenging gymnastics. And Chester's 'go button' definitely returned when we started jumping—he was back to dragging me to the fences!"

Return to Competition

Beginning in June, Amy began taking Chester to local dressage and jumping schooling shows. In August they competed at Novice Level at the Penny Oaks Horse Trials in Indiana. "Chester felt great and it reminded me of the reasons I bought him—how much I love the way he looks and the way he goes. All the long months of rehab were worth it."

Chester Today

Amy and Chester continue to compete at Novice Level and are making plans for the move up to Training Level.

CHESTER'S RECOVERY TIMELINE

March 4	Injury likely occurred.
March 30	First ESWT treatment. Prescribed stall rest and hand-grazing only.
April 13	Second ESWT treatment.
May 1	Third ESWT treatment.

June 13	Stem cell therapy and annular ligament release surgery.
June 18	Returned home. Prescribed 10-day course of bute and stall rest, sterile gauze, and pressure bandaging for 3 weeks with hand-grazing 2 times a day for 15 to 20 minutes.
July 10	Began hand-walking 5 minutes each day plus hand-grazing for up to 30 minutes.
August 1	Increased hand-walking by 5 minutes each week until walking for 15 minutes a day.
August 22	First ride at the walk. Began with 15 minutes and increased by 5 minutes each week until walking for 35 minutes.
October 3	First ride at the trot. Began with 2 minutes and increased by 2 minutes per week until trotting for 15 minutes.
November 22	Divided trot time into 2, 8-minute "blocks" with 5 minutes of walk between them. Added 2 minutes to each trot block, each week, until doing 2 trot blocks of 15 to 16 minutes each.
January 14	First ride at the canter. Began with 1-minute canters, 3 times per workout, and increased in 1-minute increments.

March 27	Worked for 60 minutes 5 days a week, including 3 blocks of 8 minutes of trot, followed by 3 minutes of canter, and 5 minutes of walk.
June 1	Began work over fences with low level gymnastics.
August	Returned to competition.

AMY'S TIPS

• Do not be tempted to rush the process—nobody manages to fully rehabilitate his or her horse by skipping steps.

• Never second-guess yourself, or your horse if he shows signs of fatigue. You have to have a "feel" about your horse's progress. If he trips up behind two of three times over a ground pole, he is tired. I made certain that I stopped the minute I felt Chester was tiring—no matter what the plan was for the day.

• If you're lucky enough to be offered the chance to ride another horse, grab it! It will help keep you from obsessing over your own horse's progress, and it will reduce any resentment you might feel about your time away from training and competing.

• Listen to "success stories"—another rider's ability to bring her horse back from a devastating injury will inspire you to trudge on with your own rehabilitation program.

• Don't be a martyr; ask for help with hand-walking.

TENDON INJURY CASE STUDY 5

ALLISON GAUGHAN – Event Rider

ALI – Thoroughbred

Manchester, Michigan

Lacerated Left Flexor Tendon

Allison

"I grew up riding Quarter Horses and showing in Western pleasure and equitation, along with showmanship and speed classes. I was your typical 'cowgirl.'" At 16, she switched to English tack and began taking lessons in dressage and eventing.

"I spent several rather frustrating years at Novice Level eventing while trying to find my way through college at the University of Michigan. Once I graduated I had no idea what I wanted to do, and so I turned to what I loved most—horses. I made a new commitment to my riding, my horse Ali and I made the leap from Novice to Training Level, and as the end of the season approached, we began to talk of the transition to Preliminary Level.

"As fall came, the mission became apparent: a long hard winter lay before us if we wanted to move up. I was excited with where we were heading and perhaps ignorant, too, of how lucky I was to be doing it with a horse that was my best friend. Ali has been the steady constant in my life—the source of my greatest frustrations but also the recipient of my fiercest love."

Ali

A 16.1-hand Thoroughbred mare, Ali was purchased by Allison from her trainer, Sue Moessner, when Ali was six.

"She has always been the true definition of the word 'diva.' Ali is a princess who wants things her way, or God help the person who disagrees! But she has a huge heart and has guided me safely through so many things. With Ali, it didn't seem to matter if my body was on 'auto-pilot' at an event or not—she would always find a way to make everything work. I trusted her to do everything and she trusted me to never question her. (In the jumping phases, that is. Dressage was never easy for us!) Ours was, in my mind at least, a perfect partnership."

At the time of her injury, Ali was 15.

The Injury

"It was 3:30 P.M. on November 12, and I'd just finished working Ali and had turned her out in the pasture. For reasons I will never know, she went 'ballistic' and jumped the pasture fence—well over 5'! She ran through an adjoining hay field, caught her leg in an old fallen cattle fence and sliced 35 percent of her left flexor tendon. When I finally caught up with her, her leg was covered in blood and she could barely walk back to the barn."

Diagnosis and Prognosis

"The rest of that night was surreal: my vet, Dr. Kara Salek, came out and debated putting Ali down. Then, we decided Ali should go to Michigan State University (MSU) for surgery. My mom asked if Ali would ever jump again. Dr. Salek emphatically said, 'No,' and there was the realization that the promising career I'd been dreaming for Ali was over. I remember saying to myself on that late drive to MSU's large animal hospital that she was 'done.' She was done. I just kept repeating that over and over. Ali went into emergency surgery at 9:00 P.M. that night."

When the surgeon emerged from the operating room, she brought promising news. Ali would recover and with proper rehabilitation, she might even jump again. But there were no promises—it would be a difficult recovery and would require a certain amount of luck if Ali were ever to return to eventing.

"I don't remember most of the rest of that week—except for the angry look in Ali's eyes that said, 'Why won't you take me home?' It was easier for Ali to blame me than comprehend what was happening to her."

Rehabilitation

Early Days

Stall rest for six months was prescribed, as well as an aggressive regimen of care. "In addition to two weeks of cold-hosing, icing, and DMSO application (see p. 365), there was also the 'wrapping'. In Ali's case, six months of wrapping—I should have bought stock in Vetrap™! I also had to keep gauze over the area of the incision for a while because it was seeping synovial fluid" (the fluid in the tendon sheath).

Not surprisingly, being stall-bound did not sit well with Ali. "She kicked down stall walls and agitated every horse in the barn and every human within a five-mile radius with her loud hysterics. Two days after her arrival home, she knocked me unconscious when her swinging head collided with mine. We had been thrust into a situation that neither of us wanted to be in; there was not going to be any 'coming to terms' with it or 'accepting' it. We were both dreadfully unhappy and uncertain.

"Ali and I were both desperate for consolation and I came to realize that no matter how much my family loved and supported both of us, Ali was the only other being that truly understood what I was going through. I would find excuses to stay in the barn almost all day so I could be with her, even on sub-zero Michigan winter days. Finally, it wasn't the other

"My mom asked if Ali would ever jump again. Dr. Salek emphatically said, 'No,' and there was the realization that the promising career I'd been dreaming for Ali was over."

horses coming into the barn at night that calmed her down and made her happy, it was *me*. I was no longer simply the rider in her life—I became her life just as she had always been mine. Our new partnership was formed that winter."

Another unexpected bright spot during Ali's recovery was Allison's purchase of Roscoe, a six-year-old off-the-track Thoroughbred gelding.

"She kicked down stall walls and agitated every horse in the barn and every human within a five mile radius with her loud hysterics. Two days after her arrival home she knocked me unconscious when her swinging head collided with mine."

"I was supposed to look at him the evening of Ali's accident, but obviously didn't make it. Two days later, I finally went to see him. Roscoe had been bounced around to three or four different racehorse trainers in six years and never really had a home. Roscoe needed a family and I was looking for a lesson horse, so I wrote the check and he came home with us. In the first week it became apparent that he wasn't lesson horse material, but I remembered my mother's words—'What else are you going to do all winter besides take care of Ali?'—and began training Roscoe with the intention of selling him in the spring. Well, he's still here and will be forever. Roscoe taught me a whole new way of riding. He made me more sensitive and taught me to really ride from my seat. Roscoe is definitely not the easiest horse to ride, with lots of insecurities and quirks, but he's made my riding a-thousand-percent better."

Allison finally got the okay to begin hand-walking Ali in early March, four months after the accident. "This was no easy task at the tail end of a Michigan winter. There were still days when the yard was too icy and we were forced to stay inside. Ali was surprisingly calm for our daily walks and more interested in the rare find of early spring grass than anything."

Back to Ridden Work

Thirty days later, Allison began "walking Ali around the yard with me on her bareback. My parents and friends were amazed that I could get on her bareback without a second thought, but it never seemed like a big deal to me. Ali wouldn't do anything to jeopardize herself or me—that I knew for certain. I started at five minutes and moved to 10, 15, and then 20 minutes of walking over the next six weeks."

In April, six months after the injury, a series of ultrasounds showed that the tendon had healed, despite the mass of scar tissue that now covered the back of Ali's leg. In May, Allison began light trot work (now under saddle) along the same lines she had scheduled Ali's walk work—increasing the time by five-minute increments until they were trotting for 20 to 30 minutes in a 40-minute ride. "Each time I rode her I felt like I was sitting on heaven. But as her recovery continued, I realized I would never be able to ride her in the same way again. Before, I'd ridden her in a sort of absent-minded bliss; I now couldn't ride without monitoring her every step and feeling for the one that was 'off'. Every time I got on her I worried that this might be the day that she started limping again and our hopes would once again be dashed.

"Each time I rode her I felt like I was sitting on heaven. But as her recovery continued, I realized I would never be able to ride her in the same way again."

"And after months of riding only Roscoe, Ali felt completely foreign to me. Nothing was as I remembered it: where Ali has always been a bit downhill, Roscoe is very uphill and requires a quiet, subtle ride. What it did was make me a better rider for Ali. In other words, Roscoe changed my riding immensely and made me a more deserving rider for the mare that had always done so much for me."

In July, Allison began asking Ali for brief bits of canter. "I felt (and I'm sure she did as well) like a fish out of water. Whether it was because she was so unbalanced from the loss of strength or because I had now become accustomed to Roscoe's more powerful canter, or both, it felt strange to me. I came to realize as we cantered more, that her muscle and balance would come back, but that it would take time."

Allison spent the summer carefully and slowly bringing Ali back. She scheduled "countless" ultrasounds to check on the tendon. They worked in the sand arena and went for hacks around the farm. One day, she was sitting on Ali while teaching a jumping lesson, and "Ali casually turned toward a fence and before I knew what was happening—she jumped it!

My first reaction was, of course, fear for her tendon, but it was quickly replaced by a feeling that she wanted to get back to jumping just as much as I did. I didn't tell her to jump—she did it on her own. I think it was the first moment I realized that everything might work out after all.

"The one thing that surprised me was how much Ali wanted to get back to where she had been. I've had trainers tell me that most horses really don't care about being ridden and improving, but Ali's entire demeanor suggested that she wanted to event again. Whenever she would see me ride another horse, especially Roscoe, she would go into hysterics in her paddock. One day, when she had access to the arena while I was riding Roscoe, she walked in and as I passed by, cow-kicked him. Normally, she and Roscoe are good friends, but she didn't want me to ride him instead of her. It's almost as if she felt all of my time should be devoted to her career instead of another horse.

"The one thing that surprised me was how much Ali wanted to get back to where she had been. I've had trainers tell me that most horses really don't care about riding and improving, but Ali's entire demeanor suggested that she wanted to event again."

"The day in October I first asked Ali to jump again, 11 months from the day she was injured, was terrifying. I was absolutely petrified that she would break down. Ali, on the other hand, was in fighting form and dragged me to everything that I pointed her at. She felt better about it than I did. I started with very small fences and slowly worked my way up to low Training Level height. Eventually, I got up the nerve to take her to a lesson with my trainer, who set up some jumps that I hadn't seen in quite a long time. Ali attacked them with the same glee that I was feeling."

It was during Ali's recovery that Allison finally realized what she wanted to do with her life—"anything and everything equine." With her parent's support, they built an indoor arena and additional stabling and Allison went into the business of training, boarding, and teaching. "I love every minute of what I do and now wonder why I waited so long to figure it out. Every day my students reaffirm what Ali taught me from the start: riding is more than competing and winning—it's all about the relationship you create with your horse."

Return to Competition

A year-and-a-half after Ali was injured she returned to competition at the Encore Horse Trials in Ann Arbor, Michigan, competing at Novice Level. "I was surprised that I wasn't more nervous than I was about her leg holding up," says Allison. "But it was actually very comfortable and 'familiar.' Ali felt the way she always had—strong, eager, and ready to go; as though she had missed it and wanted nothing more than to be back on a cross-country course."

Ali Today

Ali and Allison returned to successfully competing at Training Level before Ali retired from eventing at age 18. She and Allison now spend their time together "trail riding and competing in an occasional dressage schooling show just for fun."

ALI'S RECOVERY TIMELINE

November 12	Injury and surgery.
November 22	Returned home. Began 2 weeks of cold-hosing, icing, and DMSO application, and 6 months of wrapping.
March 3	Began hand-walking with 5 minutes, gradually increasing to 20 minutes per day.
April 3	Began riding bareback at the walk for 5 minutes, gradually increasing to 20 minutes.
May 14	First ride at the trot. Began with 5 minutes and increased in 5-minute increments until trotting for 20 to 30 minutes in a 40 minute ride.

July 8	First ride at the canter.
October 11	Began schooling over fences.
June	Returned to competition.

ALLISON'S TIP

- Expect to experience the most wrenching emotions you can think of. I will never forget that winter. I felt raw inside. At times I would sit with my parents or my boyfriend and absolutely wail. I didn't know that I could feel so much grief and anger. Most non-horse people would equate it to losing a loved one and probably wouldn't understand how someone could feel the same way about a horse. But the emotions are just as strong. I can't lie and say it made me a better person. I know it made me stronger. I can't imagine feeling as strongly and powerfully as I did that winter ever again in my life. It's okay to cry, scream, throw things—whatever it takes. It's not just a horse. It wasn't just a horse. It was my Ali.

Hoof
DY

Sara Edelston Lieser — Event Rider
Mort — Thoroughbred

Hampden, Maine, and Boyce, Virginia

Bowed Tendons

Sara

"I always rode. My mom bought me a pony before I was born. She was crazy about horses—she'd ridden her stepfather's polo ponies as a child and bought a horse for foxhunting as soon as she graduated from college. My mother was determined that I would have the advantages, like riding lessons, that she didn't have as a child."

Sara joined Pony Club at age eight and graduated as a C-3 at 21. She evented through Training Level in her early teens and got Mort, her first "made" horse, when she was 17.

"I was so pleased with Mort and so excited about eventing that I decided to take a year off between high school and college. I couldn't see wasting his talent by going to college and letting him sit for four years. So after graduation, I packed my bags and took Mort to Denny Emerson's Tamarack Hill Farm in Vermont, where I spent a year as a working student. I had no idea how much I had to learn!"

Sara and Mort completed their first One-Star at the Radnor Hunt International Three-Day Event in Pennsylvania and soon made plans for the move up to Intermediate. "My first Intermediate with Mort was at the Morven Park Horse Trials in Virginia. So what if I fell off and had two stops. . . I was thrilled to be at that level."

Mortimer aka "Mort"

Sara's mother bought the 12-year-old, 16.1-hand Thoroughbred from a

Pony Clubber who had competed him through Intermediate Level. "At the time I was a bit at loose ends. My last horse had to be put down after a pasture accident, and I was involved with school and not certain what my goals were for riding. When my mom brought Mort home I wasn't even sure if he was for me or for her. Slightly sway-backed even then, with a full Maine winter coat, he certainly didn't look too impressive—that was, until I took him for my first jump school and he nearly jumped me out of the tack!"

The Injury

In mid-April, going Intermediate at the Menfelt Horse Trials in Maryland, Sara remembers "forcing Mort into an awkward distance in a combination cross-country. He scrambled over but I didn't stick with him and came off. Mort galloped the rest of the course handily and jumped clean in show jumping the next day, but a few days later I noticed his front legs didn't look quite right."

Home Facility

At the time of Mort's injury, Sara was living in Southern Pines, North Carolina, the winter home of Tamarack Hill Farm. "It's a professional facility with a cross-country course, several sand riding arenas, an indoor ring, and miles of trails on the Walthour Moss Foundation. The stalls all face the outside in shed-row-type barns."

Diagnosis and Prognosis

"There had been some swelling in his front legs on the morning of show jumping, but I hadn't worried about it, because he often 'stocked up' after a night in a stall. But I was concerned when the filling in his legs didn't go away after two days off in Southern Pines. I jogged him, but he still looked sound. Luckily, there was always a vet on the farm, so I asked him to take a look. He palpated his legs and told me that we would need to do an ultrasound. It showed that Mort had bowed both front tendons. I was absolutely and completely heartbroken."

Rehabilitation

Early Days

Sara decided on tendon splitting surgery, which was recommended by her vet to relieve the pressure on Mort's tendons and increase circulation to areas of the legs that receive poor blood flow.

Mort was put on stall rest for a month, allowed out only for brief periods of hand-grazing. Sara, who had been working a second job as a cashier at Wal-Mart as well as at the farm, quit so she could concentrate on Mort's recovery.

In May, about a month after the ill-fated cross-country go in Maryland, Mort and Sara returned to Vermont with the rest of Tamarack Hill Farm. Sara hand-walked Mort during her lunch break, going for rambling walks on the quiet dirt roads near the farm.

In June, she moved Mort home to her family's farm in Maine. "Mort was a horse who had always lived out 24/7, so being confined to a stall was driving him nuts. Once we arrived home, the vet agreed that we could try putting Mort on very restricted turnout—a tiny paddock with absolutely no running around. But the first time I turned him out, he began galloping wildly and calling for his friends. I panicked because I couldn't catch him and I couldn't stop him. I finally opened the paddock gate so he could gallop off to be with the other horses. Once he got to them, he stopped running, so I never tried to keep him by himself again.

"I hand-walked during my lunch break, going for rambling walks on the quiet dirt roads near the farm."

"I was extremely lucky that Mort didn't reinjure himself in the incident or during the time he was turned out with the other horses, and I would not recommend that anyone turn his or her horse out so early in his rehab—except under extraordinary circumstances and with the consent of a vet. If I could do it over again, I would find a way so that Mort could be confined and yet still have interaction with other horses." (For one way to allow restricted turnout near pasture buddies, see p. 276.)

By mid-August, instead of continuing Mort's rehab, Sara was packing for her freshman year at Amherst College. "I wish I could have done things perfectly, but that wasn't an option. For me it was always a question of what we could manage. My mom worked full time as a lawyer and I was about to be in school. We didn't have the funds to pay someone to start him back to work, so I knew Mort's rehab would have to wait until I came home for the summer. At that point in my life, at 19 years old, I wasn't used to making my own decisions concerning my horses, and it was really difficult to leave Mort at home without knowing if he was going to recover and be 'eventable' again.

"I wish I could have done things perfectly, but that wasn't an option. For me it was always a question of what we could manage."

"Despite gamely trying, I found that I was miserable at school without horses. I did join the equestrian team and competed in hunter and equitation classes on the collegiate circuit, but they laughed at my equitation and it was obvious to the judges (and to me) that I was an eventer. So I stopped showing and just worked at the school barn, cleaning stalls and riding some of the coach's horses."

Back to Ridden Work

In April, a year after Mort bowed his tendons, Sara's mother began hacking him, walking him on a road near their home so Mort would have a base of fitness when Sara returned from college. "Our local vet had ultrasounded him and the results were positive—he said Mort was good to go. His tendons had healed very well, with little of the 'cross-hatching' in the fibers that would signify that the healed tendons wouldn't be flexible."

When Sara returned home in May, she knew she was going to start riding Mort, but "had no idea what he would be able to do. I decided to treat Mort like a horse coming off a long layup instead of an injury and focused not just on strengthening his tendons, but on building strength throughout his body. My program was similar to my vet's suggested regimen—just many months later than I was supposed to start it! We began the 'legging-up' work by going on trail rides. Mort took going back to work as he took everything, with his good-natured enthusiasm. He wasn't a terror, although my mom did take him on a trail ride down by the coast where he jigged the entire time. Basically he was happy to be wandering around with a rider on his back again.

"I began by flatting him at the walk, trot, and canter. It was 'mud season' in Maine, so finding appropriate footing was a real challenge. I became paranoid about wet sloppy footing and always checked his legs for heat or swelling. I vowed never to jump or gallop him without sports medicine boots and to cold-hose him after every strenuous workout. Every time he came back with cold hard legs, I cheered.

"In late June, I took a jumping lesson with a friend who is a Pony Club instructor, and she said we both looked great. Mort is a talented experienced jumper, so it was more about getting in shape and working on *me*, rather than him.

"I decided to treat Mort like a horse coming off a long layup instead of an injury and focused not just on strengthening his tendons, but on building strength throughout his body."

"I have to say that this program—one with a long downtime between the injury and really getting back into work—is far from ideal and not one I would recommend. Mort—as always—tried his heart out for me, and he really wanted to get better. Throughout the process he was my inspiration."

Return to Competition

Sara and Mort's first event post-bowed-tendons was at the Huntington Farm Horse Trials in Vermont in July. Sara decided to go out Preliminary (down a level from where they had been competing) "because if Mort wasn't going to hold up to Preliminary, I wasn't going to continue eventing him. After a year off, you get to the point where you just want to know—will we sink or swim?

"Of course, it rained. The footing wasn't great, so I went slowly and didn't try to make the time. We didn't win any ribbons and we did have a lot of time penalties, but Mort was fine afterward. I carefully iced his legs after cross-country and had him ultrasounded when we got home. His legs would forever 'look' ugly (the original swelling never left) but they felt good and were strong on the inside.

"I took him to another Preliminary event in August at the GMHA (Green Mountain Horse Association) Horse Trials in Vermont—and it rained again! This time I went for time, had a great ride, placed third, and his legs were still fine at the end. It was only then that I really felt we had made it back."

Over the next three years, Sara continued to compete Mort. She brought him to Amherst and worked multiple jobs—everything from cleaning stalls to being a museum guard—in order to pay to keep him there until she graduated. Eventually, they moved back up to Intermediate, doing three or four events a season.

"Mort—as always— tried his heart out for me and he really wanted to get better. Throughout the process he was my inspiration."

"After I graduated, I decided to have one last really competitive season with Mort. I took him to two Preliminary events and two Intermediate events and placed second at our last one—the Seneca Valley Pony Club Horse Trials in Maryland. That weekend was as muddy as any event I have ever attended, and I knew it was a risk, but it was our last event and I went for it. Mort was fabulous, his legs never swelled. And, he carried my mom around Training Level a few weeks later."

Sara is now member of the editorial staff at the *Chronicle of the Horse*. She has a new horse, Cat's Pajamas (aka "Sam"), a Thoroughbred by Denny Emerson's stallion, Loyal Pal. She competes Sam at Preliminary Level and "rides before work, or after work, and sometimes I take on extra jobs to help pay his competition expenses. I enjoy Sam and have a special relationship with him, but no horse will replace Mort in my heart. Mort was my best friend. I never felt like he owed me anything. If he couldn't have continued competing, we wouldn't have. But the fact that he could and clearly enjoyed it was a gift."

Mort Today

"Mort evented at Novice and Training Level with my mother until the ripe old age of 20 and is now—at 22—retired at my home in Virginia. While other small lameness issues have cropped up, I can honestly say that his tendons never bothered him again."

MORT'S RECOVERY TIMELINE

April 15	Injury and surgery. Stall rest and hand-grazing until mid-May.
May 18	Began hand-walking, starting with 15 minutes a day and working up to 30 minutes a day over the next 30 days.
June 7	Returned to Maine. Continued hand-walking.
April 5	Began hacking out at the walk.
May 20	Returned to work on the flat at the walk, trot, and canter.
June 25	First jumping lesson.
July	Returned to competition.

SARA'S TIPS

- It's okay to be emotional when your horse suffers a major injury. I know that the veterinarians, my trainer, and other barn staff all felt I was making too big of a deal about the whole thing. For them it was just one more horse with bowed tendons. For me it was my best friend suffering from an injury that was probably my fault, and I couldn't do anything to relieve his misery. Mort couldn't understand why he'd gone from "Three-Day-fit" to standing in a stall with no turnout, and I couldn't explain it to him so I felt awful. In such situations, it is important to surround yourself with friends who will support you instead of people who just tell you to "get on with life."

- Take the injury one day at a time. Don't waste time figuring out how quickly you can get your horse back into competition. Each horse is an individual and it's more important to listen to your horse than it is to follow a regimented rehabilitation schedule. If you think your horse is being pushed in his rehab, back off. Rushing things will only make it take longer and increase the chance of reinjury.

- After your horse is back at work, ride with confidence. You want to protect your horse, but at some point you have to let go of that, because it will get in the way of your riding. If you're constantly looking for signs that something's wrong, you'll drive yourself crazy. That's not to say that you shouldn't make compromises after an injury. I never pulled Mort from a competition, but I did run him slowly if the conditions required it. I paid attention to his legs, but when I was on his back it was important that I rode him confidently. I remember one event where he stopped at an oxer in the warm-up. Since Mort is a horse that doesn't stop, I immediately worried that he was lame. In truth, I just wasn't riding him forward, giving him the confidence to jump a big jump. I got over the oxer and went to ride cross-country. I decided that Mort would tell me if there really was a problem, so I kicked on and had a great ride. Eventing requires a full commitment, and if your heart isn't in it, it isn't safe for you or your horse.

Chapter 4

Laminitis

Because laminitis has multiple causes, as well as an equally confusing number of treatment and rehabilitation options, it can be one of the most challenging illnesses faced by horse owners. One of Dr. David Ramey's extremely useful Concise Guides (for others in the series, see *Resources*, p. 372) offers the latest research on the disease's prevention, causes, and treatment—as well as a discussion of how owners can best manage it long-term. I have included an excerpt from the *Concise Guide to Laminitis in the Horse* with the hope that Dr. Ramey's explanations of the disease and laminitis-related issues, simply stated in language any horse person can understand, will help alleviate some of the usual confusion and promote successful rehabilitation of afflicted horses in the future.

INTRODUCTION TO LAMINITIS

by David W. Ramey, DVM
(excerpt from *Concise Guide to Laminitis in the Horse*)

What Is Laminitis?

Laminitis is a potentially devastating disease of the horse's feet. While many horses can recover from an episode of laminitis uneventfully, the disease can also end a horse's career, or even his life. It's a bane to horse owners, farriers, and veterinarians alike (not to mention the horses).

Fortunately, intensive investigations have shed light on what's underlying this troubling condition. While a sure cure is still just a dream, many serious cases are now being saved that might not have been in years past. And, good strategies for prevention exist in many cases. While it's likely that laminitis will always be a concern, good management and good care (and some good luck) give you the best chance to overcome this frustrating disease.

Dr. **David Ramey** is a 1983 graduate of Colorado State University. After completing an internship in equine medicine and surgery at Iowa State University, he entered private equine practice in southern California in 1984. Dr. Ramey's practice is devoted to caring for sport and pleasure horses of various disciplines.

Dr. Ramey is also a noted author and lecturer, having written for and spoken to professional and lay audiences around the world on many topics pertaining to horse health. His "Concise Guide" series to equine health was a landmark when first published, and new and updated versions of these books are available (see p. 372).

Laminitis is a disease that appears to occur largely because people have domesticated the horse. By taking him out of his "natural" free-ranging situation, the horse has become overfed and under-exercised. He no longer follows his normal feeding or activity patterns—his situation has been changed to accommodate the needs of his owner. The price for this convenience seems to be an increase in a variety of medical problems, including laminitis.

The horse has been domesticated for centuries. Without a doubt, laminitis has been a problem for just as long. Over the years, there have been countless attempts at fixing the problem, including various medicines, surgical approaches, and innumerable shoeing techniques. These approaches have all had their vocal proponents and "successes" and they have all had complete failures. It's only been a relatively short time that good scientific investigations have been directed at the problem; as a result, knowledge about the condition has increased dramatically. With all of the eager and well-meaning attempts to solve this troubling problem, there's a witches brew of scientific data, clinical impressions, and old myths that you'll have to sort through when trying to understand what's going on in a horse with laminitis.

The word roots that give meaning to the term *laminitis* are really quite simple. And, when you know something about the anatomy of the foot, they're also quite descriptive. Any time that you see the suffix "-itis" added on to a word, it means that something is inflamed. In the case of this disease, that something is the laminae of the hoof, which are the connections that bind the bone of the hoof to the hoof itself (you'll read all about them in a bit). Still, even though inflammation does occur in the foot of the horse with laminitis, there's a good bit more to the condition than just treating and attempting to relieve inflammation. In fact, laminitis is a complicated condition that may progress to involve virtually all of the anatomical structures of the horse's foot.

Historical Aspects

Diseases predate people's understanding of them. Nevertheless, people have apparently always wanted to put a name on disease conditions, probably just so that they could identify them and call them *something*. As a result of this eternal attempt to put a name on things that they didn't understand, people are still using terms like malaria (the "mal" means bad and the "aria" refers to the air) or influenza (implying that the disease comes from evil influences). In the case of laminitis, people didn't always know about the laminae of the hoof and they didn't always understand the process of inflammation. So, over history, there have been all sorts of terms used to describe the condition. For example, the ancient Greeks referred to laminitis as "gout" or "barley disease." Of course, these terms aren't used anymore, but some old words do seem to have a way of stick-ing around. In the case of laminitis, there is a very old word that's still in use. That word would be "founder."

The word "founder" apparently first showed up in Geoffrey Chau-cer's writings from the thirteenth century. People who study the origins of words think that "founder" most likely comes from an Old French verb that meant "to sink." And, as such, it's really not such a bad term. In fact, in some horses—those in which the coffin bone "sinks" into ground (and out of the hoof)—it sometimes describes the situation pretty well.

Some people have tried to make a distinction between the terms founder and laminitis. For example, for a while, *laminitis* was the veter-inarian's term and *founder* was the term used by everyone else. Others have tried to say that a foundered horse is one in which there is chronic lameness, accompanied by changes in the anatomical structures of the foot. In my opinion, such distinctions really aren't particularly useful and they can be quite confusing. In fact, they're simply all just different de-grees of the same thing.

To begin to understand what's going on inside the hoof of a horse with laminitis, you have to know just a little bit about the structures that become involved with the disease process. Once you know a few basics about the relevant anatomy, you're on your way to understanding why this can be such a difficult and complicated disease.

A Brief Anatomy of the Horse's Foot

While the anatomy of all of the structures that are hidden inside the horse's hoof is certainly quite complex, the anatomy that's relevant for an understanding of laminitis, and for understanding the rationale for its various treatments, is really not all that complicated. In fact, it comes down to a few key structures.

The Hoof

The horse's *hoof* is a marvelous structure that's flexible, renewable, and invaluable. It's a remarkable configuration that is uniquely strong and shaped so as to carry the great load of the weight of the horse. It grows down from the coronary band (located where the hair meets the hoof) and totally replaces itself every four to 12 months. At the heels, where the hoof is shorter, it takes less time to replace itself than at the toe, where it is longer.

Hoof grows down from the coronary band in small little tubes. These tubes are oriented vertically, roughly perpendicular to the ground. The tubes grow down in a solid sheet, like a wall. In fact, the portion of the hoof that you can easily see when the horse's foot is on the ground is called the *hoof wall*.

Ordinarily, you can get some indication that the wall is made up of little tubes by two kinds of lines that you normally see on the hoof wall. If you look closely, you'll see regular fine lines that run perpendicular to the ground, called the *tubules*. Then, there are more variable, irregular lines that parallel the coronary band. These parallel lines are the rows of the cells that lock the tubules together.

In abnormal hooves, you'll sometimes see larger, irregular lines around the hoof wall that run at right angles to the tubules, or roughly parallel to the coronary band. These lines appear as "rings" around the hoof. The rings may be normal. For example, normal rings in the hoof wall may occur as a result of such things as changes in the seasons or with changes in nutrition. Rings in the hoof wall can also be abnormal, occurring after such things as fever or infection. But in all cases, rings reflect the fact that something happened to the horse in the past, and, in particular, hoof rings may also be seen after episodes of laminitis (so keep an eye open for such things in a horse that you may be looking to buy).

Laminitis affects the strength of the hoof. Therefore, trying to protect and restore hoof strength becomes fundamental when trying to treat horses with laminitis.

The Coffin Bone

Inside the hoof sits the *coffin bone*. It's called the coffin bone because the bone appears as if—according to an eighteenth century source—it is inside a coffin (morbid, but true). The main function of bone—all bone—is to serve as the structural framework for the horse's body. Bones support the massive weight of the horse and also serve as attachments for all sorts of other tissue.

So it is for the coffin bone, which is particularly critical because all of the weight of the horse ultimately comes to bear on it. Accordingly, it's subject to tremendous stresses. Although it may not look like it, bone is a living and very active tissue, and when stress is applied to it, the bone changes. Laminitis causes additional stresses; thus, laminitis may be associated with any number of changes in the coffin bone.

The Laminae

The hoof and the coffin bone are connected. These connections, called the *laminae,* are the only things that keep the weight of the horse from driving the coffin bone right on down into the ground. The laminae link up like Velcro; some of them arise from the inner part of the hoof wall and others come from the living tissue that's attached to the surface of the coffin bone. The laminae are the key areas affected in laminitis.

These attachments between bone and hoof are simply thin little layers (in fact, the word *lamina* is Latin for "layer"). They interlock with each other in a manner not unlike the paper that's around a popular peanut-butter-and-chocolate candy cup. There are hundreds of them inside each foot. A thin sheet of tissue known as the *basement membrane* keeps these layers attached. The basement membrane is the glue that holds the laminae of the hoof to the laminae of the coffin bone. When laminitis occurs, it's this basement membrane that seems to be the target of the initial damage. When the basement membrane starts to fall apart, the connections between the hoof and the coffin bone may begin to give way, with some potentially devastating consequences for the poor horse to which those connections are attached.

The Deep Digital Flexor Tendon

A tendon connects a muscle to a bone. In the particular instance of laminitis, the muscle involved is the deep digital flexor muscle and the bone involved is the coffin bone. The deep digital flexor muscle starts up behind the horse's forearm; as it continues down the leg the muscle becomes a tendon, beginning at about the level of the horse's knee (carpus). The tendon of the deep digital flexor muscle drops down the back of the leg and attaches at the bottom of the coffin bone, underneath the toe. When the muscle contracts (which is the only thing that muscle can do) it allows the horse to pull his foot up and back during his stride.

In the normal horse, this muscle-tendon system exists under tension, much like the string on an archer's bow. So, in addition to making the movement of the horse's leg possible, the system acts like a supporting cable for the horse's leg. The horse's weight wants to push everything down into the ground; the muscle-tendon system resists the downward force on the leg that comes from the weight of the horse above it. Unfortunately, the normal tension that exists in the deep digital flexor tendon can become something of a problem in laminitis.

The Blood Vessels

Finally, just a quick word about the blood supply to the foot. Of course, blood is critical for any living tissue. Blood, containing oxygen and other nutrients, is carried to the foot in *arteries*. It's taken away from the foot in *veins*. There are two big arteries that run down the back of the horse's pastern; right next to them are two big veins. In between arteries and veins are very small blood vessels called *capillaries*. Capillaries get the blood into every nook and cranny of the foot.

Having veins, arteries, and capillaries does not distinguish the horse's foot from any other tissue in the horse's body. However, in the foot, the circulatory structures have some very special and unique functions. For one, the blood itself helps to cushion the structures of the hoof. The blood in the vessels appears to act very much like the water in a waterbed, cushioning the horse on a liquid foundation. Damage to these little vessels can affect the ability of the horse to comfortably support himself.

But there's another really interesting thing about the blood supply to the horse's foot. In addition to the capillaries that run throughout the foot, there are other direct connections between the arteries and the veins. These connections, called *shunts*, are found at about the level of the hairline, at the top of the foot. The shunts allow the circulating blood to bypass the foot.

Of course, normally, blood doesn't bypass the foot, but the shunts do serve a useful purpose in certain circumstances. It is thought that the shunts are there to help the horse regulate the temperature of his feet. They allow the horse to adjust the flow of the warm blood to the hoof, allowing for more or less blood as environmental temperatures dictate.

The shunts can become very important in the horse with laminitis. Under the abnormal conditions associated with the disease, the shunts appear to allow blood to bypass the feet (which is most likely a bad thing, although no one knows for sure). In any case, it's fair to say that the unique and special features that characterize the blood circulation to the horse's foot also make it a target for the numerous problems that can occur in laminitis.

So What Happens?

At its simplest level, laminitis is the failure of the attachments—the laminae—between the coffin bone of the foot and the inner surface of the hoof wall. If the bone of the hoof isn't properly attached inside the hoof, the weight of the horse and the enormous forces associated with normal movement can drive the bone right down into the ground. In the process, virtually all of the important tissues inside the hoof can potentially be damaged. This damage is in large part responsible for the unrelenting pain and lameness that is often associated with the condition.

The clinical disease of laminitis is commonly broken down into three separate phases:

1 *Developmental:* The separation of the laminae attaching the coffin bone and the hoof begins. Unfortunately, you may not know that this phase is occurring because horses in the developmental phase of laminitis generally won't show any obvious clinical signs of the disease, such as pain.

2 *Acute:* This phase lasts from the time the first clinical signs of foot pain become evident until such time as changes in the foot can be seen on X-rays, or, if such changes don't occur (and, happily, they don't always occur) the horse gets better. It's generally felt that prompt and aggressive treatment, as early as possible in the acute phase of the disease, gives you the best chance of success in treating laminitis. This makes some sense of course; the sooner you get on with the job of putting out a fire, the less damage is likely to be done.

3 *Chronic:* This phase can last indefinitely. Clinical signs of chronic laminitis may range from a persistent, mild lameness, to severe, unrelenting foot pain; from no noticeable abnormalities after a successful recovery, to permanent hoof deformities; to loss of the whole hoof. Many horses affected with laminitis recover; some never return to normal; some may even die.

The Root of the Problem

As I mentioned earlier, the end result of laminitis is a spectacular disintegration of the laminae that attach the coffin bone to the hoof. This disintegration starts during the developmental phase of laminitis. You will not even know that it is happening. The breakdown of the hoof architecture that may result from laminitis can turn a system that is normally remarkably resilient and trouble-free, into one that is virtually useless, in a relatively short period of time. Exactly what happens is still a puzzle. Fortunately, however, some of the parts of the puzzle have begun to come together.

There are currently three prevailing theories that attempt to describe what's going on in the earliest stages of laminitis. The first, and oldest theory, suggests that laminitis results from changes in the circulation of blood to the foot. The second theory suggests that laminitis is a result of trauma, which directly damages the structures of the hoof. The third and newest, theory, suggests that laminitis is a result of out-of-control enzyme activity in the hoof. There is some overlap among the theories. There are observations that support each of them, although none of them appears to completely explain what's going on.

As Time Goes By

There's really not any controversy at all about what happens to the horse's foot as laminitis progresses through its phases. Of course, it doesn't always progress. A good number of horses will get better (in some cases, perhaps even in spite of treatment). But, if laminitis does progress and become chronic, to a certain degree, the foot falls apart. Depending on how badly the foot falls apart, the horse may be able to recover, at least partially, or he may be damaged for the rest of his life. Some horses may have permanent changes in their feet, as shown on X-rays, and yet still may be able to perform as useful athletes. Others may hurt so badly that the only humane thing to do is to put them to sleep.*

REHABILITATING A HORSE FROM LAMINITIS

by David W. Ramey, DVM

No one yet understands why horses get laminitis. Once horses do get laminitis, the success of *any* rehabilitation program largely depends on how bad the problem was in the first place. Happily, there are also a significant number of cases that get better on their own.

---

* From *The Concise Guide to Laminitis in the Horse* (North Pomfret, VT: Trafalgar Square Publishing, 2003) vii–18.

Therein lies the rub. If a horse's laminitis is terribly severe, if there is massive destruction of the attachments of the bone inside the hoof, no matter how sincere and dedicated your rehabilitation program, failure may be inevitable. Conversely, if the initial insult is relatively minor, and the horse is going to get better anyway, just about any thing that you choose to do will appear to "work."

Given the possibilities of almost certain failure and almost certain success, an almost endless number of techniques and approaches to rehabilitating the horse with laminitis exist. These possibilities range from the simplest, such as a bit of rest and some trimming and shoeing of the hoof, to the more complex, such as special diets, wooden shoes, and a drawerful of medications. Indeed, one of the greatest challenges is trying to choose from all of the different treatment and rehabilitation options.

The fact is that, insofar as laminitis goes, no single approach to therapy and rehabilitation has been shown to be effective in all—or even most—cases. Nor have any studies been done to compare the usefulness of one approach to another. Thus, your decisions concerning the "proper" rehabilitation program for your horse are going to be mostly based on the experience of the person(s) taking care of him (your veterinarian, farrier, etc.) Furthermore, since each case of laminitis can be a little different, there probably is no "ideal" rehabilitation program. So, as much as it would be great to have a single program that fits every horse, some trial and error may be inevitable.

It's also a fact that while there are many different approaches to rehabilitating the horse with laminitis, the ability of particular individuals to use any of these approaches may vary. Not every veterinarian is comfortable performing unusual surgeries and not every farrier has made every possible shoe. Indeed, more complicated and difficult cases may require some considerable teamwork and it will be up to you to keep everyone working together.

That said, some general principles for rehabilitating a horse with laminitis would seem to be applicable.

- Try, to the best of your ability, to keep the horse out of pain. Management of the pain of laminitis is important from many standpoints, not the least of which is a humane one. It may not be possible to keep a horse that is recovering from laminitis pain-free, but it is certainly something you can try to do. Pain management may include drugs, particular bedding, or special shoes; work with your veterinarian and farrier to come up with a program that seems to best help your horse.

- Monitor the status of the horse's foot. This generally means that you should "look inside" it on a regular basis with radiographs (X-rays). By following the status of the horse's coffin bone, you'll be able to get a pretty good indication of how things are going inside the hoof.

- Some shoeing and trimming of the horse may be necessary. The possibilities are almost endless. However, in other cases, less is more—that is, many cases of laminitis do well with *no* shoes and need little more than to be left alone.

- Wait at least 30 days after your horse appears to be normal before resuming any sort of normal work. Laminitis can cause some permanent changes inside your horse's hoof, and for a horse to completely recover, some significant growth and healing has to occur. Laminitis can leave the foot structurally weak, and it takes time for the horse's body to repair the weakness. If you appear to have won the battle against laminitis, don't assume that because he looks good, everything is now okay. Be patient and let things stabilize before getting your horse back to work.

Still, no matter what rehabilitation approach you choose, caring for horses with laminitis is more than just finding the best approach. There are a few important considerations beyond the medical ones.

- Keep in mind that, with laminitis, you're not just rehabbing a foot; the foot has an entire horse attached to it! You must understand that many other issues can be associated with laminitis, and if you're going to have a successful outcome for your rehabilitation efforts, you must address the primary problem (if possible).

- Understand that it's simply impossible to predict how an individual horse with laminitis is going to respond to your rehabilitation efforts. There is a wide variation in the signs of disease, as well as in the extent of the underlying problem. The mechanism and development of laminitis has not been fully worked out. There are a lot of theories, and some facts, but as yet an incomplete understanding of the condition. No one has all the answers.

- Recognize that the clinical signs of the disease and the amount of pain associated with laminitis do not necessarily correspond to the amount of damage in the foot. Furthermore, so much damage may occur from the initial onset of the disease that healing of the foot is impossible. So, depending on what happens, and regardless of what you do and how well you do it, you may not have a successful outcome, no matter how early in the course of the disease you start treatment. Try to keep your expectations realistic.

- Know it may not be possible to determine the exact cause of your horse's laminitis. It's not always someone's fault. Complex problems, such as laminitis, don't necessarily have simple solutions. Sure, in some cases you're going to find out that your horse managed to break into the feed bin or a serious illness or surgery caused the disease, but in other cases, your horse will have been normal and there will have been no obvious changes in his feeding, exercise, or grooming routine. If you start speculating as to what caused the problem, you may find that all you end up doing is placing blame somewhere that it doesn't belong.

- Remember that the success of your rehabilitation program is probably going to be most directly influenced by how bad the problem was in the first place. By the time someone recognizes that your horse has laminitis (that is, your horse is in pain or is showing lameness) structural changes within the foot have already occurred. As a result, you're in a difficult position when it comes to trying to rehabilitate your horse because the disease has a head start. Treatment and rehabilitation then becomes a matter of "damage control." The longer the problem has been going on, the harder it is likely to be to repair damage already done. Furthermore, in horses in which the damage to the foot has been extensive, it may not be possible to fix things at all.

The best that you can do is attack the condition to the best of your ability, and hope that everything turns out well. You may end up feeling like a hero and get a sound riding horse back. On the other end of the scale, your efforts may be futile, and your horse may have to be put to sleep for humane reasons.

Then, there's the middle ground. In spite of your best efforts at rehabilitation, you could also end up with a permanently lame horse, or one with chronic problems. That is, even if your initial treatments stop the progress of the disease (or it stops on its own), you still might end up with a horse that requires constant attention. This attention might include regular visits from your veterinarian and/or farrier, special medication, custom horseshoes, or specific feed and bedding requirements. Otherwise stated, no matter how diligently and sincerely you rehabilitate your horse with laminitis, you could end up with a lifelong problem on your hands. There's a cost for this—before you undertake extensive rehabilitation efforts understand that managing laminitis can be very expensive.

Even if things go well initially, it's possible that other foot problems may crop up later. These problems include such things as foot abscesses, separations of the hoof wall ("seedy toe"), abnormal hoof growth, lameness, or additional episodes of laminitis. It's been said that once a horse has laminitis, he always has laminitis—even if a horse appears to have gotten completely better, he still has some risk of developing the condition again at some point in the future.

One of the most difficult issues to deal with is a horse that is not responding to any rehabilitation efforts, and, as a result, is in chronic pain. The horse's well-being *must* be kept at the forefront of your rehabilitation efforts. Most horses that have laminitis also have a significant amount of pain, lameness, and/or structural change within the hoof itself. This is an inevitable part of dealing with the condition. However, it is important that the horse not be allowed to suffer unduly.

Unfortunately, there's almost never a point at which you can say, "Now's the time." Most people hold onto some hope for recovery, even in the most severe circumstances. Someone is always able to recall a horse that made a seemingly miraculous recovery from a devastating case of laminitis. But, in cases where a horse with laminitis is *not* responding to treatment and rehabilitation efforts, you may need to ask yourself, "Is this horse being kept alive for its sake or for my sake?" Clearly, making a decision to end a horse's life isn't easy. It's a decision that should be made by all of the parties involved in the caring for the horse. But, keeping a chronically suffering horse alive just because someone thinks that the horse is "irreplaceable," or because there is some "new" approach to rehabilitation, is not kind—it's cruel.

Finally, if someone tells you that if he or she had started their particular approach to rehabilitation "in time," your horse would be much better, you're either dealing with a charlatan, an egomaniac, or a fool. Laminitis is a humbling disease and anyone who claims universal success simply hasn't treated enough horses.

Horses with laminitis can be difficult to treat and rehabilitate even under the best of circumstances. Unfortunately, at this time, there is simply no single "optimum" approach to rehabilitation for each horse. Most of the things that people do to rehabilitate horses with laminitis seem to *some* value, at least *some* of the time, but no one procedure is clearly superior to another. To succeed in rehabilitating a horse with laminitis, you should try to learn as much as you can about this condition. If nothing else, no matter what the outcome, you'll be able to feel good that you did everything that you could for your horse.

LAMINITIS CASE STUDY I

BETSY CLARK – Dressage Rider
ALEX – Swedish Warmblood

Haymarket, Virginia

Betsy

As a junior high school student, Betsy took weekly riding lessons at a local hunter barn near Schenectady, New York. But by the time she reached high school, she rode "only periodically," concentrating instead on studies and friends. Her horse passion was reignited while she was getting her doctorate in cognitive psychology at the University of California—Berkeley. "I saw a notice tacked on a bulletin board that offered dressage lessons, and it wasn't long before I was once again taking weekly lessons."

But, after only six months Betsy finished her Ph.D., moved to Northern Virginia, and began her career "studying what makes software programmers more productive." Riding lessons were left behind while she concentrated on building her business.

In her early thirties, Betsy decided it was time to return to riding and get a horse of her own. "I often traveled to Sweden on business, and one day I read an article in an airline magazine about dressage rider Anne Grethe Jensen and her horse, Marzog. Jensen talked about the joy she found in riding dressage and partnering with Marzog. She had even turned down an offer of $2 million for him—although she worked as a secretary. I thought, 'Now there's a happy woman. *I* want a life like that, where no amount of money can replace doing what I love.'"

Betsy soon bought her first horse, a Swedish Warmblood named Lotus that she took from an unbroken three-year-old to Intermediaire I.

He was soon followed by another three-year-old Swedish Warmblood named Timor that she competed to Intermediaire I.

Alex

The 16.2-hand Swedish Warmblood was bought as a yearling from the same breeder from whom Betsy had purchased Timor. "Alex was very difficult as a youngster. I tried to start him, but everything went downhill very fast. He began bucking, and I was scared to death. Thankfully, I had the good sense to send him to Olin Armstrong, from Staunton, Virginia, who is known for his skill in working with young horses. Alex came back a different horse."

Home Facility

Alex lives on Betsy and Brad Clark's 20-acre farm in Haymarket, Virginia. At the time of his illness, Alex lived with four other horses, including two Swedish Warmbloods that Betsy was competing in upper level dressage. The farm has seven stalls and both an indoor and outdoor arena.

Betsy gives much of the credit for Alex's progress to Libby Anderson, a trainer and Fédération Equestre Internationale (FEI) dressage judge with whom she worked from the time Alex was a four-year-old until he was 10. "Libby knew how to 'puff Alex up' and make him feel so good about himself."

At 10, he earned Betsy her United States Dressage Federation (USDF) silver medal and was competing at Grand Prix in Wellington, Florida, with Danish Olympic rider, Bent Jensen. "Bent is such an elegant, effective rider. I thought that Alex deserved the opportunity to be with a top-level rider who could show what he was capable of." Alex was ranked third nationally in the USDF standings at Intermediaire I and earlier that year had won the Volvo World Cup qualifying Grand Prix freestyle in Raleigh, North Carolina.

Diagnosis and Prognosis

"In early December the farrier wasn't able to get shoes on Alex and thought it might be symptomatic of laminitis. This was very surprising as Alex had not shown any signs of lameness, and we were never able to track down what might have triggered it. The same day, X-rays were taken by Dr. Rob Boswell in Wellington, and Alex was diagnosed with laminitis and accompanying founder—rotation of the coffin bone in all four feet right down to the soles. Dr. Boswell was very surprised to see the severe nature of the founder. Alex's prognosis was in the bottom 10 percent survival range."

Betsy, at home in Virginia, asked that the radiographs be sent to a local veterinarian. "This vet told me there was no hope, that Alex was in a great deal of pain and would not recover. I called Dr. Boswell, very upset, of course, and he said, 'I'd say the same thing if all I saw were the radiographs, but I'm treating the horse, not the X-rays. This horse has never stopped eating, and he has a good attitude—I believe attitude is more than half the battle. I can't promise you anything—his days as an athlete are over—but we may be able to get him home, and he may recover enough to go out in the pasture and be reasonably comfortable.'

"I was told there was no hope; that Alex was in a great deal of pain and would not recover."

"So that became my goal. Dr. Boswell recommended having Dr. Ric Redden from Kentucky, one of the foremost laminitis experts in the world, travel down to Wellington to look at Alex, which he did. And he absolutely saved Alex's life.

"Dr. Redden saw that Alex was fitted with special orthopedic shoes to stabilize the coffin bone in each foot, prescribed a course of medication, and told me that Alex had to be on strict stall rest indefinitely. Dr. Redden asked that I continue to send him periodic radiographs, and every two months, I was to send him a video of Alex walking down the barn aisle and then turning around. He also cautioned me not to be fooled by what might 'appear' to be soundness—he said that Alex had an incredible tolerance for pain and a huge heart."

Rehabilitation

Early Days

In March, three months after his diagnosis, Alex was allowed to travel from Florida to Betsy's farm in Virginia. As soon as Alex returned home, Paul Goodness, a farrier from Round Hill, Virginia, well known for working with special cases, began shoeing him "I was very fortunate to have a farrier of Paul's caliber in the area. He was the farrier onsite at the Atlanta Olympics in 1996 and has a number of famous clients. I called him in desperation and asked him to take Alex on. Paul consulted with Dr. Redden on how Alex should now be shod—he used shoes with two bars running parallel to the side hoof walls. The purpose of these bars was to stabilize the lateral (sideways) stresses to the hoof when turning. The shoes also were built up in the frog area to take stress off the front of the hoof. The objective was to minimize movement of the coffin bone to allow for the strongest possible reattachment of new laminae growth between the coffin bone and the new hoof wall.

> Don't listen to bad stories or negativity. If your horse isn't going to recover, you will know that in due time—but negativity just completely saps your energy.

"I ignored the local vet who had given me the very pessimistic prognosis after seeing the X-rays and enrolled the help of my regular vets, Drs. Broaddus and Newcomb of Herndon, Virginia. I told them that I knew there wasn't a lot of hope but I didn't want to hear any bad stories or negativity. I just felt that, if Alex wasn't going to recover, I would know that in due time—but negativity just completely sapped my energy. They were wonderful in providing excellent care throughout the entire process."

Unfortunately, this "process" included emergency colic surgery in May. "Prolonged stall rest for any horse always poses a risk of colic, and we were very lucky that Alex came through the surgery so well. It is very telling of the strength of Alex's personality that, when I went to the hospital five days after his surgery to bring him home, he was so feisty and full of himself that it took several attendants to get his leg wraps on! I've found over the years that the 'brattier' Alex is, the better he feels, so this was a good sign."

In June, my vets called and asked that I come into their office. This time it was good news—the X-rays showed that Alex's coffin bones were reattaching. "I cried with joy when I saw the X-rays because they were proof-positive that the therapeutic shoeing and stall rest was working. This was the first hope I had that Alex might really recover, although I didn't dare dream he would ever return to Grand Prix competition."

In September, nine months after diagnosis, Dr. Redden gave Betsy the okay to begin began hand-walking Alex. "During my first attempt in the indoor arena, I almost got knocked over! It was apparent that for my own safety—and his—Alex needed to be tranquilized. This proved more difficult than expected as we had to try several tranquilizers before we found a combination that worked for him.

"I was very lucky that I could have absolute control over the environment—it was my own indoor arena, and I could shut the doors and have the place entirely to myself. I don't think I could have managed it if I had been in a busy boarding facility."

"I cried with joy when I saw the X-rays because they were proof-positive that the therapeutic shoeing and stall rest was working."

Betsy hand-walked Alex every day, beginning with five minutes and working up to 30 minutes a day over the next month. In October, Alex was turned out (again with the help of a tranquilizer "cocktail") in a 20- by 30-foot paddock. "The first day, he was very quiet; then he exploded in bucks and I saw a shoe go flying. But he eventually settled down, and I gradually reduced his tranquilizer until he was able to go out without it and remain quiet. It was at that point, I knew I could safely ride him. Dr. Redden had actually encouraged me to ride him sooner, but I knew I wouldn't be safe until Alex could be turned out without a tranquilizer."

Back to Ridden Work

In November, 11 months after the onset of his laminitis, Betsy began riding Alex at a walk. "He was so weak from the almost year-long stall rest that he felt wobbly under me. And so skinny (from the weight that we had to keep off of him to reduce the stress on his feet) that he was nothing but ribs and backbone—I felt badly about putting a saddle on him. But Alex is a horse who loves to work and he loves attention. And after 10 months doing nothing but stand in his stall, he was very happy to move again, whether out in the pasture or under saddle. And I, who never ever thought I would be able to ride him again, was unbelievably grateful to just be able to sit on him, even at a walk."

"I was cautiously optimistic, but in the back of my mind, I still feared that Alex might go downhill."

Betsy began walking Alex under saddle every day for five minutes and gradually increased the time until they were walking for 30 minutes each day in her indoor arena. "We walked on straight lines and only made large turns following the outside track of the arena because small circles put additional lateral stress on the feet."

In December, Betsy added trot to Alex's workouts. "I began by trotting once around the arena and over the next two months, I very gradually increased his trot time to 15 minutes. I rode Alex on a long rein, did some stretching, and made certain I never pushed him. If he felt tired, we stopped. I was cautiously optimistic, but in the back of my mind, I still feared that Alex might suddenly go downhill."

In February, Alex had his first canter once around the arena, and Betsy added more canter in small increments until they were cantering for five minutes in a 40-minute ride. "By June, I could do anything with Alex; there were no restrictions. But I always felt for a digital pulse rate after riding him as a strong pulse might be an indication that his feet were being stressed.

"I then spent six months doing nothing but simple transitions and stretching through his back, riding 'long and low' to build up Alex's topline again. I worked with a local trainer, Marina Genn, focusing on getting Alex fit and strong before asking for advanced movements. And when I did, Alex remembered everything!"

Betsy's demanding career as a computer software consultant and president of a small consulting company didn't deter her conscientious efforts to rehabilitate her horse. "Although I have always been a hard worker career-wise, I never missed a session with Alex. He was a real focal point in my life. I didn't understand why he had gotten laminitis, but I felt terrible about it. His rehabilitation helped me focus on doing something positive with those feelings.

"I took it one day at a time and never tried to project into the future—that would have been overwhelming. I followed instructions from my farrier and veterinarians religiously. Fortunately, during the period of Alex's struggle with laminitis, I didn't have to travel at all. I was just very devoted to him—I was prepared to spend any amount of dollars and time on him. I've always felt he was very special and I just wasn't going to give up as long as he didn't give up."

Return to Competition

Two-and-a-half years after Alex's diagnosis, he and Betsy returned to competition at Intermediaire I, and four years after Alex's days as an athlete were thought to be at an end, they earned their USDF gold medal. "One of my best friends, Ann DeMatteo, who boards at my barn and watched the whole process, encouraged me to stop treating Alex like a fragile little flower and enjoy him and show him and just have a great time—and she was right!"

"Even today, a decade later, I view every ride as a miracle."

Alex Today

Alex, now 22 years old, "is in regular work and still does all the Grand Prix movements. I ride him in clinics and just have a lot of fun with him—and he's still full of personality!

"Alex did have a second, but minor, bout with laminitis 11 years after the first. Again, he was never lame, but this time I picked up really subtle signs when I was riding, and it was caught very early.

"Alex is still shod by Paul Goodness. He now wears normal shoes that are set back on the front to minimize stress on that part of the hoof wall. His X-rays are completely normal and the coffin bone in all four feet remains parallel to the hoof wall.

"Even today, more than a decade later, I view every ride as a miracle. I never in my wildest imagination thought Alex would come back 100 percent as an athlete. I just wanted to see him comfortable out in the pasture."

ALEX'S RECOVERY TIMELINE

December	Diagnosis made, stall rest, medication, and orthopedic shoeing prescribed.
March	Moved back to home to Virginia.
May	Emergency colic surgery.
September	Began hand-walking 5 minutes daily and increased to 30 minutes daily over the next 4 weeks.
October	Allowed turnout in size-restricted paddock.
November	Began walking under saddle on straight lines only, beginning with 5 minutes daily and increasing to 30 minutes a day over the next 4 weeks.
December	First ride at the trot, beginning with once around the arena and gradually increasing to 15 minutes of trot and 30 minutes of walk per workout over the next 8 weeks.

February	First ride at the canter, beginning with once around the arena and increasing to 5 minutes of canter in a 40-minute ride.
June	Back to full work.

Betsy's Tips

- If you make the decision to bring a horse back to work from a serious injury or illness, seek out the best possible help. If you live in an area without first-rate veterinary care, use the Internet to find a world-class expert to consult. Don't be shy and don't settle for less than the best. Once you find the best, follow their instructions to the letter.

- Seek help and support from friends who are *positive*. Don't listen to negative "I knew a horse that had...and he never recovered" stories. And remember to be positive if you know someone who is dealing with a devastating illness or injury (to herself or to her horse). This doesn't mean denying the seriousness of a situation, but no one knows the end result, so it's always better to assume the best.

- Realize that bringing your horse back will require an extraordinary commitment of time and money—and emotional energy.

- Take it one day at a time...otherwise the whole process can be overwhelming.

MEGAN GEORGES – Dressage Rider

QUIMERO – Lusitano

Georgetown, Texas

Megan

"Beginning at age six, I begged my parents for riding lessons and was constantly drawing pictures of horses," remembers Megan. "Finally, my mother tracked down Kathleen Johnson, the woman who had given her riding lessons when she was a teenager. I began riding saddle seat and by the time I was 16, I was giving lessons to others in both hunt seat and saddle seat.

"After high school, I took a break from riding and worked in local bookstores. But it wasn't long before I found myself gravitating to the horse section in the store. I finally looked up dressage trainers in the Houston phonebook and chose the one (of two) who had lesson horses. I loved dressage from my first lesson. It was such a challenge! I'd stay awake at night thinking about how I could keep from bouncing at the sitting trot.

"At 20, I got my very first horse—Quimero. He was a belated wedding present from my husband Joel. Instead of a fancy ring, I got a horse!"

Quimero

The 16.2-hand Lusitano gelding was bought by Megan when he was two-and-a-half. "A friend was looking to purchase an Andalusian, and Quimero happened to be on the sales tape the breeder had sent her. When she went to the breeder's farm to see the Andalusian, I went along, and while I was there, I stopped by Quimero's stall—he looked so gangly and immature, but it was love at first sight for me."

Home Facility

Quimero lives on Megan and husband Joel Mickey's farm, Phoenix Rising Equestrian, in Georgetown, Texas. The five-acre facility is home to Quimero, a Freisian mare named Amanda, and Toodles, the Miniature Horse.

Megan brought Quimero home to Houston and boarded him at a friend's barn. "I was the first one to tack him up, the first one to ride him, and the first one to be bucked off. But the second day I got on him, he behaved as if he'd been ridden all his life."

Diagnosis and Prognosis

In late September of Quimero's eighth year, he and Megan were competing at Intermediaire II when he came up lame in his right front leg during a daily school. After five days of stall rest and "bute" (see p. 365), he had not improved. A week later, the lameness had spread to the left front leg. X-rays showed some sidebone and navicular changes and a bone chip in the right front fetlock, but no rotation of the coffin bones. "My vet and I had laminitis in the back of our minds, but with all the other little arthritic changes, we just assumed the lameness had to be caused by one of them."

In mid-October, Megan consulted a second veterinarian, who thought it might indeed be laminitis and encouraged her to take a new set of X-rays. "This time, the X-rays showed a bit of rotation and I panicked. We pulled his shoes, put him in a deeply bedded stall, and started him on a course of Banamine® and bute."

A month later, Quimero showed little improvement. "I was very scared. Everyone I talked to seemed to have a different idea on how to treat him and I didn't know who to trust."

Megan then called in a third vet, who put Quimero in a reverse shoe. "Three days later, on November 21, Quimero's condition reached a crisis point when the soles of his front feet developed large cracks—a sign that his coffin bones were now progressing downward."

Megan's contacted her original vet, who referred her to Ron Marshall, a local farrier who specializes in shoeing horses with laminitis. Ron recommended that she take Quimero to see Dr. Bruce Lyle, a specialist in laminitis, whose practice was five hours north in Aubrey, Texas. "To ensure that Quimero would be able to stand the journey, Ron designed and made a special pair of wooden—yes, wooden—shoes. They were to protect his coffin bones and keep him comfortable enough to stand in the trailer during the trip.

"But as I was loading Quimero, he stepped in a crack in the concrete driveway and 'sucked' one shoe off. I'll never forget the look on his face; it was heartbreaking. He was confidently heading toward that open trailer, so proud that he was able to move, and when that shoe came off and his hoof hit the ground, he had a look of absolute terror and immediately broke out into a sweat. Thank goodness Ron was there—and my vet, who came running with a shot of Banamine®!"

"There was a good chance that within days, I could lose him."

Once they made it to Aubrey, Dr. Lyle explained to Megan that a tenotomy (a surgical procedure that transects a tendon, in this case, the deep digital flexor tendon, which runs down the back of the horse's leg and attaches to the bottom of the coffin bone) was her horse's best hope. Megan immediately agreed to the surgery. "I thought about how Quimero had always taken care of me in the show arena and that it was now my turn to take care of him.

"It was the day before Thanksgiving. I stayed and watched the surgery, then tucked him into a stall, told him I loved him and that he was going to get better from here on out—there was no way he *couldn't* get better. As I drove to my hotel in town, I gave myself the same speech. But I was crying so hard I drove 20 miles past the hotel."

Shortly after New Year's, about a month-and-a-half later, Megan was able to bring Quimero home. "When I went to pick him up, he had this 'wild' look in his eyes—not unlike a fire-breathing dragon. And he was also clearly mad at me—he looked away when I put his halter on. When I unloaded him at my barn, he ran backward out of the trailer, dragged me down the aisle way to his stall, and threw himself down into the shavings and rolled about three times. He was very happy to be back!"

Rehabilitation

Early Days

In early February, after five weeks of stall rest, Megan was allowed to hand-walk Quimero for 10 minutes a day. "I'd done a lot of research to find out what the dream footing would be for a foundered horse, and then I made it happen by adding an inch of crumb rubber (made from recycled tires) to the sand footing in my arena. Quimero was also shod in Ron Marshall's handmade aluminum heart bar shoes with rocker toes. The heart bars provided support and protection not only for his soles and coffin bones but for the tendons that were healing from his surgery."

At first, she was uncertain about what would happen once Quimero was freed from the confines of his stall. "I was so sure that he'd get away from me after all that stall rest; I put a chain on his nose and attached a longe line. If he tried to run off, I was going to hold onto that longe line with all my strength and throw myself on the ground—he'd just have to drag me with him! Luckily, he never did try anything.

Do some research to find out what the "dream footing" would be for a foundered horse, and then make it happen.

"He walked slowly at first, never putting any pressure on the line. After a few weeks he started to gain confidence and would walk very briskly as if on a mission. Quimero took his rehab very seriously. I really think he sensed my worry, because whenever I'd hand-walk him, he'd turn his head toward me the whole time. I think he was watching my expression, as if to say, 'Are you sure this is okay to do, Mom? Did Dr. Lyle approve it?'

"As he felt better, he began to liven up our walks with a few gymnastic displays. He'd do this grunt/squeal noise to warn me and then jump up and down a few times. Then his expression would go back to normal and he'd continue walking. I began to expect these outbursts and we made a deal...as long as he didn't pull on the longe or get too close to me, he could grunt and jump up and down on his hind legs all he wanted. Luckily he was out of shape, so his acrobatics were usually very short-lived."

Back to Ridden Work

On March 9, they had their first walk under saddle and it was a memorable one. "We began at the precise moment the neighbor kids decided to try out their new skateboard ramp. And what happened? Absolutely nothing! I was shocked! I probably developed an ulcer in about 30 seconds, but Quimero didn't seem to notice…phew!"

Megan began with 10 minutes of walking two or three days a week, gradually increasing the time over the next four weeks until they were walking for 20-minute periods. The first week of April, she began adding five minutes of trot to their walks, and by the beginning of May, Quimero was trotting for more than 15 minutes in his workouts.

"At first, he was incredibly protective and wary of his 'new' feet. My farrier said he had completely different hooves than the last time he trotted, and it was going to take time for him to get used to the new mechanics. To this day, Quimero is very aware of new footing (at shows or clinics) and very careful."

The first week of August, Megan began adding small amounts of canter, at first cantering him just once down the long side of the arena. "I also began adding circles smaller than 20 meters and simple lateral work. I just took it slow and listened to my horse. I'm still very careful with him, and I hope I always will be. And I also hope I always remember what I almost lost—and how blessed I am."

Return to Competition

Quimero returned to the show ring in late September, 10 months after his surgery. "He did First Level at a schooling show with Caris, one of my students. He did give us a little scare though—in the first test, he took off at a canter and threw a shoe into the audience. But Quimero went back to the show the next day—with a new shoe—and helped Caris get her very first score towards her USDF bronze medal!"

The experience of caring for and rehabilitating Quimero has profoundly changed the goals Megan set for herself and her horse. "Before this all happened, I told myself that scores and ribbons were secondary to my love for Quimero. But there was always this secret part of me that wasn't so sure. Things had been so easy with him from day one, I didn't know if I might be confusing love with success.

"I still wake up and think of him first thing, but now the thoughts are different. Before the laminitis, I would have been thinking about a training issue, planning how I could add more jump to his flying changes. Now, I wake up caring about nothing but his health and happiness. I say, 'Quimero is healthy again, another day another gift,' throw my clothes on, and run to the barn—and he's there, sound and seemingly oblivious to all his body has been through. Now I know that scores and ribbons are just pieces of fabric and marks on paper; the day-to-day companionship and the training are what are important."

Quimero Today

Three years after his diagnosis, Quimero and Megan qualified for and competed at Intermediaire II at the Region 9 Championships. "Looking to the future, I would like to try for a USDF gold medal and a regional championship at Grand Prix; maybe a Grand Prix Freestyle as well," says Megan. "But I plan on being very careful about it—Quimero and I well be very 'gently' chasing those dreams. The most important thing is to have fun!"

QUIMERO'S RECOVERY TIMELINE

November 22	Tenotomy surgery.
January 5	Returned home.
February 8	Began hand-walking for 10 minutes each day.

March 9	Began walking under saddle, beginning with 10 minutes of walk, 2 to 3 times a week, and increasing to 20 minutes per workout over the next 4 weeks.
April 12	First ride at the trot, beginning with 5 minutes and increasing to 15 minutes in a 35-minute ride.
August 1	First ride at the canter, beginning with a canter down the long side of the arena and gradual addition of circles smaller than 20 meters and simple lateral work.
September 25	Returned to competition.

MEGAN'S TIPS

- Stick to good science when looking for a plan to treat laminitis. There are a lot of trends out there that come and go, and everybody seems to have an opinion about what's the worst and best thing to do—especially on the Internet!

- Try not to kill your horse with kindness. I couldn't figure out why Quimero was still gaining weight after I cut his grain—I didn't realize that five pounds of carrots a day contained so many calories! Go over your feeding program (including treats and supplements) with your vet.

- Laminitis can be a terribly expensive disease to treat, so use your funds wisely! Vets, X-rays, and farrier-work are worthwhile expenditures—

→

steer away from high-priced supplements and formulas that claim to "cure" laminitis and reverse its damage. Horses all heal differently and at varying rates, and it takes a vet and farrier team with many years of experience to be able to monitor and treat this disease.

- The biggest mistake I've seen people make with their recovering horses (and I've seen it over and over) is to turn a horse out in a field before the vet approves it. Horses with laminitis tend to have "good days" before their feet are truly stable enough to support them, so don't let your horse convince you to let him go outside before his body is ready.

Chapter 5

Best Tips, Treatments, and Therapies from Riders and Experts

After the diagnosis has been given or the surgery performed, horse owners with limited experience rehabilitating their equine partners are faced with a tidal wave of questions and challenges: "I can't get to the barn every day—who'll wrap my horse's legs or administer his meds?"; "What if my horse goes ballistic confined to a stall?"; "Should I change my horse's feed?"; "To my horse, 'hand-walking' means 'airs above the ground'–how can I safely walk him while he's on stall rest?"

While the best source of advice is always your veterinarian, the experience of other riders who may have survived a similar experience (and lived to tell about it!) is invaluable. In this chapter I've compiled some of the therapies available and recommended by experts, tips for general management and ways to keep your ailing horse as comfortable and sane as possible, as well as "been there—done that" wisdom from riders of all disciplines and levels.

STALL REST

Bedding

"A horse needs to be properly cushioned and bedded so he can rest," says KESMARC's (Kentucky Equine Sports Medicine and Rehabilitation Center) Kirsten Johnson. "If he doesn't have enough bedding, he'll fight to keep himself comfortable. It's essential to have a deeply bedded stall, even if you have stall mats. Do not skimp—use at least 10 to 12 inches of bedding.

"We think the best bedding—and the healthiest because it produces minimal dust and allergens—is cardboard. We use bedding from Hunt Club (see p. 367). Straw, because of mold, mildew, and allergens and its overall negative effects on a horse's airway, is the single worst choice for long-term bedding.

"The stall should be cleaned out thoroughly at least once a day and picked out regularly throughout the day. Horses sleep longer, more often, and sounder on a clean bed. And rest is essential to any recovery."

Diet

"Horses that are confined to stalls or small paddocks during their rehabilitation," says Kirsten, "need diets that provide less energy but not less nutrition—a feed that is fiber-rich and low in carbohydrates.

"My first choice would be a good high-fat/low-carb extruded feed. If you don't have access to extruded feeds, you can use a senior feed. Gradually introduce the new feed over a period of seven to 10 days. You can continue to top-dress with your horse's regular supplements.

"Never simply cut back on the quantity you're feeding your horse. He will feel deprived and unhappy and keeping your horse emotionally healthy is an important part of a successful rehabilitation program.

"If you are unable to hand-graze, it's important that your horse still get a daily supply of fresh grass. All you need is a weed whacker, a rake, and a clean muck bucket."

Fasting

by Mary L. Brennan, DVM

Fasting is sometimes a normal response to illness; a horse instinctively stops eating while his body focuses his energy on recovery. During fasting, his body goes through a normal detoxification process as it expels wastes and cleanses organs, glands, and cells. But a total fast should be avoided. A horse's digestive tract depends on roughage to continue to function in a normal manner. If no food or water is taken, the food already in the system may move along too slowly. If the food stops moving altogether, it can become impacted in the digestive tract. That's why it is important to encourage a horse to at least eat small amounts of hay during most illnesses. Consult your veterinarian immediately if your horse is not eating or if you have any specific questions on feeding a sick horse.

Always supply plenty of fresh water to horses that are not eating well. Your veterinarian may recommend adding electrolytes to the water to support your horse's body during a stressful period. But don't just add electrolytes to the water and assume that your horse will drink it. Many horses are unaccustomed to the taste and may decrease their water consumption when the electrolytes are mixed in it. For this reason, it is important to monitor the water consumption carefully so the horse is guarded against dehydration. If your horse goes more than three hours without drinking, provide fresh water without electrolytes.*

* From "Nursing Your Horse" in *The Complete Holistic Care and Healing for Horses*

Limited Turnout

Most riders will tell you that the most difficult part of any rehabilitation program—for both human and equine—is the weeks or months their horse was confined to a stall. But with a little imagination and some heavy lifting, you can—*with your vet's approval*—create a moveable and size-restricted turnout that will allow your horse to graze near his buddies without jeopardizing his recovery.

Size-Restricted and Moveable Containment

Dealing with a fit, stall-bound Training Level event horse is not for the faint of heart, discovered Diane Francisco of Monroe, North Carolina, when Stryder, her 10-year-old Thoroughbred/Appaloosa cross, was recovering from a torn check ligament.

"He bolted, kicked, and dragged me—and once, my husband—whenever we took him out of his stall," remembers Diane. "Trying to hand-walk Stryder was a disaster." To save "a little of our sanity and prevent more injury to all of us," Diane devised a system that allowed Stryder be out of his stall in a safe, grass-filled environment.

In one of their paddocks, Diane set up round pen panels and sectioned off a 20-foot area where Stryder could graze in semi-freedom. She made certain the footing was good and hole-free, and additional panels were set up next to Stryder so that Rusty, his "pony pal," could graze near him. The panels were moved each day so that Stryder would always have a fresh supply of grass. Diane began with 30 minutes of turnout for Stryder and worked up to five hours a day over the next two weeks.

When Stryder was finally cleared by the vet for turnout with the rest of Diane's horses in her 35-acre pasture, she once again put the panels into service. "We hoped it would desensitize Stryder to being in a large area again so he wouldn't go crazy and run forever once we let him loose." She began by partitioning off a 30-foot corner of the

Diane Francisco

Diane's relationship with horses began at five years old when she begged for rides on a neighbor's retired plow horse. She didn't begin eventing until her thirties, when she and her Thoroughbred/Appaloosa named Stryder entered a local, unrecognized horse trial. A wife and full-time mother to a son, four dogs, and two cats, Diane is also an equine and canine massage therapist. While she and Stryder are no longer competing, they are enjoying trail riding and teaching her son the joys of horse companionship.

pasture and then gradually added additional panels making the area larger and larger. "By the time we had used all the available panels, Stryder was in an area approximately 60 feet wide. One day I just left a panel open. Stryder casually grazed his way out of the pen and joined his buddies.

"Using the fence panels was probably the best idea we had throughout Stryder's rehab. Since Stryder was so fit and used to a more hectic schedule, combating boredom was a major part of his care, and being able to graze kept him reasonably calm and occupied while giving him some time out of his stall. Everyone was happy and safe."

One option for size-restricted turnout is Port-A-Paddock™ (see *Resources*, p. 367). This moveable pen can be positioned within a standard paddock or pasture area and your horse can have access to both grass and his friends while still being safely contained in a limited space. This is a viable option *only* if your horse remains quiet.

Herbs to Keep Your Horse Calm

Four months after winning the Tevis Cup, Benjih, Judy Reens' nine-year-old Arabian, became lame during a 50-mile race in northern California. The diagnosis: tendonitis in his right superficial digital flexor tendon and a core lesion in his right front distal sesamoidean ligament.

While Benjih was started immediately on a controlled exercise program of hand-walking and then

Judy Reens

Judy grew up in New York City and learned to ride at summer camp when she was 11. She began endurance riding in 1987, winning the Tevis Cup in 2000 (see photo), finishing fifteenth in the 2003 Pan Am Endurance championships, and riding her homebred half-Arab to a "Top 10" finish in her division at the 2006 Arabian Horse Association (AHA) National 100-Mile Championships. Judy lives on a ranch "with my husband, two dogs, two cats, one goat, and nine horses—with two foals expected in the spring!"

An International Success Story

As head groom for international eventer and three-time Olympic medalist Karen O'Connor, Max Corcoran is lucky enough to care for Karen's— and her husband's (Olympic gold medalist David O'Connor)—top hors-

es, including Upstage, a 15.2-hand Thoroughbred known in the barn as "Woody." An example of the ultimate rehab success story, Woody recovered from a fractured leg and came back to compete for the United States at the FEI World Equestrian Games in 2006.

In August 2004, Woody was on track to compete in September at the Burghley CCI**** in England, when he hit a cross-country fence at a horse trials, fracturing his left hind tibial tuberosity (the lower bone of the stifle joint).

Then, just 90 days later, Woody rolled in his stall and colicked. Surgery to untwist and de-gas him was performed, and six days later, Woody was able to return home to the O'Connor's farm in The Plains, Virginia.

Max began hand-walking Woody, then ponying him behind Joker's Wild, Karen's now retired, Pan-Am-silver-medal partner. By late January, Woody was trotting, and by mid-February, he was able to school over fences. In April 2005, Karen and Woody finished seventh at the Rolex Kentucky CCI**** in Lexington, Kentucky. He was clear cross-country and had one of the only clear show jumping rounds.

MAX'S TIPS

- Be patient. Bringing a horse back to work too quickly can backfire. It makes no sense to rush him back to work and competition only to have him reinjured and then need even more time off. Make your horse the priority, *not* your show schedule.

- Be smart about footing (and this includes turnout footing) once your horse is back at work and competition. Hard ground can be bad for feet due to the concussion it causes. Wet ground and deep footing can be bad for horses coming back from soft tissue injury, as unstable ground can cause extra stress on tendons and ligaments.

- Know your horse. When you go into his stall during the rehab, make sure you can understand his "subtleties," so if he's a bit off-the-mark, you can catch things early. Check to see if he's been eating, going to the bathroom, and drinking water. Is there a reason to check his temperature? If you're concerned for any reason, call your vet.

- While Woody's fracture was healing and he was confined to his stall and unable even to be hand-grazed, we took a weed whacker out to a nearby field every morning and cut and raked up enough fresh grass to fill (as in "packed down") a muck tub. Having this daily tub of grass was important, not just to Woody's digestive system, but to his overall state of mind.

- On days that are freezing cold or pouring rain or terribly hot…do the best you can. If the weather is truly awful, you may need to hand-walk your horse instead of riding him. When hand-grazing in the rain, throw a waterproof turnout on your horse, bundle yourself up in rain gear, and think about how great it will be when he's sound again. On cold days, give your horse a good curry before you ride to get his blood moving. You'll warm up and so will he.

- Consider using alternative therapies during your horse's rehab. Massage therapist Joanne Wilson saw Woody once a month. Keeping his muscles in proper working order insured that his body would be operating efficiently when he returned to work. We also used a magnetic blanket with stifle wraps twice a day and lasered the area of his fracture three times a day (see *Resources*, p. 370).

- Keep your horse's stall clean. How would you like to spend weeks on end in a dirty room? When Woody was stall-bound, we mucked twice a day and picked out several more times.

exercise under saddle, his rehabilitation also called for him to be confined to a 12- by 16-foot paddock for the next eight months.

Judy, a small animal vet with a practice in Concord, California, decided against relying on drugs to keep Benjih mellow. "I don't even do that with my small animal patients during recovery unless it's absolutely necessary." After consulting with her trainer and coach, Donna Snyder-Smith, Judy decided to use Hilton Herbs Confidence Plus. She added it to Benjih's feed once a day and found "it took the edge off my fit horse without making him dull and sedated. It was rather like Celestial Seasonings Sleepytime tea for horses" (see *Resources*, p. 367).

Hand-Walking

Hand-walking is a crucial part of your horse's rehabilitation program, but it can also be one of the most hazardous to your horse's recovery and your own well-being. If you have even the smallest doubt about your horse behaving himself, do not take *any* chances. Know your level of handling skills and be honest about your limitations.

Discuss with your vet the possible short-term use of sedatives, such as acepromazine (see p. 365), if you feel your horse is in any danger of hurting himself—or you—while being hand-walked. Ask your trainer or another qualified horse person to give you a hand-walking lesson.

At KESMARC (Kentucky Equine Sports Medicine and Rehabilition Center), the staff regularly handles young race-fit Thoroughbreds worth millions of dollars. "Being able to safely lead horses in our care is a top priority," says Kirsten Johnson. "A horse that gets away from his handler not only can injure himself, but puts the people around him at risk of injury."

When hand-walking, Kirsten recommends the following:

- Until you are absolutely confident in your ability to safely hand-walk your horse, make certain a friend or fellow boarder is nearby and confine your walking to enclosed areas such as a fenced outdoor arena or indoor arena.

- Do not attempt to control your horse by hanging on to him. If you get into a tug-of-war, he'll win.

- When your horse begins to get revved up or you feel you're losing control, move *immediately* to an enclosed area.

- If you need more control over your horse, use a correctly applied chain over your horse's nose or a lip chain with a stopper. If your horse is not accustomed to a chain, you must ask your trainer or vet for guidance *before* using it.

"We always introduce horses to nose or lip chains in their stalls," says Kirsten. "Make it a slow process with petting and rewards. The goal is to *acclimate,* not terrorize your horse. Only when he respects and understands the purpose of a chain should you lead him outside his stall wearing it.

"You can wrap the lead chain in Vetrap™ to cut down on any scrapes or cuts on his nose or gums should he act up. As a health precaution, never share 'Vetrapped' chains between horses.

"*Never* put a chain *under* a horse's chin. It's the quickest way to flip a horse over backward."

Get Help! It Can Take a Village to Hand-Walk a Horse

When Tiny, Teri Bernstein's 14-year-old Quarter Horse gelding, arrived home after a grueling eight days in intensive care after colic surgery, Teri knew she would need help with the weeks of hand-walking that were ahead.

A wife and mother of small children, Teri lived 28 miles and a 45-minute drive from her barn in Golden, Colorado. "I couldn't physically be there to hand-walk Tiny three times a day as prescribed by his vet

Teri Bernstein

Teri grew up on a ranch in Colorado and was a rodeo pole bending champion in high school. "From there, I went on to study fashion design and took a long break from riding." Not until her daughter began taking lessons did Teri get back in the saddle—this time, an *English* one. "I had great fun competing in hunters, but my primary focus these days is supporting my daughter's aspirations to be an Olympic rider. I've started a party planning business to help defer the costs of this expensive habit and look forward to the time I'll ride again—soon I hope!"

without camping out and forgoing all of my other responsibilities.'"

Asking for help did not come easily to Teri. "I like to control my own life and those closest to me—my children, friends, and animals. I call it 'quality control.'" But with Tiny's recovery on the line, Teri knew she had to reach out to her fellow boarders for assistance. On the large white board at the barn's entrance, Teri tacked up a plea for help with Tiny. She explained that she needed volunteer hand-walkers and let people know that they could help as little or as much as they wanted.

She put together a plastic three-ring binder that contained calendars and a notepad, attached a pen with a long ribbon, and tied it all to a halter hook outside Tiny's stall. "I asked volunteers to sign up next to a calendar date, either A.M., Noon, or P.M. They were asked to let me know on the notepad how long Tiny was walked and anything else I might need to know."

A group soon known as "Tiny's Aunties" began to fill up the gelding's rehab calendar. "I was very fortunate that not only was there a group of young show riders at my barn but a huge group of 'mature' women who came and went at all hours. While there were several wonderful junior riders who signed up, it was largely the older women in the barn that stepped up—much to Tiny's delight, as he seemed to find comfort in their quiet natures and their mothering of him."

Tiny's favorite "Auntie" was a woman in her sixties named Sam, who not only walked him, but massaged him and did a series of exercises to help break down the scar tissue caused by a hock injury Tiny received while he was in intensive care. "To this day, Sam and Tiny have a special bond. Tiny hears her voice and comes right over. Without her I would not have been able to get it all done.

"We've always tried to help each other out at our barn, but this was the first time we had to deal with a major long-term medical issue. I learned to reach out—I now have a motto, 'All they can say is no'—and I learned that it's okay to give the reins over to others, even if they don't do it my way. People have good hearts and they want to be needed. All you have to do is ask.

"Tiny has since retired and found a second career with his new owner, a psychologist, helping her patients overcome road blocks in their recovery. He lives in the Rocky Mountains with a beautiful pasture and a lovely barn, and he goes on trail rides and is truly loved!"

TERI'S TIPS

- Meet personally with those who want to help and show them exactly what needs to be done and, if you're using a calendar or journal, how to log in walking times and progress updates.

- Have a backup "go-to" person. Janet, our barn manager, was always there if anyone had questions or if something didn't seem right with Tiny. I trusted her judgment without hesitation.

- Check in with your horse's "Aunties" every week. Let them know how much you and your horse appreciate their help and ask for their input on how your horse is doing.

Adventures in Hand-Walking

While hand-walking is often described as week after week of sheer boredom, it can be a time—with some imagination and a cooperative horse—for remedial lessons in ground manners, an introduction to a particular

Anna Schierioth

"After high school I attended the Morven Park Equestrian Institute in Leesburg, Virginia, and from there I went to Germany for a year to study at a Trakehner breeding farm. But after a number of disappointing jobs in the equestrian field, I returned home to New Hampshire and joined my family's real estate firm."

Anna didn't ride again for more than 10 years...until she was offered a free horse—a Thoroughbred mare that would become Godiva's dam. Nine years later at age 45, Anna competed in her first One-Star at the Kentucky Horse Park in Lexington, Kentucky, on her Quarter Horse, Evil Zipper. She counts herself lucky to have "a husband who is supportive (considering he is allergic to the horses) and thinks that riding is good mental heath medicine."

training methodology—such as clicker training (see *Resources*, p. 372)—or an initiation to foreign environments.

When Anna Schierioth got the go-ahead to start 30 days of hand-walking with Godiva, a two-and-a-half-year-old homebred Thoroughbred/Hanoverian coming back from colic surgery, she decided to put the weeks to good use. "Godiva was bred to be an event horse, and I thought an early introduction to the potential terrors of the outside world might really pay off when it came time for her to tackle a cross-country course."

A hardy New Englander, Anna was undeterred by November temperatures that ranged from the high twenties to the low thirties and set about showing Godiva the wonders of rural Fitzwilliam, New Hampshire.

For safety, Anna gave Godiva a dose of acepromazine (see p. 365) prior to each walk—"It may not have helped, but a little 'fairy dust' made me feel safer"—and also walked the mare with a chain over her nose. Her goal: walks that were interesting but not over-stimulating for a young horse. At first, remembers Anna, "she'd shy at anything. As you can imagine, we raised more than a few eyebrows in the neighborhood."

But it wasn't long before Godiva settled in and Anna expanded their walks to include the local fire department's training station. She and Godiva would explore its ladder tower, dirt parking lot, pond, outbuildings, and trailers before heading down a small trail to an abandoned summer camp complete with rusting camper. One Sunday, they even took in the "very spooky" sights at a nearby lumberyard that was closed for the day.

At four, Godiva completed her first Beginner Novice horse trial and is now competing at Training Level. And did Godiva's hand-walking outings pay off? "Absolutely," says Anna, "Her first time going cross-country, she didn't even look at all the new things—she just jumped them!"

Back to Work

Managing Rider Anxiety

As any rider will tell you, those first days back in the saddle are a roller coaster of emotions—an unsettling combination of elation that you are once again able to ride (even if it is only at the walk) and anxiety about what might happen next. Is your horse (despite the weeks and weeks of hand-walking) so fresh that he's likely to explode? Are you so tense he'll pick-up on your nerves and have meltdown?

It's not only amateurs who have to deal with settling their nerves. Even a gold-medal winner can have some tense moments when starting a horse back to work under saddle.

Connie Walker of Plainfield, New Hampshire, is an experienced endurance competitor. But despite her international successes, she still had to contend with a bout of nerves while rehabilitating her seven-year-old Anglo Arabian stallion, VSF Otis, after a leg injury.

During Otis' first 100-mile ride, the Vermont 100 Mile Endurance Ride, he fractured a long pastern bone in his left hind leg. "We had been

Connie Walker

Connie has been involved in distance riding for 20 years and has logged more than 7,000 miles between competitive trail riding and endurance riding. She won individual and team gold medals at the 1999 Pan American Games and competed at the 2000 World Endurance Championships in Compiegne, France, finishing eleventh on her gelding DML Smoke Silver.

Married and the mother of three adult children, Connie is a professional dog groomer and breeds German Shepherds with which she does search-and-rescue training and obedience trials.

in a brook getting a drink and when he turned to come out and go up a bank, his foot was apparently lodged between rocks, and he twisted and yanked it at the same time."

Connie describes Otis as "being on his best behavior while stall-bound and he actually started out quietly when I began riding him at the walk, but the more stimulus, the more excited he got. Once his adrenalin started flowing, it was hard to overcome and he really just wanted to rip-roar!"

For Connie, the first week of walking Otis under saddle was "like riding a keg of dynamite ready to go off. I was apprehensive—thinking too much about the possibility he might hurt himself again—and that made me tense. And that tension was coming through to Otis." Adding to their problems was the fact that it was winter and the footing in her paddock wasn't always good. Connie's only option was to take him out on the neighborhood roads. "Fortunately, I could get out of the residential area—where we'd face dogs, people shoveling snow, and traffic; all reasons for Otis to blow up—within 10 minutes."

To calm herself and her horse, Connie used a technique she had learned while attending a clinic with Daniel Stewart, a United States Equestrian Federation (USEF) endurance clinician and coach for the

United States Endurance Team at the 2002 World Equestrian Games. "During stressful situations, Daniel recommends verbalizing simple one-syllable words, numbers, letters, or even songs: 'Row-row-row your boat'; 'One-two, one-two'; 'Tick-tock, tick-tock'; or 'Ho-hum, ho-hum', which I used. In addition to being a relaxation technique, it also helps to create a rhythm and tempo in your riding."

By the end of the first week and after a symphony of "ho-hums," Otis had settled into "a good flat-footed walk." The experience, believes Connie, "was a great training opportunity. Learn how to deal with challenges like this at home and you can reap real benefits when it comes to dealing with your horse in stressful situations like the beginning of a big ride."

A year after his injury, Otis and Connie returned to Vermont and "not only completed the 100-mile, one-day ride, but Otis was sound and absolutely phenomenal throughout the race. And he looked like a million bucks for his final trot out."

Two years after the injury, Otis and Connie were in the "Top 10" in four 100s—the Old Dominion 100, the Vermont 100, the Northwinds Challenge Canadian Championship 100 and the AERC National Championship 100.

Riding in Pairs

We are most familiar with polo ponies and Thoroughbreds on the track being "ponied," but horses of all disciplines can benefit from the practice. In some cases, it can be a particularly useful method of integrating under-saddle work into your rehab program and exercising two horses at once when your time is tight.

Endurance rider Mike Maul was concerned about the strain his weight might put on his 16-year-old Arabian/Thoroughbred gelding as he was just coming back from colic surgery. "With all my tack and gear, I weigh about 220 pounds, almost 25 percent of Rroc-my-Sol's weight.

"While I could have taken off some pounds by removing gear, it wouldn't have helped that much. I felt it would be easiest on Rroc if I po-

Mike Maul

Vice-President of the American Endurance Ride Conference (AERC), Mike learned to ride after age 50 (on a 28-year-old Arabian broodmare) and did his first Tevis at 60. He has since earned 8,000 miles in AERC competition. Retired from the semiconductor electronics industry, Mike is presently teaching computer science at a community college. He and his wife, who competes in dressage, share their lives with seven horses.

nied him under saddle at the walk rather than rode him. I'd never rehabbed a horse from colic surgery before, so I had no previous experience, but it just seemed to be the right thing to do."

Mike saddled up his other endurance horse, Monterey PH ("Thor"), an 11-year-old Arabian gelding with 2,300 lifetime AERC endurance miles, and began Rroc's ponying program. He rode alone—"I wanted to keep stress levels low and not have any competitive behavior show up where Rroc might exert himself more than I wanted him to."

Mike began with 10-minute walks and worked up to an hour over the next 30 days. Rroc, Thor, and Mike walked county roads near his home outside Houston and along stretches of grass on the berms next to the bayous. "Thor is very competitive and never wanted Rroc to get even an inch in front of him while Rroc was being ponied. Thor would arch his neck, pin his ears, bare his teeth, and make vicious faces at Rroc to make sure he knew his place—one step back. Rroc is very laid-back and pretty much ignored him, but he did stay at least that one inch behind."

Their only mishap—"Roc stops completely when he poops, no matter how fast or slow he's going. I was almost jerked off Thor the first time it happened. It was hard to watch for because Rroc was always a little behind me. I had to let go of the lead rope several times to avoid going off. Most horses can poop and walk but Rroc apparently can't—or doesn't want to!"

After a month of ponying, Mike continued Rroc's

rehab under saddle—this time, without Thor. In the remainder of the season following his surgery, Rroc completed 575 endurance miles and now has 5,000 lifetime AERC endurance miles. "He's completed the last 22 rides without even a pull."

MIKE'S TIPS

- Use a cotton lead rope when you pony your horse. It's easier on your hands—especially when your horse stops unexpectedly.

- Partner your horse with another horse he likes. And make sure it's one that doesn't kick.

- Always ride on a good surface with no holes or slick spots. If possible, pick a route for your rides that your horse is already familiar with and avoid places where he might be tempted to spook.

- Do it some place other than an arena so your horse (and you!) are not bored. Exercise your horse's mind as well as his body.

Rehabbing without an Arena

Contrary to popular belief, not every competitive rider has regular access to an arena with Fibar footing, lights, and letters perfectly stenciled on wooden flower boxes. For some riders, the challenge of bringing a horse back to work includes finding safe and suitable footing while rehabbing their horses.

Julie Wright, a Second Level dressage competitor from College Station, Texas, lives on 11 acres, but rides her horses at home "only when it's not too dry or too wet or I'm in a time crunch. Even then I can basically only walk and trot due to the slope of my place."

When Julie was ready to rehab Tomboy, her seven-year-old Belgian/Warmblood mare, from a severed superficial digital tendon and an 80-percent tear in her deep digital flexor tendon, she knew that much of the work would have to be done away from home.

Julie Wright

Julie began her riding career on her grandparents' Quarter Horses and Shetland ponies. She currently owns five horses (all mares) and is "a small-scale breeder." In 2001 Julie and her homebred mare Inca were United States Dressage Federation (USDF) All-Breed Award First Level Reserve Champions for the International Sport Horse Registry. Julie and her husband (both graduates of Texas A&M) live in College Station, Texas, where she works as the controller for a statewide chain of restaurants. When not riding or working, you can find Julie and her husband in the stands cheering on the "Aggies."

Once Julie began hand-walking and hand-jogging Tomboy, they trailered every weekend to arenas at local stables and friend's barns. When Tomboy was back under saddle, she and Julie headed out at least two or three days a week.

"It was very tough to be married, work full-time as controller of a state-wide restaurant chain, care for my other horses, and rehab Tomboy. There were quite a few times I was in tears just from the stress of it all—especially when my other mare stepped on a nail and infected her coffin bone. During the week it seemed like I got up, cared for horses, went to work, came home, cared for horses, maybe ate dinner, went to bed, and then started all over again!"

As Tomboy's rehab progressed and Julie began cantering the mare, she made the decision to move Tomboy to a nearby boarding barn for two months so she could ride in their covered arena and get in the four or five rides a weeks that Tomboy needed. "The barn was on my way to work so I could stop by in the morning and check on her. And, of course, I would go every evening, even if I didn't ride that day."

Despite the difficulties of trailering so often, Julie feels it benefited both her and Tomboy and highly recommends it—even to riders who have arenas on site. "Getting out and about meant that I was able to regularly see my horse friends and Tomboy got a change of scenery. Not only was it good for Tomboy's mental health, it made me feel like things were returning to normal because that is what we did before her injury—we loaded up and went places several times a week."

The At-Home Dressage Arena

Once dressage and event riders progress far enough in their horse's rehab that 20-meter circles, movements across the diagonal, and downward transitions at "M" are once again part of their training program, they need a proper arena. But for riders who keep their horses at home, an arena is often something that's a trailer-ride away.

As anyone who has tried to jerry-rig a dressage arena in a field can tell you, it's not a pretty sight. Converting feet into meters, trying to get the sides straight (impossible) and the letters in the right position is often an exercise in futility.

Anna Marie Urquhart of Tampa Bay, Florida, developed a simple, one-person-can-do-it, at-home arena that she used while rehabbing her Hanoverian gelding Flavio (also known as "Bear") from a torn check ligament. "Since my grass dressage arena shared space with turnout for Bear and my 24-year-old Arabian mare, Sheba, I could never put up a traditional dressage arena with letters and ropes. My arena setups have always been homemade and this one proved to be both the safest and the least likely to be demolished by a horse."

Aside from an occasional tooth mark on a letter, Anna Marie's arena survived Bear's rehab and one season after his injury, Bear and Anna Marie were Region 3 First Level Adult Amateur Champions and Open First Level Freestyle Champions.

Anna Marie's Arena Tips

- Site the arena in an area with a stable base and good drainage. Keep the grass cut at two or two-and-a-half inches to speed drying.

- The Arena Layout Tool from Silk Tree® (see *Resources*, p. 367) produces straight sides, square corners, and accurate letter placement for both large and small arenas. And, it can easily be used by one person—no more begging your friends to help you haul around a tape measurer and convert feet into meters.

- The plastic picket fencing used for flowerbed borders makes easy and inexpensive corners. I also put the fencing on either side of letters down the long side to help Bear visualize a straight line.

- Bold, easy-to-read letter markers can be made from squares of corrugated plastic and stick-on letters that you can order from Dover Saddlery (see *Resources*, p. 367).

Anna Marie Urquhart

"I'm pretty adventurous and have done a lot of mountain climbing, hiking and scuba diving and even jumped out of an airplane once. I'd love to be on *Survivor* and tried out for the third season—incorporating horses into my audition video, of course! My other hobby is photography and I'm a huge football fan."

Anna, who is a single mother to a dog and two horses, works as a contract manager in the aerospace industry. She and her Hanoverian, Bear, are planning the move up to Fourth Level after winning the United States Dressage Federation (USDF) All-Breeds Hanoverian Year-End Second Level and Third Level Freestyle Championships.

Rehabbing and Schooling on the Trail

For many horses and riders, monotony is one of the greatest challenges in the rehabilitation process with weeks, and sometimes months, spent walking and trotting in the same arena or small field. But once your rehab is almost completed—and with the consent of your vet—think about moving your flatwork onto the trail.

When Kirsten Lotter's Thoroughbred event horse, Taylor, was nearing the end of his rehabilitation from a fractured splint bone, she devised several exercises that could be done on the trails surrounding her barn in Austin, Texas. These exercises not only sharpened Taylor's dressage skills, they gave him a break from weeks of working in an arena.

"The most important thing about doing dressage on trails is to know your own skill level and your horse's reaction to new environments. Don't take foolish risks. If in doubt, don't go or take someone with you. Enjoy your ride and realize that your horse will probably perform better when he's back competing since he's learning to focus on you while the trees are rustling and wildlife is present in the bushes!"

Kirsten's Exercises

Trot Logs

Using logs as trot poles provided a great change of pace for Taylor and paid off with real improvement in his strength and balance at the trot when we worked in the arena.

A neighbor had recently cleared some trees, so I

Kirsten Lotter

A Registered Nurse who works in central booking at the Travis County Jail, Kirsten is single with a dog, a cat, and a retired horse named Riley. Between 18 and 30, Kirsten took a hiatus from riding and cycled competitively (in mountain and road racing) in Canada and Texas. Currently, in addition to showing Taylor she is training for the Austin Marathon and hopes to complete the Austin Distance Challenge—seven races that total over 100 miles of running.

managed to get six logs, four to six inches in diameter and eight feet long. If you don't have logs, regular ground poles are fine. The important thing is for the horse to be out of the arena and having a good time.

I set up two groups of three logs that were five heel-to-toe steps apart. This suited Taylor's long stride, but everyone should determine what's right for her horse. I shortened the distance to three-and-a-half steps apart to work on collection and put them six steps apart when I wanted to work on lengthening Taylor's stride.

I would trot the poles three or four times at the five-step distance, then would either shorten or lengthen them—usually just once to reduce the number of times I had to get on and off!

Gates

Opening and closing a gate is a great way to improve obedience to your leg, seat, and hands. Always remember to be patient; most horses won't master this in one day but if you try a little every time you go out, eventually it will be easy.

Opening a Gate: Settle your horse so he is standing comfortably beside the gate. You should be able to back a few steps or move forward a few steps if necessary. You need to be close enough to the latch so you only have to reach a little bit to open it. Trust me, if you are halfway off your horse straining to reach the latch and a bunny jumps out of the bushes, you're going to fall off! Once the latch is open, carefully leg-yield your horse far enough away so the gate can swing open—don't let it bang into your horse.

Closing a Gate: Line your horse up so he's standing parallel to the open gate. Push the gate away from you (toward the fence) and ask your horse to take a few steps sideways and move closer to the gate. Repeat this until the gate is lined up with the fence and in a position to be latched. If you can't easily reach the gate closure, carefully ask your horse to take a few steps forward and back until you are in the right place to secure the latch.

If things are getting into a mess and the horse seems confused or scared, move away from the gate, reassure him and get off to open or close the gate with him standing beside you. It's just not worth getting into a wreck and there will always be another day.

Lateral Work

Before you go out on the trail intending to work on lateral movements, make sure you have a clear plan as to what you want to work on that day. Start out with something your horse is good at and don't be afraid to experiment—you'll have lots of space to work in and your horse will be more tolerant of your mistakes than when he's trotting endless circles in an arena.

Leg-Yielding: A really fun and easy exercise at the trot is to go straight down one side of the trail and then leg-yield across to the other side. Straighten your horse, go straight, reorganize yourself, and leg yield back the way you came. Remember to try and keep your horse soft in the bridle—this will become easier as the horse becomes more relaxed about doing this on a trail. Once you can easily leg-yield smoothly from one side of the trail to the other, try leg-yielding just a few (two or three) steps in one direction, straightening the horse and then leg-yielding a few steps the other way. This becomes a leg-yield-zig-zag. Again, to get the maximum benefit, your horse should be soft in the bridle—flex his jaw softly in the correct direction and stay straight.

Shoulder-In/Renvers/Shoulder-In: Working in the arena, we often ran out of space during this exercise. On the trail, I had time to fix my leg when I made a mistake and more time to transition between shoulder-in and renvers. I worked mostly at the walk so I could focus on making sure my aids were correct. When we got back to the arena, I didn't have to concentrate as much on what I was doing but could focus on making sure my horse's bend was correct and that he was using his back.

Back to Work Bareback

"I was not one of those kids who galloped madly around bareback, but I always wanted to be," says Carol Federighi, an attorney for the Department of Justice in Washington, DC. "Perhaps I like riding bareback as an adult because it enables me to fulfill those childhood fantasies." But before she was faced with rehabbing Rupert, her Novice Level event horse, not once but *twice*, she had only ridden him bareback when they went out grazing. "I'd sit on his back reading a book while he munched—always with a helmet on, of course!"

After Rupert's first suspensory injury, Carol rode him bareback—using a Toklat CoolBack® double-fleece bareback pad (see *Resources*, p. 367)—almost all the time during the 90-day walking period prescribed by the vet. Once they started trotting, his "added friskiness" sent Carol back to riding in a saddle.

When she rehabbed Rupert for the second time—another suspensory injury *and* surgery for fractured withers—Carol decided she would again do most of his walk rehab bareback as the scars from his surgery were still too tender for a saddle. That went so well that she did two months of his trot and canter work bareback, and even took him over some tiny jumps. When Rupert was well along in his recovery and needed to begin building fitness, she added work on the 13 miles of trails in Rock Creek Park in Washington, DC.

"If you feel your horse's temperament is suited to doing portions of his rehab bareback, I would highly recommend it. When we started schooling dressage again, my seat and sitting trot had improved tremen-

Carol Federighi

Carol grew up in Schenectady, New York, the child of non-horsey parents who nevertheless found her a place to Western trail ride. Today, she works as an appellate attorney for the United States Department of Justice in Washington, DC, and competes as an eventer.

dously. I could really feel my position at leg-yields and shoulder-ins; what my seat was doing and what was correct. Rupert got used to me scrambling to get on his back and using all kinds of banks and branches to do so, and he became much more responsive to my leg aids as a result of the time I had practiced 'putting my leg on' his naked side."

A year and five months after Rupert's suspensory injury, he and Carol were on the winning Novice division team at the USEA Adult Team Championships.

TREATMENTS

TOOLS AND TECHNIQUES FOR REHABILITATION

As someone who has always kept a supply of homeopathic remedies in my tack trunk, it's not surprising that Dr. Mary Brennan's *Complete Holistic Care and Healing for Horses* became an indispensable part of my horse library (see *Resources*, p. 372). Dr. Brennan's book offers not only a comprehensive and user-friendly guide to a wide range of alternative therapies (from acupuncture to Bach Flower remedies) but also practical advice for anyone whose horse is recovering from an illness or injury.

Managing Pain

Dr. Brennan writes, "Treat your horse with just as much respect as you would want if you were ill or injured. Remember that just because horses can't talk and tell us about the pain they are experiencing doesn't mean they don't feel it. Most horses recover from illness or injury much more quickly than people and can return to exercise gradually. However, each case is unique. Watch your horse for signs of discomfort, including lack of appetite, stiff movement, or uncharacteristic behavior, such as not wanting to be touched or brushed.

"If you suspect your horse is in pain, do not jump to the conclusion that medication must be administered immediately. There are times,

Dr. Mary Brennan has a holistic veterinary practice based in Blairsville, Georgia. Her practice is multifaceted and includes acupuncture, chiropractic, homeopathy, herbs, essential oils, Bach Flowers, nutritional evaluation, and patient management. She has worked with a variety of performance horses, including individuals competing in the Olympics, Thoroughbreds racing in Breeders' Cups, barrel racers, ropers, endurance horses, and halter horses.

Dr. Brennan is a member of the American Veterinary Medical Association, the American Holistic Veterinary Medical Association, the International Veterinary Acupuncture Society, the United States Equestrian Federation, and the United States Dressage Federation. In addition to running her holistic veterinary practice she is a competitive dressage rider.

with tendon or bone injuries, for example, when it is best that your horse experience a little pain so he will limit his movement and allow healing to take place. If you medicate a horse that should not be moving around, he will be without pain and may exercise more than he should, possibly doing more damage. This can be a very fine line for some horses because pain can sometimes lead to colic or laminitis. You need to consult your veterinarian whenever your horse is in noticeable pain.

"Following a surgical procedure, horses are often very uncomfortable. The best medication to help relieve this distress is *Arnica montana*, a homeopathic remedy that decreases inflammation and pain. It is very effective and is my treatment of choice both for horses and myself for many types of pain. A potency (see p. 299) of 30X up to 30C is sometimes effective in alleviating pain and helping to diminish bruising and inflammation that occurs after minor surgery. Give these potencies five times the first day, then three times a day for the following seven days.

"If the procedure was major, such as surgery for colic, then a higher potency of arnica—200C, 1M, or 10M, may be called for. Give the higher potency of arnica three times a day for the first three days, then once a day for seven days. Arnica will not upset the stomach and can be given long-term with no ill effects. Higher potency homeopathics such as these are often only available through a homeopathic veterinarian or homeopathic pharmacist and they will also be able to advise you on the frequency of doses for your horse's specific needs.

"Another alternative (or, in addition to the arnica) is to give phenylbutazone, sometimes referred to as "bute" (see p. 365). Bute is available in tablet, paste, or powder form and does not interfere with arnica. Bute often irritates the stomach lining and can sometimes lead to gastric ulcers if given long-term. It is not recommended to control pain and inflammation following surgery for colic."*

> **Caution**
>
> Always consult your veterinarian before giving any medication for pain, especially following surgery.

Explaining Potency

"Homeopathic remedies are diluted many times and "potentized" through a method of vigorous shaking between dilutions. This process is known as 'succussing.' The potencies of homeopathic remedies refer to how many times the medicine has been diluted and succussed. They usually range from the low potencies of 3C, 6X, 6C, 12X, 12C, 15X, and 15C to higher potencies such as 200C or 1M. The difference between potencies of 'X' (dilutions of 10), 'C' (dilutions of 100), and 'M' (dilutions of 1,000) is based on the dilution of the original tincture. For example, a potency of X means one part of the medicine was mixed with nine parts of a dilutant...After the first dilution is made, the mixture is shaken (succussed)...This dilution and succussing (potentization) is done a total of six times for a 6X potency."†

Cold Hose/Ice

For many injuries, an immediate course of cold hosing or icing is prescribed. The prompt application of cold therapy will constrict ruptured blood vessels and slow hemorrhaging and bruising.

---

* From "Nursing Your Horse" *The Complete Holistic Care and Healing for Horses* (North Pomfret, Vermont: Trafalgar Square, 2001) 161.

† From "Alternative Treatments," *Complete Holistic*, 41.

Fortunately, there are now effective and efficient alternatives to simply hosing your horse with water that may or may not ever get cold enough to do the job, or trying to wrap a package of frozen peas around his leg. Numerous varieties of gel wraps (which can be stored in the freezer until needed) are sold by tack stores, catalogs, and online vet-supply companies. And, hi-tech whole-leg cold therapy systems are built to continuously pump ice water into specially designed leg wraps (see *Resources*, p. 367).

As advised by Dr. Richard Markell of Rancho Santa Fe, California, earlier in this book (see p. 88), it is important to note that one needs to be careful not to overuse ice during the more active phase of rehabilitation (i.e., hand-walking and work under saddle) as it can cover up signs of overwork. "Let the injury and your horse 'talk to you' and tell you if you've been doing too much walking or trotting," Dr. Markell recommends. By using ice only moderately and consciously monitoring your horse's body's reaction to your work schedule, you can avoid straining or otherwise reinjuring the problem area. "If the injury becomes swollen and hot the day after you increase your horse's work," says Dr. Markell, "it's likely saying, 'Hey, that's too much! Time to slow down.'"

Bandaging

As Mary Brennan, DVM, explains in her book *The Complete Holistic Care and Healing for Horses*: "There are various bandages and bandaging methods, including stable, exercise, polo, shipping, and other specialty wraps. All horse owners should have basic bandaging supplies on hand, and the knowledge to apply them.

"Stable (sometimes referred to as 'standing') bandages are commonly used for many purposes: after strenuous work to prevent swelling ('stocking up'); to prevent a fractious horse from injuring himself in a stall; to protect an injury; and to hold a dressing in place. The materials you need are:

- "Four pads of cotton sheeting or quilted fabric sized to fit the horse's legs.

- "Four non-elasticized bandages made of cotton or polyester with Velcro™ closures, or string ties. (If they do not have Velcro closures, you need masking tape or safety pins at the ready.)

"To begin the bandaging process, have all your supplies ready. The pads should already be neatly rolled, as should the bandages. Be sure the closures are rolled into the bandages correctly. There is nothing more frustrating than getting a horse's leg all wrapped and then discovering that the Velcro is the wrong way up!

"Stand your horse in a clean place and be sure his leg is clean also. Wrap the pad around the leg so it is positioned smoothly between the knee (or hock) to just below the fetlock joint.

"Start to bandage over the pad at mid-cannon on the outside of the leg, tucking the end of the bandage under the edge of the pad. As you wrap, it's very important to remember to only apply tension to the bandage when passing over the front of the cannon, and not at the back of the leg, or over the tendons.

"Make one wrap around the mid-cannon, and then begin wrapping downward over the fetlock joint until you've covered all but a half-inch of the pad that will be showing. At this point, wrap back up the leg to just below the knee (or hock), again leaving a half-inch of pad showing on top.

"Now wrap a few turns back down the leg to use up the bandage. Always finish the bandage on the outside of the leg, mid-cannon. Fasten it securely with the closure you have at hand. If you are concerned that your horse might fiddle with the wraps, you can apply masking or duct tape over the closure for extra security. Always use tape in a 'barber-pole' fashion to prevent constriction on the leg.

"When you use stable bandages to protect an injury, be sure to first clean the wound and apply any topical remedy. Then you can place a non-stick gauze pad over the wound before bandaging in order to prevent the wrap from sticking to the wound."*

---

* From "Nursing Your Horse," *Complete Holistic*, 156.

Rehabbing with Heart Monitors
by Jeannie Waldron, DVM

One constant fear among riders rehabbing their horses is that they may ask for too much, too soon, or fail to recognize their horses are experiencing pain. While top human athletes, endurance riders, and trainers of Thoroughbred racehorses have long used heart rate monitors to aid them in developing training schedules, many riders are still unfamiliar with their extremely beneficial use as an early warning system for sickness, pain, and fatigue.

Q&A

What are heart rate monitors?

Heart rate monitors give riders the ability to monitor their horse's heart rate in a "real time" manner. Most monitors have "leads" that are attached to the horse's girth, and each time the heart beats, a transmitter sends a "pulse" to a wristwatch worn by the rider. The watch's wireless receiver counts the pulses, calculates heart rate, and displays it.

What can a heart rate monitor tell me about my horse that I can't feel or my trainer can't see?

A horse's heart rate can increase from illness, fear, fatigue, or pain. If your horse's heart rate spikes from fear (which would include momentary spooking), it will increase dramatically but quickly return to normal. If his heart rate remains elevated, he may be ill, tired (working beyond his fitness level), or in pain. Remember: what makes the heart monitor so valuable is not that it shows how high your horse's heart rate goes, but that it tells you how fast it returns to normal.

How do I know if my horse's heart rate is normal?

"Normal" is not about specific numbers, it's about a *range* that is normal for your horse at the walk, trot, and canter. I explain how to establish a range for the horse you are rehabbing from injury or surgery in the answer to the next question, on p. 303.

Dr. **Jeanne Waldron,** uses heart monitors both as a veterinarian and as a medal-winning endurance rider. She has been elected to the American Endurance Ride Conference (AERC) Hall of Fame and serves as a member of the United States Equestrian Federation (USEF) Endurance Committee. She holds eight FEI medals, including individual silver and team silver at the 1986 World Endurance Championships; team gold at the 1987 European Endurance Championships; individual bronze and team gold at the 1988 World Endurance Championships; and she is a three-time winner of the Old Dominion 100. She served as head veterinarian at the 2001 Pan Am Championships and as a team vet at the World Endurance Championships in Jerez de la Frontera, Spain, and Dubai.

Dr. Waldron's practice is located at the Rector Equine Center in Rectortown, Virginia.

The most important thing to look for when using a heart monitor to detect fatigue or pain are numbers that are outside the *upper levels* of that usual range. Has the horse's heart rate suddenly increased? Is it going up, then down, and then up again?

A *too low* heart rate is not an issue. The lowest numbers will be generated while the horse is at rest. Any work will raise the pulse above the resting pulse, and in the physically prepared horse, this pulse will return promptly to the normal range.

How do I use a heart monitor during my horse's rehab?
You can begin during the hand-walking stage for a suspensory or tendon injury. After colic surgery, wait until your horse is walking under saddle.

Start by checking your horse's heart rate in his stall, then again after a few minutes of walking. Check it again every few minutes. Keep a written record of your horse's "ranges" during your first few days of hand-walking. These should give you his "normal" range—a range that your horse will generally fall into, which will become second nature to you after a very few sessions.

When you begin the walking, trotting, and cantering under saddle stages of your horse's rehab, you must always take a few days to establish a new "normal" range.

While working, if your horse's heart rate remains elevated or becomes erratic, back off, decrease his work, and see if the numbers stabilize. If they don't, consult your veterinarian.

Should my horse's heart rate decrease as he progresses through each stage of his rehab?
Absolutely. Lower numbers will reflect his increasing fitness.

Throughout the rehabilitation process, remember to continue to use your *senses*, including *sound* (to help detect lameness), *sight*, and *feel* to determine whether your horse is improving or losing ground.

THERAPIES FOR REHABILITATION

Swimming

Any rider who has brought a horse back to work after a long layoff knows how unsettling those first rides can be—"Like riding wet spaghetti," or "I felt as if I was on a drunken sailor." Today, horses coming back from injuries or surgery can be conditioned while they are healing—by swimming.

The swimming facility at the Kentucky Equine Sports Medicine and Rehabilitation Center (KESMARC) includes both a circular pool and an Aquatred—an underwater treadmill. "Both the pool and the Aquatred are safe alternatives to hand-walking," reports Kirsten Johnson, "offering less chance of reinjury, better healing quality, and an eventual return to normal activity."

The circular pool is used for event, endurance, and racehorses recovering from suspensory and tendon injuries, and various problems of the foot. Work in the pool has more cardiovascular and respiratory benefit than work on the Aquatred, and it produces no "concussive" effects on the legs and feet.

The Aquatred is used for hunters, arena jumpers, and dressage horses rehabbing from injuries, as it works the same muscle groups the horse would use on land and produces "controlled concussion." Post-colic surgery cases from any discipline are worked in the Aquatred.

For a list of swimming facilities, see *Resources*, p. 370.

Massage
by Richard Valdez, LMT, ESMT

Why do horses coming back from an injury or surgery need massage? Whatever the performance level of your horse, an injury or insult to a muscle will result in a deterioration of the muscle(s) within 48 hours. The old saying "use it or lose it" really applies here.

Massage stimulates circulation in the tissues and in the lymphatic system, which in turn reduces swelling and speeds the healing process. Massage also keeps the tissues supple, reduces stress, and aids the body in releasing its own natural painkillers called *endorphins*. While there are many books available that describe various massage techniques and intense, complex massage sessions, I've designed a simple "10-Minute Massage" that can be used both during the healing process and after a horse has returned to full work (see p. 308).

Caution
Never massage an area that is hot or swollen. If you feel heat or swelling, contact your veterinarian.

Before beginning any massage program on your horse, you may want to consult a licensed professional massage therapist who can help evaluate your horse's needs.

Richard Valdez, LMT, ESMT, served as the official massage therapist for the United States Endurance Team at the 2002 World Equestrian Games and as a massage therapist at Devon. Richard lives outside of Nashville, Tennessee, with his wife, two children, and a menagerie of animals.

Q&A—*General Massage Guidelines*

How often should I massage my horse?

There is no limit to how often. If possible, you should try and give your horse a daily 10-minute massage session.

When is the best time to massage my horse?

The best time is before he's worked—it's much easier to find problem areas before a horse is warmed up. Your horse will be more sensitive to your touch and this will allow you to recognize any feedback he's providing on how he feels that day.

Should I massage my horse in his stall on cross-ties?

I prefer working in a stall using a halter and a loose lead rope, as this helps your horse be more relaxed. I rarely secure a horse in cross-ties or to a post; you want an honest response to your touch. Over the years, I've found the best way to accomplish this is with simply a halter and lead rope.

If it's your first time, you may want to have a friend hold the lead rope. I generally toss the lead rope over my shoulder, which gives me the ability to grab it if need be. If no one is available to help you, then try it my way.

How do I begin?

Begin by learning three basic massage techniques: *compression*, *friction*, and *glide*.

Compression is applied with an open palm in a twisting or rotating motion. Imagine that you are kneading dough; as you press down, rotate or twist the lower part of your palm to the right and left. The pressure you apply will vary from a medium "currying" to a heavy currying pressure. At first, this technique may seem awkward, but you soon get the hang of it.

In the *friction* technique, you use your fingertips in a circular motion. Imagine your hands on a keyboard. But instead of typing, you're moving your fingertips in a circular motion while applying light to medium currying pressure.

When you use the *glide* technique, think of "sliding." Apply a light to medium pressure with the base or palm of your hand as you slide down the musculature of your horse.

When massaging your horse, assume an "archer stance": stand with one foot forward and the other slightly behind—as if you are shooting a bow and arrow. Whichever foot is forward will also be your lead hand—the hand that will be applying most of the pressure (i.e. left foot, left hand).

Remember, you are trying to create a smooth, rhythmic action of *twist-and-push.* Lean into the horse with your body and create a rhythm—*twist-and-push, twist-and-push, twist-and-push.* Your arm should be extended and slightly bent at the elbow. Use your body weight, not your arm, to leverage into the horse. Again, it may seem awkward at first, but practice makes perfect.

If there is a change in your horse's body language, such as leaning into you, relaxing a leg, dropping his head, licking, or chewing, you're heading in the right direction. As you work, you may find that he flinches when you are concentrating on a certain area. This is considered a *restricted area,* which is an area that lacks sufficient blood flow and has become "tight." You might want to do some extra compression in this spot. Start with a light pressure and gradually increase it as your horse can tolerate it.

It's important to keep your eye on your horse's eye and watch for either a "softened" or "panicked" look. If it looks soft—great job, keep on working. If it appears panicked, lighten your touch. As a horse gets used to the pressure, you can increase it, but always be mindful of his response.

How do I know if what I'm feeling and how my horse is reacting is "normal"?
No one's tissue is the same, be they horse or human. Healthy tissue is firm

yet supple to your touch. Tender tissue usually feels tight and restricted. The horse will respond to tender tissue by flinching, moving away, biting, kicking, or any combination thereof.

If you find an area that your horse responds favorably to, you may want to focus on this area for several minutes and increase the pressure as tolerated.

How To: The 10-Minute Massage

1   Begin at the poll (noted by a black dot in Fig. 5.3A)—it doesn't matter which side. Find the "soft" area behind your horse's ear and using the *friction* technique, do gentle circles with your fingers. This sets the stage for him to relax and get accustomed to pressure from your fingers and hands. After about 30 seconds, look for his head to drop and his eyes to "glaze" over. This indicates you're going in the right direction. If your horse is sensitive at the poll, lighten your touch so the pressure is not so threatening, and try again. If he still resists, just skip to the next section.

2   Using the *glide* technique, apply light-to-medium currying pressure with your open palm and, following the arrows in Fig. 5.3A, "slide" down his neck, over the withers, down the back, and then down his butt. Do this three to four times.

3   Using the *compression* technique—an open palm with light-to-medium currying pressure—start behind the poll and follow the arrows in Fig. 5.3B as you move down the neck to the withers, down the front of the shoulder and then return to the poll and follow the lower path of arrows to complete the set. Do this two to three times.

4   Starting at the top of the withers, use the *compression* technique and follow the arrows in Fig. 5.3C as you go down the back of the shoulder all the way to the elbow. Do this two or three times using mild curry-

ing pressure. If your horse is a little "girthy," rest your hand in the area noted by a black dot in Fig. 5.3C until he gets used to the pressure.

5   Following the arrows in Fig. 5.3D, use a circular motion with your open palm and apply light-to-medium *compression* to the top of the shoulder and down toward the top of the foreleg in three separate paths. Do this set two to three times.

6   Beginning at the wither and using *compression,* a circular motion, and light currying pressure with your open palm, follow the arrows in Fig. 5.3E in two separate paths down his back, over the top of the hip, and down behind the back of the leg. Do this set three to four times.

Repeat on his other side. When you finish, use a treat to stretch your horse's neck from side to side—such as like dangling a carrot in front of his nose, but just out of reach. And don't forget to give it to him when he finishes stretching!

Caution

The hind end can be very sensitive when your horse is sore and may cause him to strike out. Use care when working around this area.

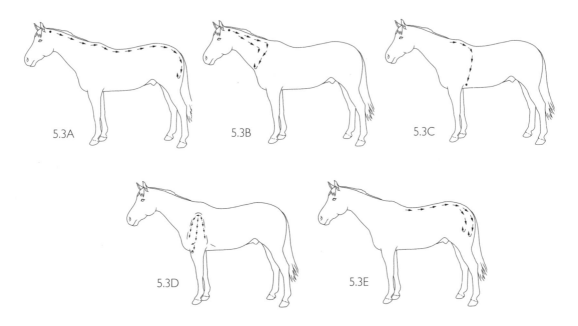

5.3A   5.3B   5.3C

5.3D   5.3E

Maintaining Mobility with Massage

"My job as a Trauma Critical Care nurse and Nursing Instructor at the University of Maryland," says Suzanne Sherwood, "has taught me that every system in the body (pulmonary, gastrointestinal, muscle, skin, and even the emotions) is affected when people—and horses—can't maintain their mobility. When my dressage horse, Absolute Mazeppa, a 10-year-old Thoroughbred/Quarter Horse, fractured a hind leg, I was determined to find a way to maintain his mobility while he was confined to his stall."

Suzanne's solution was massage. "Massaging Absolute helped to relieve his boredom, and it certainly helped relieve my stress from working with trauma patients." The effect was so positive that Suzanne continued massage as part of Absolute's rehab once he was back under saddle.

Suzanne learned basic techniques by watching the massage therapist she hired to work on Absolute. "I asked lots of questions and watched how Absolute responded when she worked on each part of his body. After every session, she gave me diagrams that pinpointed where Absolute was stiff or sore and I used them when I did follow-up massages. I also read books: *The New Equine Sports Therapy* by Mimi Porter and *The Complete Holistic Care and Healing for Horses* by Mary Brennan, DVM, were particularly helpful" (see *Resources*, p. 372).

After Absolute was back to work, Suzanne did a light massage before and after riding and scheduled weekly massages with the therapist as they progressed through his rehab. "I still have a professional do deep massage—that's not something that an amateur should tackle—but I do the light-to-medium massages for minor aches and pains and to prevent muscle injury. I ride four to five days a week—Absolute is an athlete and I treat him as one."

Two years after Absolute's injury, they won the Adult Amateur Training Level division at the Bengt Lundquist Memorial (BLM) Championships at the Horse Park of New Jersey.

Suzanne Sherwood

Suzanne rode as a child but didn't own a horse until she was 29. "Riding has been a
passion ever since." After trail riding, jumping and driving horses, Suzanne began
competing in dressage when she bought her Thoroughbred/Quarter Horse, Absolute.
Since his injury, Absolute and Suzanne have won the Maryland State Quarter Horse
Association Dressage Achievement Award and were Reserve Champions for First
Level Pas De Deux at the BLM Championships. Absolute has recently been joined by
Worthy, a Hanoverian Suzanne is now competing at Third and Fourth Level.

Chapter 6

Riders Get Back to Work

Although this book's initial premise was bringing *horses* back to work, it wasn't long into the writing that I began to hear stories about riders who had themselves made extraordinary comebacks from injuries and illnesses. With great humor and uncommon insight, these riders recounted the unexpected challenges (is it possible to clean five stalls with only one good arm?), how they dealt emotionally with long months away from the sport they loved, and the enormous generosity of friends and barn mates.

Because for many riders recovering from injury or illness means dealing not just with physical limitations, but also combating anxiety or fear when they begin riding again, I've turned to sports psychologist and jumper rider Dr. Janet Sasson Edgette for her recommendations for "overcoming the psychological challenges of riding." And, as you'll find in the excerpted article from the *Chronicle of the Horse* included in this chapter, it's not just the amateur rider who must conquer her fears after a bad fall—some of the most accomplished riders in the world have had to battle their nerves when they first returned to competition.

The inspiration provided by the remarkable equestrians in this chapter holds lessons not just for the riding arena but for life itself.

INTRODUCTION

by Janet Sasson Edgette, Psy.D.

Having recovered myself from a variety of injuries (separated shoulder, broken rib, etc.) and three ambulance rides (at least three that I remember), you can believe that I understand the challenges riders face when they go back to riding again after a mishap.

You can tell yourself all you want that you're ready to pick up right where you left off, and maybe you are. But the moment of truth comes when you are invited back out on that trail where your horse took off and left you to walk home, or you are asked by your trainer to jump the wall that spooked the daylights out of your horse and made him spin like a cutting horse, or you are sitting on your pony only to find yourself thinking that he feels as fresh as that day he tossed you like a referee tossing a coin. And if that moment reveals some trepidation on your part, well, welcome to your personal tutorial on human nature. Your mind is doing one of the jobs it is charged with—protecting you. Granted, sometimes it gets overzealous. Sometimes it's right on the money. But, what it wants is to be heard, and what it wants most is to be respected.

Rarely should anxiety have to be the problem it so often becomes for riders returning to the saddle after a frightening incident or serious injury. It becomes a problem when a rider believes that she *shouldn't* feel anxious about riding. The reasons given include anything from "I've done this a million times before without any problem" to "I've fallen lots

Dr. **Janet Sasson Edgette** is a sport psychologist practicing in the western suburbs of Philadelphia, Pennsylvania. She is the author of *Heads Up! Practical Sports Psychology for Riders, Their Families and Their Trainers* and was the consulting sport psychologist and columnist for *Practical Horseman* magazine for eight years. She is a successful competitor of jumpers for Edgette Equestrian, LLC.

of times and haven't been hurt yet" to "I don't have time to get anxious." Some riders are downright offended by their own anxiety, taking umbrage with it and proclaiming to everyone how ridiculous it all is because they've been riding their entire lives.

Most of the time, we can quell our mild-mannered, background concerns about riding and risk with the kind of statements noted above—if they even come into our awareness at all. But when our sense of risk has been heightened by an in-your-face reality check—be it something that happens to us or something we see or hear about happening to someone else—it can raise the body's alert level just as if it were its own national security system, mobilized after attack. Eventually, when days come and go without incident, and one's attention turns more toward the future than the past, the vigilance and anxiety subside. And you are okay again.

SHOULDN'T I BE OVER THIS BY NOW?

by Janet Sasson Edgette, Psy.D.

(excerpt from *The Rider's Edge*)

Dear Janet: Recently I asked my horse for a canter on a loose rein to warm him up... I got him with my spur, and he picked up speed until we were in a full, out-of-control gallop...finally bucking me off! Broken bones, weeks of bed rest...It's been two weeks since I started riding again...And then my horse tripped and I went flying off...no damage, just a good scare. Now I'm terrified...try to pretend nothing is wrong, visualize myself riding safely, but it's not working. Instead of concentrating on my serpentines, I'm wondering how far the hospital is from the barn...Need help! —Liz

It's through no fault of your own that you still feel frightened riding, worrying that at any moment your horse may run off again. That's how people who've had something bad happen to them *react*. They're always feeling that the "bad thing" could happen again, that they must be on the lookout all the time. Ironically, getting over this kind of fear involves accepting it and understanding why it can't be wished away. First, it serves an evolutionary purpose: Eons ago, those cavemen who respected their fear survived the best. Of course, the dangers were a little different (rock avalanches, mountain lions), but our bodies are still pretty much wired the same way. Second, we have vivid memories; we *remember* the panic of the runaway, the pain of our injuries, the frustration of being laid up. And finally, as creatures with forebrains, we humans attach meaning to incidents and put them in a larger context. A fall isn't just a fall but a month out of work, a month without income, a month with no one to muck or feed or tend to the rest of the family.

Pretending that something didn't happen or didn't affect you doesn't work; the larger part of you always knows what's true and what's not. And visualizing yourself riding safely won't do a thing until you really *feel* safe riding again. Visualization can't overpower a worry (and shouldn't in case it's a "good" worry). I prefer you use visualization to enhance or enliven a feeling you *already have*.

So, what can you do? I recommend what I'd tell anyone who suffered a trauma—take a deep breath, pat yourself on the shoulder for trying to get back in the game, and become as supportive and patient with your own self. You start slowly, you take your time, you stick to gaits and exercises you're comfortable with, and you build from there.

In this case, the sequence of steps might be: With your trainer or a knowledgeable friend present as long as you need her, ride comfortably at the walk; ride on a loose rein at the walk; trot comfortably; trot circles at each end of the ring without worry; trot a serpentine of just two loops; then trot on a loose rein; trot a three-loop serpentine; and so on. Wait until you *want* to take each next step; when you feel ready and eager, take it and see if it's okay. If you become nervous, back up; try again another time. Your trainer or friend can help you decide when to try and can provide the encouragement you may need to get over the hump. How long should each step take? As long as it takes. Learn to value moving toward goals as you value attaining them.*

---

* From "Shouldn't I Be Over This By Now?" *The Rider's Edge: Overcoming the Psychological Challenges of Riding* (Gaithersburg, MD: PRIMEDIA Equine Network, 2004), 44–5.

Sometimes It's Not Easy to Get Back up and Kick on

by Beth Rasin

(Reprinted by permission of *The Chronicle of the Horse.*
Visit www.chronofhorse.com to subscribe.)

When Darren Chiacchia fell at the 2002 Bromont CCI** in Quebec, he knew he couldn't linger in bed for long. Despite cracking one side of his hip and breaking off a piece of the other side of his hip (as well as tearing muscles, cracking ribs, and bruising), he wanted to be riding in the World Equestrian Games three months later.

"The goal of the WEG gave me a single-minded focus to get back in action," he said. "I was convinced that was going to happen. The doctors didn't agree, but it happened."

In Chiacchia's case, he thinks his extensive experience in the sport helped him move on quickly, without any lingering nerves after his fall. But for others, especially amateurs, he says, "It's not like you can shake it off, get back on, and ride. When you're laid up, the fall is the last thing that happened. When you have a fall and don't know what you could have done differently or why, it's hard to process, and it can make you intimidated."

For Chiacchia, the most frustrating part of his fall was being physically sub par for months afterward. "I had residual problems for a long time—my leg was numb for months," he said. Still, he said, he "just sort of did it."

But not before giving the accident some thought. "You always learn from it," he said. "If you don't, you're stupid, and I've never met a good rider who's not intelligent. You've got to be honest—did I ride too fast or was it too difficult for my horse? Sometimes it's just a misstep."

Chiacchia tried to get back in the saddle a week after his fall. "That was not a good idea, so I waited another week," he said. Within five weeks, he was competing again, which secured him a spot on the WEG squad with RG Renegade. "From a young age, I haven't lived in the past," he said. "If there's a lesson to learn, I make a mental note and go forward."

He sees a big advantage, though, for riders who have more than one horse. "I've had competitions where I've fallen from the first horse and had to ride more, and that's a huge benefit. You can't spend two weeks stewing over what happened," he said. "It's great when you can jump on the next one and just go do it."

Stephen Bradley also kept his goal—the 1992 Olympics—foremost in his mind while recovering from a fall at the 1992 Rolex Kentucky CCI. Bradley had fractured a rib and suffered a compression fracture in his back after falling with Hy Flying Brent. But he rode Sassy Reason—and won—at the Checkmate CCI*** in Canada six weeks later, securing his spot on the Olympic team.

"I didn't actually get back on until I got up to Canada," he said. "It was very nerve-racking thinking of going to a Three-Star without getting on for six weeks, but I had all kinds of history with him. I wasn't concerned because it was Sassy. If I'd had to ride the same horse again, I don't know if I could have done it, but the fall really didn't play on my mind."

Bradley didn't let himself dwell on the accident. "I knew it was a hard fall, and I knew why it happened," he said. "I made a point not to think about it because I couldn't remember it well anyway. I didn't look at pictures or videos, and that was very helpful. Any time I started to think about it, I made myself stop."

Discovering Your Mortality

Karen O'Connor recalled that a fall at the 1987 Burghley CCI**** in England, where she perforated her kidney, was her first taste of her own mortality. "It's a big moment of reflection on your riding and what you can do to improve," she said. "You analyze this, then analyze that, then analyze it some more, and watch it on film. You end up thinking about how to prevent that from happening again."

O'Connor spent a month in the hospital in England and didn't return to a horse's back for almost six months. "When your body gets injured—not your arms and legs and collarbone, but your organs—those kinds of falls have a big effect on you," she said. "It really took a year for me to ride aggressively and courageously again."

O'Connor doesn't see any reason to rush things if a rider feels anxious following a fall. "You get more careful and have more time faults, but that's a state you have to allow to happen, however long it takes," she said. "If that's where you are at that moment to be a safe cross-country rider, then that's where you are. It's an individual thing, and everyone has to make their own decision."

But there can be positive repercussions of accidents too. "The responsibility you feel makes you a better rider," said O'Connor. "You make it your mission to find out your weaknesses because you don't want it to happen again."

For Buck Davidson, a serious fall at the Menfelt Horse Trials in Maryland in 2000 made him realize he had to pay more attention to his horse's balance and details on cross-country. "Before the fall I was young and dumb; a little too brave for my own good," he said. "I'd been more worried about winning than surviving. I became more conscious of doing it the right way, rather than looking at my watch."

Other injuries—such as a broken ankle (which didn't stop him from riding in a steeplechase race) and a broken collarbone—hadn't fazed Davidson, but displacing and fracturing his femur forced him to take some downtime. "That was the only time where I couldn't suck it up and keep going," he said with a laugh. "It gave me time to think."

Since his fall happened in plain view, Davidson said he was repeatedly told how scary the accident looked. "I went over what I would have done differently, and I knew what went wrong," he said.

Like O'Connor, Davidson started back slowly when he returned to competition. "I don't know that I consciously thought about it, but when I first came back, I probably did take an extra pull where I would have kicked before," he said. "I won my first event back, but I was way more nervous than I would usually be for a Preliminary event."

And in his next event, Davidson fell on an Intermediate course—and he believes that was probably the best thing that could have happened to him. "You realize every fall isn't going to really hurt you," he said. "The biggest part of healing was knowing I hit the ground and was fine."

Davidson thought his physical efforts to stay in condition while injured helped him mentally. "As soon as I could get into a pool and get myself back going, I was in there," he said. "You have to keep everything else from falling apart; get the rest of your muscles in shape. When I was physically ready to go, I was mentally ready too."

But that doesn't mean he immediately considered himself to be riding at the same level as before, partly because the leg still hurt, and he was compensating, carrying himself off-center to protect it. "Anytime you break a bone, it probably takes you a year to get back to where you feel good," he said. "Eighteen months later, when I got the rod out, then I was fully back."

And Davidson said there's one other lesson he took away from the accident, when Class Touch tried to leave out a stride on a three-stride, downhill combination. The horse started to leave the ground, then put his feet down again and hit the huge log with his chest. "I never thought he was going to fall. I believed he was too good. I dropped the reins and leaned back, so he ended up falling on top of me. When all is lost, know when to get away."

Helping Students

Just as Davidson used his fall to reexamine his own cross-country technique, he also told student Laine Ashker to take the same lesson from her fall at the 2005 Rolex Kentucky CCI, where she broke her neck. "She told me, 'This is the first time I've been nervous to go cross-country,' and I said, 'Laine, that's the best thing I've heard. Nothing bothered you before—now you have a better sense of what can happen.'

"She had a great ride at Groton House in Massachusetts, and she's back. We all need to learn; it's just that sometimes learning hurts a little. But we find out the little things matter more than we appreciated they did."

Of course, riders who didn't lean toward the bold side before a bad fall might be even more affected by a serious accident. "If I felt a fall had damaged my confidence, I would seek help in dealing with that immediately, because horses sense that lack of confidence," said Chiacchia. "Horses feed off your confidence, and when you're worried, they're worried."

If Bradley has a student battling her nerves, he makes sure to set up exercises that he knows she'll complete successfully. "You present the exercises in a building-block way and build her confidence," he said. "That's one of the most important concepts I learned when I had my fall—you need to work with someone you trust implicitly. You need to trust his or her judgment and opinion."

In her clinics, O'Connor stresses the importance of knowing how to fall. "I ask riders to re-identify with why children are given tumbling lessons, to learn to fall without injury, to take a fall and absorb the impact through your body. If you can remember why you took tumbling and what it was like to tuck and roll, that will help."

Questioning Yourself

While she never once doubted that she wanted to compete again, O'Connor did lose confidence in her abilities after her fall at Burghley. "I did think, was I good enough to continue? Was I a bad rider who'd been given good horses? My confidence issue was, was I good enough to be given the opportunity to do it again?"

Bradley's confidence was at its lowest—and his nerves at their highest—not after his fall, but in the late 1990s, when he'd gone several years without a horse at the upper level.

"When I started stepping horses back into that level, that's when I had to work through nerves," he said. "I hadn't been jumping big or going at speed, so I came out a little quiet and slow."

Bradley credited his trainer, Bruce Davidson, with helping him work through that period. "We never even had to talk about it—he knew exactly what I was going through," said Bradley. "He kicked me in the butt and said, 'Here's what you've got to do and go do it.'"

O'Connor recalled two specific periods of her career where she suffered a series of falls—one where she was working on better balance on cross-country, and one where she was trying to be more competitive and faster. "It's generally because you're working on something new, or you *need* to be working on something," she said. "Falls aren't necessarily random—in many cases it's a pattern in your riding. The sport wasn't designed to have people or horses fall."

For Davidson, the danger remains in the back of his mind—but he doesn't worry about it. "It's way more dangerous for me to drive from New Jersey to Philadelphia than to get on a horse and go cross-country," he said. "When it's your time, it's your time. I mean, you can get hurt getting out of the shower. You are going to get hurt, but you can't worry about life all the time."

Bradley definitely sees age as one of the factors that affect riders' ability to put a bad fall behind them. "When you're younger, you think nothing can hurt you, and you're certainly not going to die," he said with a laugh. "As you get older, you're more practical. You realize bad things happen to nice people. And when you think about things more, you start to worry about what could happen. I also see that with older ladies who have children. But we all have to work through certain mental things. As you get older, you can't help but have that affect you."

The biggest effect of age on Bradley has been in the selection of his mounts. "In the last few years I've decided I really don't want to ride horses who are not good athletes and jumpers. You have to be smart about picking the horses you ride, especially when you're coming back from a fall," he said. "Adult amateurs who are nervous especially need a safe horse, one who'll stop before he falls down."

When Bradley and Stonehenge fell at the 2005 Foxhall CCI*** in Georgia, Bradley rebounded to get on his second horse, Brandenburg's Joshua, and ride to the victory.

"I was nervous when I got on Joshua; it does shake you up. But after three or four fences, I realized Josh was up and pumped for the job, and he's one of the best jumpers I've ever ridden," he said. "In that case, it was my horse that helped me get my confidence back and breathe again."

Coaches, spouses, and friends can help as much as a good horse, but ultimately, said O'Connor, you have to do it yourself. "It's your own inner strength you have to draw on, to want to fix it."

Taking Responsibility

For most riders, experiencing a serious injury to their horse can be at least as mentally damaging as an injury to themselves.

"When you pilot that horse, you're ultimately responsible," said O'Connor, who has had the misfortune of losing three horses on course during her nearly 40 years of competition.

"If you're the last person holding the reins, that's a big deal. It has a big impact on you emotionally. A piece of you goes with that horse, for sure," she added.

Losing a horse can also cause a rider to reflect about what went wrong on an even deeper level. "It gives you an increased respect for what horses can do and what we ask them to do, for what they're thinking and why they react the way they do," O'Connor said. "You don't want to repeat that ever again. The times I have lost horses have been very, very big lessons in my life and very hard lessons. You think what this is all about and why horses are so generous."

For O'Connor, those lessons have contributed to the person she is. "A lot of the top people in horse sports have a lot of virtues of integrity and honesty with themselves. The horse allows you to explore your own honesty and responsibility. As you're more successful as a horse person, the responsibility within you grows."*

---

* From "Sometimes It's Not Easy to Get Back Up and Kick On," *The Chronicle of the Horse* (August 12, 2005): 36–42.

Lynne Evans – Dressage Rider

Franklin, Tennessee
Broken Hip

Lynne

"I was surprised that I was so fearful after the accident. I kept thinking I would be able to ride through Mondriaan, my young Dutch Warmblood, throwing his head in the air and bolting off. But I was emotionally paralyzed by my fears and Mondrian really took advantage of the situation. It wasn't long before I realized that I'd lost my confidence."

A dressage instructor and competitive Third Level rider, Lynne had ridden since childhood. Daughter of a former cavalry officer who was a well known breeder of Welsh ponies, she rode hunters during college and began competing in dressage after marrying and moving to Tennessee in the 1970s.

The Injury

While she'd had her share of spills—"I'd fallen off plenty, but I'd never broken anything or been seriously hurt"—nothing prepared Lynne for the challenges she would face after a student's young Thoroughbred reared over backward and fell on her.

In the emergency room, she asked the doctor how long it would be before she could ride again. "He just looked at me and told me that I didn't realize how serious my injury was—that my hip had been dislocated and crushed. He seemed very upset that I would even consider riding again. But he had no idea how determined a horsewoman can be."

Six months and two surgeries later, the injury had not healed. Facing a hip replacement and months of additional rehab, Lynne looked for an orthopedic surgeon who would support her goal of riding again. She found Dr. Michael Christie, who won her confidence by showing her a video of a rider with a hip replacement jumping a horse. "He told me I would have to be very careful getting on and off so I wouldn't twist my new hip. And he told me not to fall off! I've taken two falls since and been fine, but the first time, as I went over the horse's head, I could see myself having to start all over again. Looking back, it was probably a good thing I had those falls as it showed me how well I—and my hip—could hold up."

"The doctor seemed very upset that I would even consider riding again. But he had no idea how determined a horsewoman can be."

During her recovery from the surgery, Lynne was confronted with yet another challenge. She was diagnosed with multiple sclerosis (MS), the disease that had claimed her mother's life. "They said I had probably had it for 20 years. Fortunately, all I've had to contend with so far are mild symptoms such as occasional numbness and vertigo. But since MS is so unpredictable, I always have concerns about it in the back of my mind."

Back to Ridden Work

A year after the accident, Lynne got approval from her doctor to begin another form of physical therapy—this time atop a horse. But this was bittersweet for Lynne, who 10 years before her accident had co-founded Saddle Up!, a therapeutic riding program based in Franklin. A Special Olympics certified instructor, she had even coached one of her students, Joann Cotton, to a gold medal at the 1995 World Games. "It seemed so ironic that I had been working with disabled children for almost 20 years and now I found myself working to overcome a disability.

"I had to go through a grief process about my hip and I was angry that I could no longer ice skate or ski, sports that I loved. But my work with disabled children put everything in perspective. My problems seemed so minor compared to what they and their families face everyday. They showed me how to go on even when faced with a challenge. The children at Saddle Up! played a major role in my recovery."

Carol Monger, a physical therapist Lynne had worked with at Saddle Up!, ran a program that specialized in physical therapy on horseback for children and adults. "My doctor agreed to write me a prescription for the horseback therapy and my insurance company paid for it! Carol found me a nice quiet Quarter Horse and when I got on the first time, I started sobbing—it was so wonderful to be on a horse again. I was overly protective of my hip and experiencing some dizziness from the MS, so Carol's help was critical in my learning how to safely mount and dismount. She also taught me a series of strength and flexibility exercises specifically for riders. One thing that really surprised me was how winded I was—I'd forgotten what an aerobic workout riding is."

"We didn't do anything fancier than walk, trot and canter but he gave me my confidence back and reminded me how much I missed riding."

Lynne and Carol worked together until Lynne was comfortable working at the trot. "Then a friend brought her old Quarter Horse over to my farm and I rode him. Another friend offered to get my beloved Montreal back in shape so I could ride him." Montreal had been born at Lynne's farm and she had started and trained him through First Level. He went on to wins as First Level, and later Second Level dressage champion at the Arabian Nationals, where he was ridden by Lynne's friend Tami Crawford. (Tami would go on to compete at the 2000 and 2004 Olympic dressage trials.)

"Montreal was 19 and had been retired for several years. We were both sore and breathing heavily, but he really enjoyed having a job again. We didn't do anything fancier than walk, trot, and canter, but he gave me my confidence back and reminded me how much I missed riding."

But once Lynne began riding the now six-year-old Mondriaan, her hard-won confidence was sorely tested. "He'd always been sensible, so I was very surprised when he started challenging me. It was difficult to admit that I was frightened by my own horse and I tried to work through his behavior—and my fears—for almost six months. It got to the point that I no longer looked forward to riding him and I knew that the two of us had come to an impasse.

"I felt like such a loser and couldn't help thinking that if I'd only tried harder we might have been able to work through our problems. Over the years, I had helped so many students deal with issues of confidence and here I was unable to do the same for myself. But then I realized that my life had changed with my hip replacement and the diagnosis of MS, and while Mondriaan had been a great horse for me a year before, he was not the right horse for me now.

"It was difficult to admit that I was frightened of my own horse."

"It was Tami who finally convinced me I should buy a school-master—a good solid confidence builder who could teach me the upper level movements I wanted to learn. One of the hardest decisions I ever made was to sell Mondriaan."

While competing in Florida, Tami spotted Jandra Rava (whose barn name is "M & M"), a recently imported 11-year-old Dutch Warmblood. "She called and told me that he didn't buck, didn't shy, and was a nice mover. When I rode him the first time, it felt so right—he gave me that 'I-can-really-do-this' feeling!" Lynne calls M & M "the horse of my middle age," a reference to his dependable and solid nature.

Return to Competition

Lynne's partnership with M & M has proven a successful one. They have earned their United States Dressage Federation (USDF) silver medal and are now working at Intermediaire I. "My injury has taught me to take pleasure in every day along the way and if it takes a long time to get those pirouettes, that's just fine."

LYNNE'S TIPS

- Talk with other riders who have come back from the same injury. Tami put me in touch with two upper level riders with hip replacements as well as her own mother, a devoted horsewoman with not one, but *two* new hips. All of them assured me that they could feel no difference at all in their riding. (Just don't turn your heel out when you're putting on spurs—it can pop your hip joint out!)

- Let your friends help you. I had friends pitch in and do my barn chores, keep Mondriaan in work, volunteer to hold my horses when the vet or farrier came, even weed my garden. They'd call just to keep me up on what was going on in the horse community.

- Set small realistic goals. Don't focus on getting back to competition—be proud of what you can accomplish each day. If all you can do that day is go to the barn and groom your horse, really savor that moment. And, if the best you can do is trot down the long side, congratulate yourself and look forward to doing even better the next time you ride.

- Make a commitment to your program of non-horsey physical therapy. Be devoted, dedicated, and diligent. Take the discipline you have as a rider and apply that to your rehab. The work you do in PT will give you the encouragement that you can come back as an athlete.

- Realize that your life as a rider may have changed. The horse that was right for you before your illness or accident may not be the right horse for you now.

LENORE KREMEN – Dressage Rider

Scottsdale, Arizona

Broken Shoulder

Lenore

Lenore can't remember a time she didn't love horses. "It may be genetic. In the 1890s, my great aunt Nanajen rode horseback in what was then Persia. It was not socially acceptable for women to ride, so she took a lot of heat for it." Lenore began riding at the age of four on her uncle's ranch in California, learned English at summer camp when she was seven, and by the time she was 14, had saved enough from her babysitting money to buy her first horse, an Appaloosa/Thoroughbred cross.

"I've done everything on a horse, from cutting cattle to eventing and now dressage. I didn't even take a break from horses during my marriage or childbearing years—my kids were actually jealous.

"If you're a rider, you know that it's virtually impossible to go through your life and not come off a horse at some point. One day, I was riding out back in my arena and the next thing I knew, I woke up in Barrows Neurological Center with a severe concussion. My 15-year-old son, Antonio, had found me and I was air evacuated. We still don't know what happened.

"I've broken my sacrum, bruised a kidney and a lung, and fractured two vertebrae. I've had so many wrecks they know me by name at the Scottsdale Healthcare North Emergency Room. My family thinks I'm nuts and they've all asked me to stop. But they've finally given up and accepted—albeit reluctantly—that horses are my passion and I'm not going to stop riding."

The Injury

After a jumping accident when she was 28—"I came off, got kicked in the back and ended up with a broken back"—Lenore switched to dressage and spent the next 12 years working her way up to showing at Third Level. But it was an accident on one of her trail horses, a 10-year-old Paint mare named Cheyenne, and not her dressage horse, that nearly put an end to her riding career.

"For no reason that I could understand, Cheyenne blew up and bucked me off so hard that my zip-up paddock boot came off and landed about 60 feet away. I knew I'd hurt my shoulder, but I thought I could handle it and didn't go to the hospital. By midnight, I knew something was wrong and I called my husband, Richard, who was working on our second home in Colorado. I was flying up there the next day, so he scheduled an appointment for me to see an orthopedist.

"Cheyenne blew up and bucked me off so hard that my zip-up paddock boot came off and landed about 60 feet away."

"The doctor discovered I'd fractured my shoulder and probably torn the rotator cuff as well. The bone healed in a short time but the shoulder pain persisted and I got frozen shoulder. It was three months before I could sleep at night and five months of physical therapy before I felt totally healed."

Lenore flew home a few days later and had to figure out how to feed horses, clean four stalls, take care of two dogs and two cats, blow dry her hair, and dress herself for work as a real estate broker. "My husband would be in Colorado for two more months, so I was on my own. My boarder helped when she could, but quite frankly, I can't remember how I managed to handle it all—I just remember being absolutely overwhelmed."

Back to Ridden Work

Two months after the accident, Lenore decided that despite the pain in her shoulder, it was time to get back on a horse—but it wouldn't be Cheyenne. "The accident on Cheyenne completely shattered me. I have never had a horse deliberately try to do me harm. I couldn't even look at her. I sold her a month after the accident to a breeder. I told her what happened and she took her and tried her and loved her."

Lenore decided that her first ride would be on Sanskrit, her five-year-old, 17.1-hand Oldenburg gelding. Because she wanted someone around the first time she got back in the saddle, she trailered Sanskrit to her trainer, Cyndi Jackson's barn. "I got on him and walked around. I was only in the saddle for about five minutes, but it was too much for me to handle mentally. I was terrified. I had to be led around by Cyndi like a child on a pony. I was humiliated. The accident on Cheyenne had taken all the wind out of my sails and I wondered if I ever wanted to ride again.

"The accident on Cheyenne completely shattered me. I have never had a horse deliberately try to do me harm. I couldn't even look at her."

"I decided to swallow my pride and get real with myself and do some soul searching. I take a three-mile walk-and-run every day and use it as a time to talk to myself and sort out whatever is worrying me. I decided that yes, I wanted to ride again. And yes, it is a dangerous sport. I prayed to get my confidence back and to understand the lessons of this experience. I didn't talk much about my fears—I felt stupid and melodramatic whenever I did."

Much to Lenore's surprise, the key to regaining her confidence was found not on the back of a horse, but at the top of a ladder at their home in Colorado. "My husband needed me to get on the ladder and hold some cedar siding. I'm terrified of heights, but I got up on the ladder and made myself look down. I thought that if I could get casual about being on the ladder and pretend I was on a horse, this might be a way to get back in the saddle. I went up 25 feet to the top of the ladder and then came back down, one step at a time. I'd stop, look down, and say, 'This isn't too bad.' It was horrible at first but got better as I went down. Finally, I got to a step where I thought I might be as high off the ground as I was on my horse, and I looked down and said, 'Piece of cake.'

"I did this for three days, then flew home, put on my helmet and my eventing vest with shoulder pads and got on Sanskrit. We walked, trotted, and cantered. But although I may have had one successful ride, I still had issues with fear that needed resolving and I wasn't quite there yet. I decided I would have to take it just one day at a time."

A month after her first ride, Lenore came off Sanskrit "when my neighbor's dogs rushed the fence at us" and had another setback. She decided that at over 17 hands (she's 5'5"), Sanskrit's size was holding her back when it came to regaining her confidence. Lenore soon found and imported Rastelli, a reasonably sized 16.1-hand Oldenberg gelding that was showing at Intermediaire I in Germany.

"I pray every time I get in the saddle now. I pray for safety and fun. I also pray for an answer to my question—why did God give me such a passion for horses? I no longer have that gripping fear that choked me to tears, but I don't like the thought of the horse putting his head down and letting it rip—that's still a bit too familiar. However, my fear is gone with respect in its place."

Return to Competition

Lenore is once again riding Sanskrit and currently competing him at First and Second Level. She and Rastelli will soon be showing at Prix St. Georges.

"I no longer have that gripping fear that choked me to tears."

On a recent Mother's Day, Lenore conquered what she calls her "greatest fear" and parachuted out of a plane with her two sons. And she's now in the process of getting her pilot's license. "It's so stressful to be up there with all the air traffic around Phoenix—now the pressure at a horse show seems like nothing!"

LENORE'S TIPS

- Stay away from all negative people and situations. Do the best you can to lessen pressure—be it from people or your own mind. When things get stressful, I use two essential oils—"Peace & Calming" and "Joy"—that I get from Young Living Essential Oils (see *Resources*, p. 367). Just put them on your wrist and inhale.

- Do not push yourself—physically or emotionally. Take your time; it isn't a race.

- Get the right kind of help from a compassionate instructor. When you're overcoming fear it's essential that you work with a trainer who is kind, considerate, a good listener and motivator, and who is not a gossip.

Courtesy of connecticutphoto.com

KIM TESTER — Event Rider

Roxbury, Connecticut

Ovarian Cancer

Kim

"I was never an athlete until I bought Henry, my first horse, when I was 39," says Kim. "I'd trail ridden and shown at local 4-H shows when I was 11 and 12, but had ridden only a handful of times over the next 27 years. When I bought Henry, all I wanted was a horse to trail ride and hug. I'd never even heard of eventing until we had been together for two years and a friend suggested I might enjoy it, and I began taking dressage and jumping lessons."

Kim and Henry were eventing at Training Level when "things started happening that never happen. I was making mistakes in the studio and wasn't able to remember a jumping course." Kim, Chairman of the Fine Arts Department at the Canterbury School in New Milford, Connecticut, also remembers "other smaller instances that all said, 'Stop, something's wrong.'"

The Surgery

"During that same time Henry, my 13-year-old Mexican Mustang cross, became noticeably lame in his left front. I had him X-rayed and it showed early ringbone.

"I was devastated and frightened for Henry, as I knew nothing about ringbone. After my vet explained it to me and showed me the X-ray, he said there would be no more Training Level jumps—too much concussion—but bringing him back down to Novice Level should be okay if I was careful about footing and not over-training. We had completed four Training Level events and Henry had been jumping beautifully and really enjoyed the height. But his body didn't."

Two days after Henry's diagnosis, Kim awoke in the middle of the night with cramps and severe gastrointestinal pains. "My gynecologist saw me on Tuesday, August 12, and a vaginal ultrasound was done on Wednesday. It showed a 5-centimeter irregular cyst and surgery was scheduled for the next Tuesday. I woke up to a complete hysterectomy for ovarian cancer: Stage I tumor with Grade 3 cancer—best case for tumor, worst case for type of cancer.

"After surgery I was bent over for at least three weeks. I came up with ways to help stretch myself upright—one was to brush Henry while holding onto his mane for support. Henry knew something was wrong and he would stand very still and watch me carefully as I hung onto him. As I got stronger, he became himself and would try to bite me as usual. I was happy to see the change; it meant that I was going to be fine in his eyes, too."

"I came up with ways to help stretch myself upright—one was to brush Henry while holding onto his mane for support."

Back to Ridden Work

Kim's trainer, Sarah Dalton-Morris, thought it would be three months before Kim would be back on Henry, and other friends believed it would be even longer. Kim "internalized that as a challenge to beat the time! I was so fit before surgery, I thought the longer I waited, the longer it would take to get back in shape."

She didn't attempt mounting and riding Henry until her muscles had started to heal. "A hysterectomy for cancer opens you all the way up. In essence, I had a big 'T' cut into my abdomen so I had no connecting stomach muscles." But it wasn't long before Kim found a novel way to determine if her muscles had healed well enough to get her back in the saddle. "We have no water at the barn—that was going to be temporary—but four years later, we still carried it about 150 feet from the well." She began to practice carrying the bucket only, then filling it with an inch of water. Each week, she slowly increased the amount of water in the bucket. "When I could carry a full bucket without my belly swelling from the stress, I knew my insides were strong enough for me to get on a horse."

Kim's first ride was eight weeks to the day after her surgery. "My husband, Brian, helped me up the first time, and my neighbor, Mimi Martinelli, came over to help me get off because I couldn't slide down on my belly—it was too tender. We spent about 10 minutes with Mimi holding Henry as I practiced getting on and off. Then I told her to open the gate. She hesitated but opened it and off we went down the road. Her comment was, 'Now there go two happy individuals!' I felt free! I had been in the house for so long and I was floating."

Kim's goal was to keep both herself and Henry happy and relaxed. "Moving is much better than not moving and just standing around." She went to a Kundulini Yoga class that emphasized strength building, flexibility, and aerobic work. Henry had 24/7 turnout and was taken off all joint supplements. "We wanted him to feel where he was going and make decisions on what was a good 'step' for him. It worked. Instead of him standing 'pointing' (one front leg extended in front of the other), he eventually stood square."

Kim had three rounds of chemotherapy between October 6 and Thanksgiving and each treatment left her unable to ride for about a week. Aside from those breaks, she rode twice a week throughout the winter. "I rode in any weather. I was on Henry if it was below zero! I rode in a snowstorm. Even if it was just bareback down the road for 15 minutes, I was on." Kim walked around her neighborhood, trailered Henry for rides on the beach, and rode him into downtown Roxbury. "It's only 2,000 people and Henry loved the dogs, kids—even the trucks."

"When I could carry a full bucket without my belly swelling from the stress, I knew my insides were strong enough for me to get on a horse."

Return to Competition

In March, Kim and Henry started taking dressage and jumping lessons again, setting a goal to be ready in May for a Novice Level Combined Test at Ethel Walker School in Simsbury, Connecticut. They came in eighth. In June, 10 months after her surgery, they won the Novice division at the Mystic Valley Horse Trials in Connecticut and qualified for both the Area One and the first annual American Eventing Championships (AEC).

"Henry was sound, I was fit, and I cried when they handed me the ribbon! We were both still struggling with our problems and recovery and every week brought a surprise in terms of new emotions. Henry was now back on supplements—MSM, COR-TA-FLX®, and Adequan® when in training—and I had my medication. I used this parallel in our simultaneous recovery to help me stay focused on taking all my own pills every day, exercising, and trying to rest at regular intervals—though I'm still not very good at that!"

In September, 13 months after her surgery, Kim and Henry competed at the AEC in North Carolina. They finished eighth in the Novice/Amateur Division.

"Henry and I have both seen a big change in our bodies in the years we've been together. I like feeling strong. It gives me a sense of independence and confidence. We found eventing suited us. I enjoy setting goals and competing with myself."

KIM'S TIPS

• Don't decide to get on your horse unless you are ready mentally and physically. I knew I wasn't ready mentally if my decision was made purely with emotion. If I could back away and look at my situation with common sense and some logic mixed in, I then knew the decision would be right for me.

• Be determined to make it—"it" being any challenge (within reason) that crosses your path.

→

- Consider "alternative" means of healing. I've been seeing my naturopath for 18 years and I credit him as the main reason (besides my determination) that I'm doing so well today. I believe the supplements he gave me while I was in chemo helped my body flush the chemicals out and kept my immune system intact when my white blood counts were very low.

- Choose your friends wisely. I kept myself away from people who were a negative influence. I didn't tell everyone what I was thinking or doing. I chose one or two people who I knew would help me, not impede my recovery.

- Understand that emotional health takes time. I'm writing this 11 months after my last chemo treatment, and I am still surprised at what feelings continue to surface. See a therapist or counselor if you need to—it's been invaluable for me to have someone I can share my thoughts and feelings with who is not involved in my daily life.

HEATHER DUVERNELL – Dressage Rider

Lombard, Illinois

Severe Tibia and Fibula Fracture

Heather

"A fellow boarder recently came up to me and said 'I just want you to know how much I admire you.' I asked why and she told me it was because I was moving forward beyond my fear. The fear that came after 'The Accident,' as it's now known to my family and friends. Everything in my life is now characterized as 'Before The Accident' and 'After The Accident.' I never realized my life could change in the blink of an eye."

The Injury

"It was September 19 and I was hacking Fergus, my then four-year-old, 16.2-hand Paint/Thoroughbred/Belgian gelding. It was a beautiful fall day and my friend Elyse and I had decided to take a short ride in the forest preserve directly across the street from the barn.

"I'd ridden Fergus bareback on short trail rides when he was an almost three-year-old, and even at that young age, he was calmer and more relaxed than a lot of the older trail horses that had been out hundreds of times. So, what happened that day really took me by surprise. Fergus and I were trotting through a clearing of trees ahead of Elyse and her horse, Misty. Fergus picked up a canter and started to buck. It wasn't malicious; they were happy bucks, as if he was kicking his heels up enjoying a good run in the field. But I lost my balance and fell off, landing on my right leg.

"I tried to get up, but couldn't stand so I knew my leg was badly broken. Because I work as a medical social worker at a community hospital, I knew just enough to realize that I would probably need surgery, plates, screws, and time on crutches. I thought I would probably be indisposed for at least eight weeks. I laid back down on the ground in shock and tried to muster as much strength as I could.

"Elyse ran to call 9-1-1, and the ambulance arrived about 30 minutes later. The paramedics were constantly checking the pulse in my foot, and I realized there was a chance, if only a minor one, that I could lose my leg—and I began to be really frightened about what lay ahead. Every time they touched my foot, the pain was excruciating, and I could feel the nerves in my toes burning as if they were on fire. That ambulance ride to Edward's Hospital was the longest ride of my life."

"Everything in my life is now characterized as 'Before the Accident' and 'After the Accident.' I never realized my life could change in the blink of an eye."

X-rays showed that Heather had fractured both her tibia, the large weight bearing bone that runs from the inside of the knee to the ankle, as well as the fibula, the smaller bone that runs on the outside of the leg. In medical terms, she had a comminuted tibia fibula fracture. She was sedated in the emergency room while her leg was straightened and splinted to remove the pressure from her blood vessels and nerves. The next evening, she had surgery and her fibula was secured with six screws and a plate. Her tibia was broken in eight places and needed an external fixator—a rod was drilled through her heel and attached to two screws drilled into the top of her tibia.

Heather went home four days later. "Then the real fun began. You can't find clothes that fit over an external fixator so I was forever in my pajamas. The inability to do anything for myself left me feeling hopeless and depressed. I cried six or seven times a day, didn't have an appetite for almost two weeks, and had little energy to do anything other than obsess about complications from surgery: deep vein thrombosis, infection at the wound site, pulmonary embolism. I would wake up at 3:00 A.M. in a state of panic, intermittently sobbing to myself or screaming at my husband, John. I think the pain medication was partly to blame—that coupled with my slightly hypochondriacal personality and years of working in a hospital where, unfortunately, bad things occasionally do happen to good people.

"Going to the barn was both physically and emotionally exhausting. Up until the accident, I was there every day. If I didn't ride, I groomed or grazed my horse, or just socialized. Now when I did go, which was maybe twice a week, I was confined to my wheelchair and couldn't even manage to stand for two seconds to pat my horse or give him a treat. Fergus looked big before, but now he looked gigantic and scary. It was hard to watch my husband or Elyse ride him when I had basically been his only rider for two years. I had mixed feelings of fear, anxiety, happiness, and sadness, which left me in tears on the way home.

"I realized there was a chance, if only a minor one, that I could lose my leg—and I began to be really frightened about what lay ahead."

"I assumed that after two months, I would be back to 'normal.' But it didn't work out that way for me. Doctor appointment after doctor appointment left me with terms like 'slow union,' 'angulation,' and 'three more weeks.' The doctor said that my petite frame slowed bone growth, and since the fractures were so displaced, it took much longer than expected to heal. It didn't help that I had lost 20 pounds and was only around 90 pounds by week two, post-surgery. I looked emaciated and felt incredibly weak."

Heather returned to work nine weeks later and remembers her co-workers laughing as she "hopped" around the nurse's station on her one good leg and "crutched" into patient's rooms to do evaluations. "It was hard to tell the same story over and over to concerned people, both staff and patients who would ask me every day, 'What happened to you?' It was even more difficult to listen to their comments about how crazy I was if I ever planned to get back on 'that horse' again. In the back of my mind, I think part of me agreed with them."

By February, she had moved Fergus to a new, dressage-only barn and began walking, ("hobbling, really") without crutches. She could now longe Fergus, brush him, and even pick out his feet. "It took a while to get to know him again. I sometimes felt distant, nervous, and irritated, especially the first month, as he did not adjust well to his new environment.

He was showing an out-of-control side I'd never seen before. People asked me if he was a stallion and I could feel them talking behind my back as they witnessed me, the little, 105-pound woman, cautiously limping around the monster she described as a 'sweet, good natured gelding.' The first day he was there, he jumped a 4' paddock fence when he spooked at a huge pile of snow crashing off the barn roof."

Back to Ridden Work

Fergus soon settled into his new surroundings, and by March, six months after the accident, Heather, with her doctor's permission, decided it was time to ride again. What she hadn't counted on was her level of anxiety about getting back on Fergus. "I owned my own horse as a teenager and foxhunted, trail rode, and competed at local 4-H shows. And although I had my fair share of falls as a child, I was never seriously hurt and couldn't imagine myself as someone who would be frightened of getting on her own horse.

"Holding my breath, I slowly walked a few circuits around the arena before picking up a reluctant trot. I trotted twice around and called it a day."

"But the first time I rode Fergus was extremely nerve-racking. Holding my breath, I slowly walked a few circuits around the arena before picking up a reluctant trot. I trotted twice around and called it a day. It was hard to try to familiarize myself with Fergus again with my new limitations and sort through my fears and anxiety about it at the same time. After that 10-minute ride, I felt physically discouraged but was overwhelmed with emotional relief. I had finally done it—I got back on."

After that first ride, Heather made "rules" for herself. "Initially, I never rode alone; someone had to be in the ring with me. I kept my rides short—20 minutes of walk/trot. If I was in doubt about Fergus' mental state, or mine, I opted to longe him or groom him and try to continue 'bonding.' After about six weeks, I decided to canter. I had a friend on the ground for support and had the entire indoor arena to myself. Fergus was completely off balance and it was a really lousy canter, but I did it, and I was on cloud nine for the next few days."

One major hurdle for Heather was the first time she rode Fergus outside the secure confines of the arena. "Elyse and I took Fergus and Misty on a 20-minute walk. Fergus followed Misty obediently and we made it around without a hitch, but my heart was pounding the entire time and everything I saw (the pile of logs on the ground, the horse in the pasture that could be galloping our way any second, the open field with the bunny ready to pounce on us, the low-hanging tree branch that looked ready to snap) seemed like a possible disaster waiting to happen. But we were fine."

Return to Competition

"Fergus—now six—and I are friends again, and I look forward to the barn days and smile to myself when Fergus comes walking up in the pasture to greet me. We have been taking dressage lessons, riding in dressage clinics, and are now showing at Training Level, hoping to show at First Level by next spring. We're back hacking out on the trails around the property and we've even been taking jumping lessons—thanks to a trainer who understands my fears and knows that on some days, we need to work on grids or combinations, not entire courses.

Your emotional recovery may always be a work in progress. There are going to be days when you are going to feel brave and days when you are not.

"But it's always a balancing act. Many of the things I would love to do with Fergus I know might never happen again, like flying over a cross-country course, foxhunting, or even cantering across an open field. And while that makes me sad, it's okay as long as I am able to keep myself safe and happy. Overall, I feel that my emotional recovery is, and will probably always be a work-in-progress. There are going to be days when I am going to feel brave and days when I am not.

"Although it's been almost two years since my accident, my ankle will unfortunately never be the same. The bones have healed, but I have lost significant mobility which sometimes makes riding (and walking) difficult and painful. But in a way, it's a good reminder as to what can happen and how quickly life can change.

"For me, my number-one goal now is to stay safe. My number-two goal is to have fun. It's not all about the riding for me anymore. I need to enjoy my horse on the ground too. Eventually, my husband and I would like to buy a small farm and set up a boarding facility. Hopefully, Fergus will be a part of that dream.

"I try to concentrate on the fun aspects of riding and being around a horse that I love. This experience has given me an appreciation for what I have had all along but maybe didn't see everyday: a wonderful husband, a loving family, great friends, and a hobby that really does give me a great deal of joy and happiness."

HEATHER'S TIPS

- Be honest with yourself about your capabilities and limitations. We can't all be perfect riders, or perfect people.

- Find a trainer who is sensitive to your anxiety about riding again after an accident and who is willing to help you work through your fears.

- There are no prizes for how quickly you can trot or canter your horse again after being out of the saddle for an extended period. Take all the time you need—if all you can do is walk around the arena, then congratulate yourself and call it a day. Be patient.

KRISTINA REIMANN-MORRIS — Hunter Rider and Foxhunter

Forest Hill, Maryland

Broken Pelvis

Kris

"I love what I do," says Kris Reimann-Morris. "It's who I am; my very soul. And I almost lost it."

Kris grew up on horseback and spent "hours running and jumping everything I could find. I showed a little, mostly local, running barrels and such." At 19, she began "working for other people riding racehorses. By the time I was 24, I was married, galloping horses at Pimlico Racetrack in Laurel, Maryland, and starting horses for clients."

Kris lives with her husband, John, and their two children on a 15-acre farm. With her business partner, Laura Wright, and twin sister, Sandy Lowery, she starts and trains young horses for careers as show hunters, eventers, fox hunters, and trail horses.

The Injury

On a sunny spring day in late April, Kris and her husband were putting up fencing on their farm. "John was in the tractor punching holes with a posthole digger. My kids were three and four, so I had them in the truck with me. The digger kept kicking sideways, so I finally turned off the truck and got out to straighten it. It was a Dodge D150 stick shift, and I didn't put it in gear when I got out. The truck started rolling down a hill with the kids in it, so I chased it and tried to catch it. Instead, it caught me. The passenger door was locked and when I tried to get to the other side the left front tire hit me. The truck rolled over me and dragged me a few feet.

"When John got to me, I tried to be really calm. I told him to take the kids to the house and call 9-1-1. It was crazy all the people who showed up: police cars, fire trucks, my family, an ambulance—it looked like a 'first responders' meeting. And I guess it was! The guys from the volunteer fire department were great. They decided to fly me out because I had severed a femoral artery. The Medivac helicopter just happened to be in the area, so I was on my way to the shock trauma center at the University of Maryland Hospital in Baltimore in only a few minutes."

Kris had broken her pelvis in five places and ruptured her spleen. "My left arm had been run over and the nerves were damaged so it wouldn't work even though it wasn't broken. My lungs were bruised and bleeding so I had to suction them out a lot, and I had a lot of muscle spasms from the 40-plus staples in my stomach. Then I had an allergic reaction to my morphine that stopped my breathing a couple of times. All in all, not much fun, but I tried to have a sense of humor and see the upside. My family dubbed me 'Speed Bump'—they're a very sick group."

While the doctors predicted months of rehab and downplayed the chances of her ever riding again, the orthopedic surgeon on call that day was more optimistic. Dr. Carol Copeland specializes in trauma and has been a rider since she was eight. "Having struggled with finding my seat and balance for years, I knew how important a level pelvis would be to Kris," says Dr. Copeland. "I also knew how horses and riding become such a huge part of who you are—they get under your skin, and they stay. Taking riding away from a real horse person would be like cutting off a limb. So I wanted her to know as early as possible that we had her pelvis lined up well enough so she would be able to return to horses and riding after she healed. The residents thought I was nuts talking to her about riding on post-op-day-one; they thought it was enough for her to just walk again!"

"The truck started rolling down a hill with the kids in it, so I chased it and tried to catch it. Instead, it caught me."

Kris was in a wheelchair for two months and on crutches for a month after that. "Growing up on a farm with no brothers, my sisters and I had to learn to do a lot of things that other women really don't do and that made me very independent. 'If you can't do it yourself, don't do it.' Now I couldn't even fix my own meals, let alone ride a horse. It was really hard to see my sister and husband taking care of the horses, because they had always been my responsibility, and I'd sit in the house and cry when I watched people ride outside."

She gradually added a regimen of farm activities to help her strength and mobility. She began by taking the footrests off her wheelchair to help work her leg muscles. "Some days, I'd roll my wheelchair down the front ramp and around the house to sit by the field—problem was I didn't have the strength to get back up the hill to the house! Once I was on crutches, things got better and I could help out by watering the horses and grooming the quiet ones."

Back to Ridden Work

On July 14, 11 weeks after the accident, the pins came out of her pelvis and Kris was longing to ride again. One day in early August, watching her children ride Chance, her 22-year-old, large pony, she decided this would be the day. "I had my sister hold Chance next to the picnic table so I could use it as a mounting block. Getting on was a lot harder than I expected and it took me a few minutes, but with help, I was soon up and walking around the front yard. I was shaking and I had to hold on to the saddle horn. I'd never held the saddle horn in my life! After only a short while, I had to get down and rest for a couple of hours. It was really difficult not being able to ride the way I was used to—just get up and go."

"My body didn't respond like it always had, out of reflex. I had to teach myself how to ride all over again."

Kris began by riding only two or three times a month. Even short trail rides at a walk left her exhausted. "My body didn't respond like it always had, out of reflex. I had to teach myself how to ride all over again. The most challenging thing was retraining myself about balance and how to hold on with my legs. I'd always been so strong and I was surprised at how difficult it was to stay balanced. I rode Chance because I grew up on him. We had always been 'one flesh' and he knew that something was wrong with me just like you know when your hand or leg isn't working right. He took care of me as he always had: if we were out in the woods, he wouldn't do anything silly like jump over a log; he'd just walk over it because he knew that I wasn't secure. He's very special that way."

It was two years before Kris was back to starting young horses again. "I just went at a pace that was comfortable to me. I know that I ride a little differently now, and I walk with a limp, but I'm good at what I do. I may not look great on a horse and I may move funny, but I can, and do, work all day. Getting on a horse sure isn't as easy as it once was—I have to lay myself over the horse first then slide my leg over. I still find that a bit embarrassing at times. And I can imagine what some first-time clients are thinking—how can this woman train my horse if she can't even get up on him?"

Return to Competition

Kris now starts 15 to 20 horses a year, shows hunters, and foxhunts. Dr. Copeland regularly sees the results of her work up close and in action… she and Kris often foxhunt together with the Howard County Iron Bridge Hounds in Damascus, Maryland. "Kris has surpassed all my expectations," says Dr. Copeland. "She's been a gift to my life—seeing the fruits of one's labor is always rewarding. Even more, she's become a true friend."

"I've learned what the really important things in life are, and a traffic jam isn't one of them."

"All of this has really changed the way I look at people—and horses—with handicaps," says Kris. "My new roping horse, Tank, has an old ligament injury, but he can outwork anything half his age. Before my accident I might not have given him much of a chance, but now I know differently. He loves his job and you can't find a better horse to work with.

"And I've learned what the really important things in life are, and a traffic jam isn't one of them. A tidy house isn't either. Family, friends, doing what you love—they're what matters. One of the biggest joys in my life is being able to call someone I care about and tell them so. Life is too short to be worried over little things.

"We have been very blessed here with our farm and our business. My kids are great little riders and we have horses winning in flat races, steeplechases, and 'A' hunter shows, and going great in the hunt field. If I had given up because I was too proud to let others help me, I don't think we would be as successful as we are today. God gave me what he gave me to touch people's lives and to help horses. I'm not throwing that gift away."

KRIS' TIPS

- Find an orthopedic surgeon who understands the special needs of riders and supports your decision to ride again.

- Asking for help doesn't mean you're weak—it shows you'll do whatever it takes to accomplish a goal.

- You may not be able to do something the same way you did it before an accident, but you can still *do* the "something"! You can't give up because it hurts or it's hard.

- When the front of a truck says "Dodge"...do it!

Melanie Moehling – Dressage Rider

Bull Valley, Illinois

Dislocated Shoulder and Torn Rotator Cuff

Melanie

Melanie rode as a very young child, but developed such a severe allergy to horses that she couldn't continue. Her passion for horses never waned and she decided to try riding again when she was 34. Miraculously, the allergy had vanished (or been outgrown) and she began taking lessons and showing hunters and jumpers. Melanie transitioned to dressage a few years later when she "decided I was mortal."

The Injury

"I don't know how long I lay in the pasture, but I do remember that when I came to, I knew something was very wrong with my right arm. I squeezed my fingers, and as strange as this may sound, my first reaction was elation in knowing my arm was still attached and there was feeling in my fingers. Yes, I'd be able to ride again!"

Melanie had been leading Stoney, a Hanoverian/Thoroughbred, and Hawk, a Quarter Horse/Paint, out to the back pasture of her farm, when Hawk swung around and bit Stoney. The "bitee" reacted by running forward. Unfortunately, Melanie was directly in his path. She flew into the air—still holding Hawk's lead rope—and landed on her right side.

"It was mid-June and the early morning dew had made the grass slippery, but I managed to get up, prop the injured arm on my hip, and using my left arm, grab their lead ropes and get them safely into the pasture. But barnwork was going to have to wait, as I knew my arm needed immediate attention."

Melanie walked back to her house, awakened her sleeping (and very non-horsey) husband, and announced that she needed to go the hospital. "This was not a welcome request, as he was planning on going to a Cubs game with the children. Jim wanted to know if he had time for a shower and since I didn't think so, I hopped in my car, propped my arm on the console, and off I drove to the hospital. My husband would have to come along later.

"My first reaction was elation in knowing my arm was still attached and there was feeling in my fingers. Yes, I'd be able to ride again!"

"When I got to Centegra Hospital, a 15-minute drive from our farm, the 7:00 A.M. shift was just arriving. I must have looked a bit rocky, because several nurses stopped and escorted me into the emergency room. After that I don't remember too much except for going to get an X-ray and the doctor putting the dislocated right shoulder into place. I was quite groggy, but when it snapped into place, well, it's just a good feeling. My husband showed up just as they were trying to get my shoulder relocated." Melanie was given a sling that held her right arm against her side and instructed to call an orthopedic surgeon the next day.

The reaction of her family to this latest horse-related injury was subdued. "I think they take it all in stride by now. I've had a total rotator cuff tear in my left arm, a concussion or two, and a fractured thumb."

Once home, Melanie saw her family off to the Cubs game, retreated to bed for 90 minutes, then got back in her car and drove an hour to a friend's house to let her dogs out ("she was out of town and counting on me"). After the dogs were taken care of, she got back in her car and went to work for a couple of hours.

The next morning, Melanie had to confront the harsh realities of being injured and having five horses to care for. Any chance of her husband pitching in on the barn chores? "On what planet does that happen? I didn't know how I was going to clean stalls, scrub buckets, put halters and fly masks on, lead horses...the list is infinite—as all horse people know. I decided to see how much I was capable of, so I headed to my barn to see if I could clean five stalls with my left arm. Knees and legs become very important at this point as they can somewhat substitute for the non-working arm."

The job proved daunting, as her "good" left arm was compromised by the rotator cuff she had torn seven years earlier. "I was trail riding and came face to face with the biggest herd of deer I've ever seen. They took off and so did my horse. I'd had surgery, but it had never returned to 100 percent of its former self. Now, after years of babying it, the arm needed to be put back into service."

The next week was spent determining exactly what additional damage had been done to Melanie's right arm. Doctors discovered she had torn the rotator cuff. "Now I had a matched set." The orthopedist told her that she would be spending the summer in therapy to make her shoulder as strong as possible before the surgery that would be scheduled for early September.

"I hired someone to clean stalls during the week and my wonderful generous friend Linda helped on weekends. The rest of the chores I struggled through myself, and I learned that hurrying through barn chores was a thing of the past—everything now took at least twice as long." As for riding the trail horses she kept at home and her two boarded-out dressage horses, doctors told her it would be four to five months after the September surgery before she would be back in the saddle.

"I was used to doing some of the 'home barn' chores first thing in the morning, then driving 40 minutes to ride Fritz, my 19-year-old Hanoverian that's working at Prix St. Georges. Then I'd get Leflander, my nine-year-old Hanoverian competing at Intermediaire I, ready for my trainer Patti Becker to ride. After that, I'd go home to finish chores and get to my job at Body Chemistre®, which sells equestrian clothing." Now Melanie sat on the sidelines and watched as Patti rode both Leflander and Fritz.

"All I wanted was to get the surgery over and get on with my life and my riding. But things don't always go as planned. In late August, while

"I decided to see how much I was capable of, so I headed to my barn to see if I could clean five stalls with one arm."

carrying a bucket of water with my 'good' left arm, I felt a burning sensation in the bicep. Then I saw an orange-sized bulge just above the bend in my elbow. As my pre-surgical appointment with the doctor was only two days away, I figured I would wait and ask him what I'd done." When the doctor saw Melanie's latest injury, she was scheduled immediately for surgery...to repair a torn bicep in her left arm. Surgery on her right rotator cuff was now postponed until December.

"At this point, I was devastated; I couldn't do much of anything. My friends Jan and Linda were my salvation. They not only did the barnwork, they kept things light; calling me 'Mr. Potato Head' or 'Mr. Bobble Head.'

"At this point, I was devastated; I couldn't do much of anything. My friends were my salvation."

They were always there when I needed them. People at Fireside (where I board Fritz and Leflander) were helpful when I needed it, but I knew I had to try and do a few things on my own. I would watch Patti ride my horses and she always made me feel part of the training sessions.

"Carole Aullgauer, the owner of Fireside, had been through two hip surgeries within a couple of years and had not been able to ride for a very long time. She was a great inspiration, as she had rehabbed herself and gone on to win the Region 2 Adult Amateur Prix St. Georges and Intermediaire I championships. Carole and I have been friends for decades and when I got to feeling sorry for myself, she was always there.

"Rotator cuff surgery was performed on December 7 and I actually stayed away from my barn for two days. On the third day, I started doing simple chores like getting feed ready, cleaning buckets, and turning the horses out. I struggled through as much barnwork as I could do, and I always tried to be there when Jan and Linda came to help me. By the end of December, I would pick an occasional stall, but getting the muck cart up the ramp to the dumpster was a long way off."

Melanie continued to visit the barn four or five days a week to watch Fritz and Leflander being ridden. "All this kept me connected with what I really love." In January, Patti took Leflander to Florida and competed him in Wellington and Palm Beach.

Back to Ridden Work

In March Melanie was back on Fritz—on the longe line. "The doctor didn't want me to ride, so I asked if I could sit on the horse and walk around if I promised not to use any arm or shoulder muscles. Working on the longe line was perfect. I took lessons with Jennifer Kotylo, a certified Equilates™ instructor as well as a trainer. Fritz, who still can do all the Grand Prix movements, was a bit mystified at our lessons being on the longe line, but he was a real trooper. And I got real payoffs from my longe lessons—they helped my seat and strengthened my abdominal muscles, which had become marshmallows."

In April, Melanie was back doing all her own barn chores and by mid-May, she was officially released from the longe line. "Although I still needed to build strength, I could see a light at the end of the tunnel. Both Jennifer and Patti were always so patient with me and took into consideration my limitations while always pushing me to do a little more. They built up my confidence and were kind and encouraging in the process." While Melanie might have been back riding, she still had to make a few temporary compensations for her healing arms. "Grooming and tacking up were both a challenge as my upper body strength was non-existent. I used a stepladder to saddle the 16.1-hand Fritz and the 16.2-hand Leflander."

If you can't use your arm muscles, working on the longe line is perfect.

Melanie had physical therapy three times a week from December to May, when it was scaled back to once or twice a week. She used the discipline she'd learned over decades of riding to help her be consistent in her workouts. "Certain movements are still difficult, if not impossible, but little by little, it's all coming back."

Return to Competition

Having earned her United States Dressage Federation (USDF) bronze medal on Fritz, Melanie is now aiming for her silver medal on Leflander.

MELANIE'S TIPS

• Learn to accept help from your friends. Before the accident, I never asked people for help. Now I was asking friends to help clean my pastures—can there be a job worse than that? Friends are the ones who support you both physically and emotionally. They are the ones who don't just ask, "Is there anything I can do?" They show up and demand to be given something to do.

• Buy or borrow a recliner to use post-surgery. After shoulder surgery, your shoulder needs to remain stable, something that's hard to do when you're lying on a couch or a bed. In a recliner, you can prop your shoulder up and take the pressure off. A recliner is also a lot easier to get out.

• Try lessons on the longe line. It's a great way to rebuild your strength and work on your seat.

Afterword

This is a book of happy endings. Advances in treatment and the introduction of controlled exercise programs mean that more and more horses are returning to full work—even at the highest levels. But these happy endings also required another essential component—a passionate commitment by that horse's human partner to his recovery.

The stories in this book, and the women and men within those stories, are all very different, but common themes unite them: perseverance in the face of long odds, cold winters, and unexpected setbacks; the willingness to sacrifice one's own goals for the sake of one's horse; and most strikingly, the discovery of a deeper, more meaningful relationship (that so-often mentioned "stronger bond") with an equine partner. Their stories have provided me—and I hope you—with a foundation of experience and inspiration that is sure to support our equestrian pursuits, whatever they may be and wherever they may take us.

Treatment Options and Medication

ACell™
(see Julia Wendell and Redmond, p. 176, and Susan McNally and Cody, p. 132)

ACell™, Inc.
10555 Guilford Rd.
Jessup, MD 20794
800-826-2926
www.acell.com

Acepromazine ("Ace")
A commonly prescribed tranquilizer used to calm and quiet a horse. Note: Ace is a prohibited substance in most sanctioned competitions.

Adequan™
Used in the treatment of osteoarthritis, it inhibits cartilage damage and stimulates the cartilage repair process. For more information, see www.luitpoldanimalhealth.com.

Annular Ligament Release Surgery
(see Amy Crownover and Chester, p. 206)

During this surgery, the annular ligament (which can restrict movement as an injured tendon becomes swollen and inflamed) is severed. This allows the injured tendon to move more freely and aids in the release of toxic fluids that can impede the healing process.

Banamine® (Flunixin Meglumine)
A nonsteroidal anti-inflammatory used for pain relief (particularly in episodes of colic). It comes in injectable, paste, and granulated forms and is available by prescription from your veterinarian.

Bone Marrow Therapy
(see Nikki Husky and Buddy, p. 196)

Alamo Pintado Equine Medical Center
2501 Santa Barbara Ave.
Los Olivos, CA 93441
805-688-6510
www.alamopintado.com

"Bute" (Phenylbutazone)
A common nonsteroidal anti-inflammatory used to treat pain from an injury or infection. Available in powder, tablets, paste, or gel from your veterinarian. Extended use may have gastrointestinal side effects.

DMSO (Dimethyl Sulfoxide)
Used to treat sprains and strains and to "carry" medications such as corticosteroids into an injured area. Also used to reduce edema and inflammation.

Extracorporeal Shock Wave Therapy (ESWT)

by W. Rich Redding, DVM, MS, DACVS
Clinical Associate Professor of Equine Orthopedic Surgery
North Carolina State University College of Veterinary Medicine

Shock wave therapy was originally used in human orthopedics to break down kidney and gall bladder stones. When some patients reported improvement in unrelated orthopedic conditions such as back pain, new applications in musculoskeletal diseases were tested in humans. Recently, veterinarians have found some of those orthopedic applications beneficial in the treatment of lame and injured horses.

Shock waves are short extremely high-energy sound waves that are transmitted through the skin to injured tendons, ligaments and bones. They are generated in much the same way as a therapeutic or diagnostic ultrasound sound wave; however, they require a different machine to produce them. Once inside the body, shock waves travel through the skin and tissue without damaging it. *Neovascularization*, or the development of a new blood supply to a targeted tissue is thought to occur, especially at sites of bone-tendon interfaces, which can in turn relieve pain and improve tissue regeneration and repair.

Each shock wave treatment consists of several "pulses" of high-pressure waves. Treatments are administered while the horse is standing and mildly sedated. The number of treatments is dependent on the horse's specific injury.

Currently, ESWT is utilized for pain relief, stimulation of bone remodeling, and neovascularization of bone-tendon interfaces. Among the clinical conditions that should theoretically respond to shock wave treatments are injuries of the suspensory ligament origin (cannon bone) and attachments (sesamoids), distal sesamoidean ligament desmitis, stress fractures, bucked shins, and splint bone fractures. Unusual applications include cervical spine osteoarthritis, crushed heels, OCD lesions, and desmitis of the superior and inferior check ligaments.

(see Pat Troost and Mac, p. 114)

Fascia Release Surgery
(see Susan McNally and Cody, p. 132)

An incision through the muscle fascia that is performed when swelling is anticipated that could compromise blood flow, cause pain, and constrict tendons and ligaments.

Flucort®
Flumethazone (brand name Flucort) is an injectable corticosteroid solution used for muscular/skeletal conditions and general inflammation. Available by prescription from your veterinarian.

Hyaluronic Acid (aka HA, Hyaluronan, and Hyaluronate Sodium)
A naturally occurring substance in connective tissue, cartilage and synovial fluid, it is used to relieve pain and improve joint mobility. Hyaluronic Acid is available in a wide range of forms, from prescription injectables to over-the-counter powders and liquids.

Legend™
An injectable form of Hyaluronate Sodium. For more information, see www.bayerdvm.com.

Sarapin®
A natural anesthetic derived from the pitcher plant, most commonly given via injection.

Stem Cells
(see Fay Watchorn and Darius, p. 94, and Amy Crownover and Chester, p. 206)

Vet-Stem™, Inc.
12120 Tech Center Drive
Poway, CA 92064
888-387-8361
www.vet-stem.com

Xylazine
An alpha-2 class sedative that is very effective at alleviating symptoms associated with colic (abdominal pain). It should be noted that xylazine will also cause gastrointestinal smooth muscle relaxation and therefore decreased motility pursuant to administration.

Product Suppliers

Cold Therapy Systems

US
Game Ready™ Equine
2201 Dwight Way
Berkeley, CA 94704
888-426-3732
www.gamereadyequine.com

MacKinnon Ice Horse™, Inc.
4408 Ocean Valley Lane
San Diego, CA 92130
800-786-6633
www.mackinnonicehorse.com

UK
Horse Active Ltd.
16 New Road
Clanfield
Waterlooville
Hants PO8 0NS
United Kingdom
+44 (0) 2392 599532
www.horseactive.co.uk

Digestive Aids

US
Gastrogard®
Merial
3239 Satellite Blvd.
Duluth, Georgia 30096
678-638-3000
www.gastrogard.us.merial.com

Neigh-Lox®
Kentucky Performance Products
PO Box 1013
Versailles, Kentucky
800-772-1988
www.kppusa.com

UK
Gastrogard®
PetMeds.co.uk
+44 (0) 800 0430848
www.petmeds.co.uk

Neigh-Lox®
Saracen Horse Feeds
The Forstal
Beddow Way
Aylesford
Kent ME20 7BT

United Kingdom
+44 (0) 1622 718487
www.saracen-horse-feeds.co.uk

Dressage Arenas, Training, and Schooling Equipment

REI
Sumner, WA 98352-0001
800-426-4840
www.REI.com

Silk Tree®
1139 Spencer Road
Dillwyn, VA 23936
434-983-1941
www.silktree.com

Toklat Originals
PO Box 488
Lake Oswego, OR 97034
888-486-5528
www.toklat.com

Educational Tools

Glass Horse Project, LLC
2351 College Station Road
#574
Athens, GA 30605
770-868-7519
www.3dglasshorse.com

Health and Recovery Bedding

US
Hunt Club®, Inc.
4710 Beidler Rd.
Willoughby, OH 44094
440-946-7454
www.huntclubinc.com

UK
Ecobed (UK) Limited
Oak Tree Farm
Marsham
Norwich NR10 5PJ
United Kingdom
+44 (0) 1263 735545
www.ecobed.co.uk

Homeopathic Treatments

(Hilton Confidence Plus, Tendonil,
Traumeel Gel, etc.)

US

Chamisa Ridge™, Inc.
3212A Richards Lane
Santa Fe, NM 87507
800-743-3188
www.chamisaridge.com

Dover Saddlery
Box 1100
Littleton, MA 01460
800-406-8204
www.doversaddlery.com

FarmVet.com, Inc.
1041 Sneed Rd.
Franklin, TN 37069
888-837-3626
www.farmvet.com

Heel, Inc.
P.O. Box 11280
Albuquerque, NM 87192-0280
800-621-7644
www.heelbhi.com

SmartPak
40 Grissom Road
Plymouth, MA 02360
800-461-8898
www.smartpakequine.com

Young Living Essential Oils
3125 West Executive Park
Lehi, UT 84043
801-418-8900
www.youngliving.com

UK

Hilton Herbs Ltd
Downclose Farm
North Perrot
Crewkerne
Somerset TA18 7SH
England
+44 (0) 1460 78300
www.hiltonherbs.com

Young Living (Europe) Limited
3 Roman Way Business Centre
Godmanchester
Huntingdon
Cambs PE29 2LN
United Kingdom
+44 (0) 1480 455088
www.younglivingeurope.com

Horsemanship

US

Parelli™ Natural Horsemanship
56 Talisman Dr.
Pagosa Springs, CO 81147
800-642-335
www.parelli.com

Tellington TTouch® Training
P.O. Box 3793
Santa Fe, NM 87501
866-4-TTOUCH
www.ttouch.com

UK
Parelli UK
Brabourne House
Pilgrims Way
Hastingleigh
Ashford
Kent TN25 5LX
United Kingdom
+44 (0) 1233 750007
www.parelli.com

Tilley Farm UK TTeam Centre
Timsbury Road
Farmborough
Bath
Somerset BA2 0AB
United Kingdom
+44 (0) 1761 471182
www.ttouchteam.co.uk

Laser Therapy

US
Centurion Systems
105 Campus Plaza Dr.
Edison, NJ 08837
800-387-8326
www.centurion-systems.com

Respond Systems
20 Baldwin Dr.
Branford, CT 06405
203-481-2810
www.respondsystems.com

UK
Centurion Systems UK & Ireland Limited
51 Connor Road
Parkgate
Templepatrick
Ballyclare
Co. Antrim
Northern Ireland
BT39 0EA
+44 (0) 2894 433666
www.centurion-systems.co.uk

Magnetic Therapy

US
Centurion Systems
105 Campus Plaza Dr.
Edison, NJ 08837
800-387-8326
www.centurion-systems.com

Equine Magnetic Therapy
124 Lentz Rd.
Winlock, WA 98596
800-731-8463
www.equinemagnetic.com

Respond Systems
20 Baldwin Dr.
Branford, CT 06405
203-481-2810
www.respondsystems.com

UK
Horsefair
Hoplands
Kings Somborne
Hants S020 6QH
United Kingdom
+44 (0) 1794 389085
www.horsefair.co.uk

Swimming and Hydrotherapy

US

Byler Performance Equine
8183 Hwy 36 North
Bellville, TX 77418
979-865-5353
www.horseswim.com

Goodenough Farms Horse Spa
3365 Goodenough Rd.
Fillmore, CA 93001
805-524-2444
www.goodenoughfarms.co

Kentucky Equine Sports Medicine and
Rehabilitation Center (KESMARC)
258 Shannon Run Rd.
Versailles, KY 40383
859-873-9955
www.kesmarc.com

Northern Virginia Animal Swim Center
35469 Millville Rd.
Middleburg, VA 26117
540-687-6816
www.animalswimcenter.com

River Meadow Farm LLC
240 Palisado Ave.
Windsor, CT 06095
860-683-2386
www.rivermeadowfarm.com

Santolina Farm
5520 E. Lone Moutain Rd.
Cave Creek, AZ 85331
480-488-1444
www.santolinafarm.com

Southern California Equine
Rehabilitation Center
9301 Los Angeles Ave.
Moorpark, CA 93021
805-553-9701
www.rehabequine.com

Whitesboro Equine Therapy
390 Gunter Rd.
Whitesboro, TX 76273
903-564-9210
www.aqua-tred.com

UK

Checkendon Equestrian Centre
Lovegroves Lane
Checkendon
Reading
Berkshire RG8 0NE
United Kingdom
+44 (0) 1491 680225
www.checkendon.f9.co.uk

Equine Service Centre
Middle Hill Farm
Inglesham
Wiltshire SN6 7QY
United Kingdom
+44 (0) 1367 253929
www.equineservicecentre.com

Middleham Equine Pool and
Therapy Centre
Coverham
Leyburn
North Yorkshire DL8 4TL
United Kingdom
+44 (0) 1969 624880
www.middlehamonline.com

The Northern Equine Therapy Centre
Beautry House
Rathmell
Settle
North Yorkshire BD24 0LA
United Kingdom
+44 (0) 1729 840284
www.northernequinetherapy.co.uk

Turnout Alternatives

US
EuroXciser
Euro Gait-Master
2658 Griffith Park Blvd.
#167
Los Angeles, CA 90039
877-772-3876
www.euroxciser.com

Pasture Pal®
Applied Animal Enrichments LLC
Box 2610
Kensington, MD 20891
301-365-1265
www.horseballs.com

Port-a-Paddock
The Grazier™ System
7555 N. Greenwich Rd.
Wichita, KA 67226
877-744-6150
www.graziersystems.com

UK
Electronic Horse Fence Kit
Tack Direct
111 George Street
Edinburgh EH2 4JN
+44 (0) 131 2257830
www.tackdirect.co.uk

Recommended Reading

All About Long Reining by Paul Fiedler (www.horseandriderbooks.com)

All Horse Systems Go: The Horse Owner's Full-Color Veterinary Care and Conditioning Resource for Modern Performance, Sport and Pleasure Horses by Nancy S. Loving, DVM (www.horseandriderbooks.com)

The Art of Long Reining by Sylvia Stanier (www.horseandriderbooks.com)

Clicker Training for Your Horse by Alexandra Kurland (www.theclickercenter.com)

Complete Holistic Care and Healing for Horses by Mary L. Brennan, DVM (www.horseandriderbooks.com)

Concise Guide to Laminitis in the Horse by David W. Ramey, DVM (www.horseandriderbooks.com)

Concise Guide to Navicular Syndrome in the Horse by David W. Ramey, DVM
(www.horseandriderbooks.com)

Concise Guide to Respiratory Disease in the Horse by David W. Ramey, DVM
(www.horseandriderbooks.com)

Gymnastics: Systematic Training for Jumping Horses by James C. Wofford
(www.amazon.com)

Long Reining: The Saumur Method by Philippe Karl
(www.horseandriderbooks.com)

The New Equine Sports Therapy by Mimi Porter (www.eclipsepress.com)

*Ride Right with Daniel Stewart: Balance Your Frame and Frame of Mind with an
Unmounted Workout and Sport Psychology System* by Daniel Stewart
(www.horseandriderbooks.com)

The Rider's Edge: Overcoming the Psychological Challenges of Riding by Janet Sasson
Edgette, Psy.D. (www.horsebooksetc.com)

You Can Train Your Horse to Do Anything by Shawna and Vinton Karrasch
(www.horseandriderbooks.com)

Associations, Organizations, and Competitions

Dressage

US

United States Dressage Federation (USDF)
The United States Dressage Federation (USDF) is dedicated to education, the recognition
of achievement and the promotion of the sport of dressage in America.

Dressage "tests" are performed at the following levels:
Training Level
First Level
Second Level
Third Level
Fourth Level
Prix St. Georges

Intermediaire I
Intermediaire II
Grand Prix

USDF bronze medals are awarded for horse and rider combinations who have earned six scores of 60 percent or higher at a USDF recognized show: two at First Level, two at Second Level, and two at Third Level.

USDF silver medals are awarded to horse and rider combinations who have earned four scores of over 60 percent or higher at a USDF recognized show: two at Fourth Level and two at Prix St. Georges.

USDF gold medals are awarded to horse and rider combinations who have earned four scores above 60 percent or higher at a USDF recognized show: two at Intermediare I and/or II and two at Grand Prix.

USDF
4051 Iron Works Parkway
Lexington, KY 40511
859-971-2277
www.usdf.org

UK
British Dressage
British Dressage is the governing body for the sport in the UK.

British Dressage
Stoneleigh Park
Kenilworth
Warwickshire CV8 2RJ
+44 (0) 2476 698830
www.britishdressage.co.uk

Endurance

US
American Endurance Ride Conference (AERC)
The American Endurance Ride Conference (AERC) is the national governing body for long distance riding. It sanctions over 700 rides in North America each year in two cat-

egories: limited distance (rides of 25 miles or less), and endurance (rides of 50, 75, or 100 miles).

AERC
1373 Lincoln Way
Suite B
Auburn, CA 95603
530-823-2260
www.aerc.org

The Tevis Cup
The Western States Trail Ride (the "Tevis Cup") is the oldest modern day endurance ride and has been held annually since 1955. The 100 mile course--which must be completed in 24 hours--goes from Robbie Park (near Lake Tahoe) to Auburn, California, with riders making ascents of 15,000 feet and descents of some 20,000 feet. The Tevis Cup is awarded to the rider who completes the 100 miles in the fastest time with a horse that is deemed "fit to continue."

Western States Trail Foundation
1216 High Street #C
Auburn, CA 95603
530-823-7282
www.foothills.net/tevis

UK
Endurance GB
Endurance GB is the governing body for the sport of Endurance Riding Great Britain. Their mission is to promote and enhance the sport within the UK by providing competitions, training and development opportunities.

Endurance GB
Stoneleigh Park
Kenilworth
Warwickshire CV8 2LR
+44 (0) 2476 698863
www.endurancegb.co.uk

Equitation, Hunters, and Jumpers

US

United States Hunter Jumper Association (USHJA)

The United States Hunter Jumper Association (USHJA) is the nationally recognized affiliate of the United States Equestrian Federation (USEF) for hunters and jumpers.

USHJA
4047 Iron Works Parkway
Lexington, KY 40511
859-225-2055
www.ushja.org

Medal Finals

The two most prestigious "Medal Finals" for amateur hunt seat equitation riders are the ASPCA-Maclay National Championship and the United States Equestrian Federation (USEF) National Hunter Seat Medal Final. Riders compete throughout the year earning points which will gain them a spot in the Medal Finals.

Medal Finals classes are held over a course of fences 3'6" in height with demanding turns and other tests (counter-cantering a fence, demonstrating changes of leads, turns on the haunches, jumping a figure-eight of fences, etc.) asked of the riders.

UK

British Show Jumping Association (BSJA)

The British Show Jumping Association (BSJA) is the governing body of show jumping in Great Britain, formulating their rules and codes of practice under which all affiliated competitions are held.

BSJA
Stoneleigh Park
Kenilworth
Warwickshire CV8 2LR
+44 (0) 2476 698800
www.bsja.co.uk

Eventing

US

United States Eventing Association (USEA)

The United States Eventing Association (USEA) is the national association of the sport of eventing in America. Eventing is the "triathalon" of the equestrian competition. Horse and rider must perform a dressage test, ride a cross-country course, and compete in stadium jumping.

At Horse Trials, the dressage test, cross-country, and stadium jumping take place over one or two days. The levels are:
Beginner Novice
Novice Level
Training Level
Preliminary Level
Intermediate Level
Advanced Level

Three-Day Events take place over three or four days. The levels are:
One-Star (*)—a Preliminary Level Three-Day
Two-Star (**)—Intermediate Level Three-Day
Three-Star (***) and Four-Star (****)—Advanced Level Three-Day competitions

USEA, Inc.
525 Old Waterford Road, NW
Leesburg, VA 20176
703-779-0440
www.useventing.com

UK

British Eventing

British Eventing is the governing body for the sport in the UK.

British Eventing
Stoneleigh Park
Kenilworth
Warwickshire CV8 2RJ
+44 (0) 2476 698856
www.britisheventing.com

General Horse Sport

US

United States Equestrian Federation (USEF)

The USEF is the national governing body for equestrian sport.

USEF, Inc.
4047 Iron Works Parkway
Lexington, KY 40511
859-258-2472
www.usef.org

UK

British Equestrian Federation (BEF)

The BEF is the governing body for horse sports in the UK.

BEF
Stoneleigh Park
Kenilworth
Warwickshire
CV8 2RH
+44 (0) 2476 698871
www.bef.co.uk

PHOTO CREDITS

Page 8: Lisa P. Samoylenko

Page 14: Jamey Massey

Page 26: Flying Horse Photo, LLC

Page 36: (Top) Patricia Smith; (Bottom) Bill Gore

Page 46: Paula M. Smisek

Page 54: Sheila Ferreri

Page 62: (Top left) Lisa Byk; (Top right) Taren Hunt Photography ; (Bottom) Kim DeKett

Page 75: Photo by Pat Jarvis, courtesy of Nancy S. Loving, DVM

Page 82: Mary Cornelius

Page 94: (Top left) Bonnie Cazier; (Bottom right) Lindsey Grindle

Page 104: Hughes Equine Photography

Page 114: Jan Cohen & Carol Quall-Sanderman

Page 124: (Top) Erin Harty; (Bottom) John Lorenzen

Page 132: Lisa P. Samoylenko

Page 142: ©James Leslie Parker

Page 152: David Tanen

Page 162: Patrick Trumbull

Page 171: George Baker

Page 175: Mark Hardesty, Suzanne's father

Page 176: (Top left) Photo by Amy Coppage/GRCPhoto.com; (Bottom right) Photo by Barrett Warner

Page 186: Ken Kotylo

Page 196: (Top) AC Custom Photo; (Bottom) Courtesy of Kevan Husky

Page 206: (Top right) Lucinda Dyer; (Bottom) Shannon Brinkman

Page 216: Joan M. Gaughan

Page 226: (Top right) Herb Gelb; (Bottom left) ©www.hoofpix.com

Page 252: Brad Clark

Page 262: Images by Alice

Page 276: David Francisco

Page 277: Donna Snyder-Smith

Page 278: Lisa Barry©2006

Page 282: Leslie Britton

INDEX